Rhode Is
Civil War Dead

MW00624800

Rhode Island's Civil War Dead

A Complete Roster

ROBERT GRANDCHAMP

McFarland & Company, Inc., Publishers

Jefferson, North Carolina

ISBN (print) 978-1-4766-7871-9
ISBN (ebook) 978-1-4766-3683-2

LIBRARY OF CONGRESS AND BRITISH LIBRARY
CATALOGUING DATA ARE AVAILABLE

Front cover: (left to right) Second Lieutenant Charles V. Scott,
First Lieutenant George F. Turner and First Lieutenant Richard A. Briggs;
the Second Rhode Island Infantry at Camp Jameson,
near Washington, D.C. (Library of Congress)

Printed in the United States of America

McFarland & Company, Inc., Publishers
Box 611, Jefferson, North Carolina 28640
www.mcfarlandpub.com

For Addison Hope

"Rest Soldier, in thine honored grave,
Thy duty nobly done;
Long as thy Country's banners wave,
The land whose life thou diedst to save,
Shall bless the memory of the brave
And prize her patriot sons."
　　　　　—Inscription on the Soldier's
　　　　　Monument Scituate, Rhode Island

Table of Contents

Acknowledgments

At the Rhode Island State Archives, Ken Carlson was instrumental in finding many of these casualties. He laid the groundwork for this study through his cataloging of the Rhode Island Adjutant General papers and also doublechecked many of my figures. Ken also served on my master's thesis committee in 2010 at Rhode Island College. He has assisted in every project I have ever worked on, and is a true ally in the search for Rhode Island's past.

Captain Phil DiMaria of Battery B has been a mentor, friend, and guide for nearly twenty years as I navigated and researched the role of Rhode Island in the Civil War era. Without Phil's assistance and guidance, none of this work would have been possible.

As always, Kris VanDenBossche pointed me in the right direction, provided access to his wonderful collection, and helped in identifying casualties from south-west Rhode Island.

In Providence, General Richard Valente provided access to the Benefit Street Arsenal and its vast resources while I was working on various projects.

The staffs at the Rhode Island Historical Society, Providence City Hall Archives, Brown University, and the Providence Public Library were equally helpful.

To the clerks of every city and town hall I visited in Rhode Island, thank you. I am especially indebted to the staff at the halls in Scituate, Glocester, Coventry, Foster, Hopkinton, and Pawtucket.

Mike Lannigan, Ben Frail, Bruce Frail, Leo Kennedy, Steve Hackett, Caleb Horton, Jaime McGuire, and Tom Rousseau of the Sons of Union Veterans of the Civil War all provided assistance while tracking down the final resting places of these veterans. To Tom and Mike, I will be eternally grateful as we replaced the headstones of more than 100 Civil War veterans in Rhode Island from 2002 to 2007.

Nina Wright and the staff at the Westerly Public Library always provided access and many photocopies when I visited that wonderful institution, as did Matt Reardon of the New England Civil War Museum in Rockville, Connecticut.

At the Varnum Continentals, Patrick Donovan provided access to the collections and listened to my many stories.

Midge Frazel helped in ways too important to list.

Cherry Fletcher Bamberg of the Rhode Island Genealogical Society is to be commended for guiding my research and writing over the years as I wrote many articles for Rhode Island Roots. I am also indebted to Rachel Peirce and the other Rhode Island veteran descendants I have met through the Rhode Island Genealogical Society for providing me information on their ancestors.

Master Sergeant Jim Loffler, the historical section chief of the Rhode Island National Guard was helpful in tracking down the burial locations of some veterans.

I particularly want to thank the staffs at Arlington National Cemetery, Fredericksburg and Spotsylvania National Military Park, Richmond National Battlefield, and Petersburg National Battlefield for providing burial information on Rhode Island veterans buried there.

Furthermore, I wish to thank the many property owners whose backyards I have visited to locate cemeteries on private property. As well as the Providence Water Supply Board for allowing me to visit the final resting place of my Knight ancestors.

John Sterling and his colleagues who have produced the Rhode Island Cemetery Books provided an invaluable resource, as did the many volunteers who contribute to the Rhode Island Cemetery Database.

John Fenton, U.S. Army veteran, descendant of a Fourth Rhode Island soldier, and fellow collector helped in many ways, including assisting to locate several grave locations I had missed.

Although many years have passed, the interlibrary loan staff and Marlene Lopes at Rhode Island College Special Collections will always be remembered for their assistance in finding long lost books and articles while I was a student there from 2004 to 2010.

Many of these sources were found in various repositories throughout Rhode Island and although I may not have remembered names, I do wish to thank these institutions that assisted in this work: Langworthy Public Library, East Providence Historical Society, Foster Preservation Society, Scituate Preservation Society, Newport Historical Society, Redwood Library, Burrillville Historical and Preservation Society, Pettaquamscutt Historical Society, Glocester Heritage Society, Bristol Historical Society, North Kingstown Public

Library, East Greenwich Public Library, Westerly Armory Foundation, and the South County Museum.

Lastly, I must thank my dear wife Elizabeth. She has the patience of a saint and gladly lives with the Civil War every day.

1

How Many?

How many Rhode Islanders died in the Civil War? It is a question that I have been trying to determine for the last twenty years. How many men left their farms and mills between 1861 and 1865, and never saw the beauties of Narragansett Bay or the rugged landscape of western Rhode Island again? After nearly twenty years of study, and thousands of hours of data analysis, we finally have an answer.

From 1861 to 1865, the men who served in the Union forces from Rhode Island left an indelible mark in the crusade to restore the Union and free the slave. Rhode Island units served in nearly every major battle of the war, firing the first infantry shots at Bull Run, and some of the last by the cavalry at Appomattox. During the war, Rhode Island sent to the front eight regiments of infantry, an independent company of hospital guards, three regiments and a battalion of cavalry, three regiments of heavy artillery, the eight batteries of the First Rhode Island Light Artillery Regiment, along with two independent batteries. Furthermore, hundreds enlisted in the United States Army, Navy, and Marine Corps. It was a remarkable achievement for a state of 1,200 square miles.

Civil War historians have long quoted that 620,000 Americans, North and South died in the Civil War or as a result of their service. In 2012, Dr. David Hacker of Binghamton University, using the latest available data, stunned the Civil War community by announcing that the casualty figure is actually much higher, nearly 750,000 Union and Confederate military dead. This number was based on census data, a careful look at the casualty rates among black and immigrant soldiers, and a review of filed pension applications. Dr. Hacker's figure is widely gaining ground in the field as the true number of men who died as a result of their service. For the record, this historian agrees with Dr. Hacker's figure, however, the true number will never be known.[1]

In my research on Rhode Island's role in the Civil War, I have long had a nagging suspicion that the state lost far more men than originally claimed.

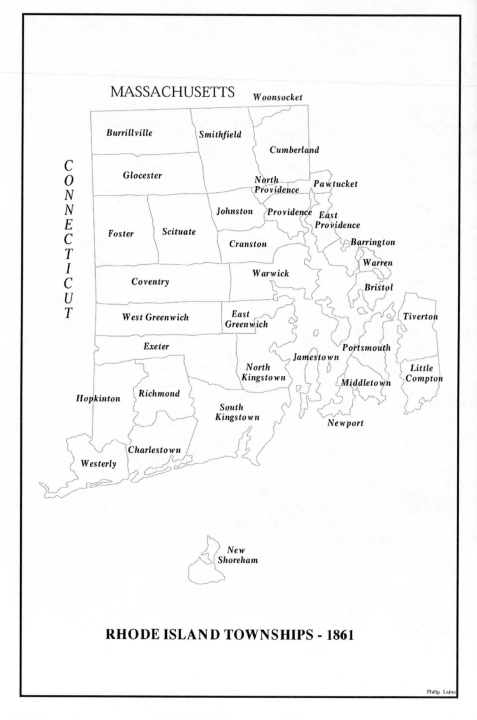

RHODE ISLAND TOWNSHIPS - 1861

Philip Laino

Map of Rhode Island during the Civil War.

According to Lieutenant Colonel William F. Fox in his massive *Regimental Losses in the American Civil War*, Rhode Island furnished 23,236 men to serve in the war. It is important to note that this figure includes all Rhode Island enlistments and not just those native-born Rhode Islanders who signed up; many men, most notably those who served in the Fourteenth Rhode Island as well as the Second Rhode Island Cavalry came from other states. Of these, according to Fox, 460 men were killed in action or mortally wounded and 861 died "from all other causes," including of disease, as prisoners of war, and in accidents for a total of 1,321 military deaths during the war. In his book, Fox offered a stern warning to future scholars regarding Civil War casualty

The Rhode Island Soldiers' and Sailors' Monument in Providence is the state's official memorial to the men of Rhode Island who died in the Civil War. It contains the names of 1,727 men.

figures. "Days, and often weeks, have been spent on the figures. It is hoped that before disputing any essential fact, careful examination of the records will be made." Despite Colonel Fox's statements, it is worth revisiting Rhode Island's Civil War casualty figures.[2]

In his 1964 book, *History of the Rhode Island Combat Units in the Civil War,* General Harold Barker, a veteran of the First and Second World Wars, whose grandfather had served in the Civil War, recorded a total of 1,685 men from Rhode Island units who died as a result of their Civil War service. The difference being that Barker included the men of the Fourteenth Rhode Island Heavy Artillery, which was later designated as the Eleventh United States Colored Heavy Artillery. Because he did not footnote his book, it is unclear how General Barker reached this conclusion.[3]

Immediately after the Civil War, the Rhode Island General Assembly appointed a committee of prominent Rhode Islanders, including Ambrose Burnside and John Russell Bartlett to find and accept a proposal for a statewide monument that would list the names of every Rhode Islander who died in the "wicked Rebellion." The monument, officially the Rhode Island Soldiers' and Sailors' Monument, would be inscribed, "Erected by the people of the state of Rhode Island to the memory of the brave men who died that their country might live." After a year-long search, the committee settled on a design from Randolph Rogers, consisting of a statue of "America Militant," four bronze panels representing War, Victory, Peace, and History, as well as four additional figures representing the infantry, cavalry, artillery, and navy. Most importantly were the twelve panels that would contain the names of every Rhode Islander who died in the war. The entire monument cost $50,000 and was dedicated in Exchange Place (Kennedy Plaza) on September 16, 1871, to much fanfare.[4]

The first step in the monument process was carefully going through the records held by the adjutant general of Rhode Island and compiling a listing of the names to be inscribed on the bronze panels. This in and of itself was an arduous task. When he inherited the records in the early 1890s Adjutant General Elisha Dyer, Jr., himself a Civil War veteran, complained about the terrible condition of Rhode Island's Civil War records. "The old and valuable records of the Rhode Island Regiments were being irreparably injured by the constant handling of those who were obliged to refer to them for information. From the close of the war until June 1883, the records were kept in pasteboard boxes in an open bookcase in the adjutant general's office, where they were easily accessible to the public, and, consequently, also in danger of being carried off and lost, as well as being spoiled or destroyed by careless handling."[5]

ERECTED
BY THE
PEOPLE OF
RHODE ISLAND
TO THE
MEMORY
OF THE
BRAVE MEN
WHO DIED
THAT THEIR
COUNTRY
MIGHT LIVE

A detailed shot of the Rhode Island Soldiers' and Sailors' Monument.

The committee only had a year to go through the thousands of muster rolls, as well as compiling a listing of men from Rhode Island who had served in the Regulars or in units from other states. Despite this momentous task, the committee completed its task and recorded the names of 1,727 Rhode Islanders who died of wounds, disease, in prisons, of accidents in the service, or of disease immediately upon returning home from the army. These 1,727 names were inscribed upon the monument in Providence. Many names were missed however.[6]

So, who is to be believed? Fox widely regarded as the leading authority on Civil War statistics, or the adjutant general's office in Rhode Island, who was responsible for recording the deaths of Rhode Island's soldiers and sailors. The discrepancy between Fox's figures and those of the state are 406; again the Fourteenth Rhode Island was not included by Fox. When one deducts Rhode Islanders who served in the units of other states, as well as in the U.S. Army, U.S. Navy, and Marine Corps, Rhode Island still records a figure of more than 300 military deaths of Rhode Islanders over the usually quoted number given by Fox. The question is who is to be believed. In the opinion of this historian, the higher number, quoted by the State of Rhode Island in 1869, the very names that were inscribed on the Soldiers' and Sailors' Mon-

A detailed shot of the panels on the Rhode Island Soldiers' and Sailors' Monument. This plaque lists the men who died serving in the Seventh Rhode Island Volunteers.

ument are the correct figure. But a deeper question remains, is the figure of 1,727 Rhode Islanders dying as a result of their Civil War service an accurate figure. Could the number be higher?

I have long held suspicion that the number of Rhode Islanders who died as a result of their Civil War service was over 2,000 and I regularly quoted the number in my books and lectures on the Civil War. In 2014, I set out to test my hypothesis, to finally determine the exact number of Rhode Islanders who died in the Civil War.

I began my study by focusing on the Seventh Rhode Island Volunteers, a regiment in which my great-great-great uncle Alfred Sheldon Knight served. According to Fox, the Seventh sustained a loss of ninety officers and men killed in action and died of wounds, as well as 109 who "died of disease, accidents, in prison &c." In his only other reference to the regiment, Fox stated that at the Battle of Fredericksburg the Seventh sustained a loss of eleven dead, 132 wounded and fifteen missing for a total of 158. While acknowledging the limited resources of muster rolls and after-action reports that Fox worked with, I knew these figures were woefully low.[7]

Based on a survey of records which have included entries in soldiers' letters and diaries, cemetery records, pension files, town clerk death listings; pretty much every scrap of paper that exists regarding the Seventh Rhode Island Volun-

Many Rhode Islanders died of illness at home shortly after returning from the front, as was the case of Private Thomas Simpson who served in the Fifth Rhode Island Heavy Artillery from Newport.

teers, I determined that the Seventh, which carried a total of 1,179 men on its rolls during the war sustained a loss of 105 officers and men who died in combat or of wounds sustained in battle, as well as 109 who died of other causes such as disease and accidents.

Not included in the above figures are the twenty-nine men from the Seventh who died after being mustered out of the army, but whose deaths are directly attributable to their Civil War service. Among them is Lieutenant Colonel Job Arnold of Providence. He was discharged for disability in May 1864 after contracting malaria in Mississippi. Arnold died in Providence in December of 1869, and as reported in local papers, he died as a direct result of his service in the Seventh Rhode Island in the Deep South; his name was inscribed on the monument.[8]

Countering Fox's claim regarding the Seventh's losses at Fredericksburg, my determination is the regiment lost three officers and forty-seven men killed in action or mortally wounded, as well as 144 officers and men wounded; in addition, three men were captured. This is a total of 197 officers and men of the roughly 570 who went into the fight. One perfect example is the case of Richard Weeden of Providence who served in Company A of the Seventh. He was wounded in action at Fredericksburg, and was later discharged for disability on March 16, 1864. He applied for and was granted a pension based on this service. However, in 1868, nearly six years after the battle, as attested in his widow's pension, Weeden died as a direct result of his Fredericksburg injuries. "Attending physician swears soldier died Oct. 4, 1868 from gun shot wounds and that he had well marked symptoms of phthisis." As in most cases, he was not listed in the "official records" as dying as a direct result of his military service in the Seventh.[9]

Lt. Col. Job Arnold served in the First Rhode Island Detached Militia, Fifth Rhode Island Heavy Artillery, and the Seventh Rhode Island Volunteers. His widow chose to engrave his memorial in North Burial Ground in Providence with the service in the regiment that took his life.

Because of the gruesome nature of Civil War combat, where minié balls and exploding artillery rounds left mangled corpses scattered around the ground, many men were simply listed as missing in action or deserted, leaving families searching, in some cases for years, as to what happened to their family member. On September 17, 1862, the Fourth Rhode Island advanced into Otto's Cornfield at the Battle of Antietam. Forming the extreme left flank of the Army of the Potomac, the Rhode Islanders were flanked in the dense corn and disintegrated under fire. According to one veteran from the regiment, "our men fell like sheep at the slaughter." After a few disjointed volleys, the men of the Fourth fled for their lives. According to the official regimental report field five days after the battle by Lieutenant Colonel Joseph B. Curtis, the regiment lost twenty-one killed, seventy-seven wounded, and two men missing in action. These figures have long been substantiated as the toll of battle for the Fourth on that terrible day.[10]

One of the Fourth's veterans who fell that day was Corporal Austin A.

Perkins of Richmond, Rhode Island. According to veteran George H. Allen in his 1887 book *Forty-Six Months in the Fourth Rhode Island Volunteers,* Perkins "deserted at Antietam." In a copy of Allen's book held in the archives of Providence College are numerous margin notes obviously written by a veteran of the Fourth who doublechecked all of Allen's statistics. In the entry for Corporal Perkins he wrote, "Later believed to have been killed at Antietam Sept. 17, 1862." Fortunately, in the early 1890s, as Elisha Dyer prepared to publish his massive *Revised Register,* it was noted under the entry for Austin, "Believed to have been killed in the battle of Antietam." Despite the official nod from the state that this soldier lost his life in combat, no additional names were ever added to the Soldiers' and Sailors' Monument. With the hindsight of a century and a half to carefully check all the records, it is now believed that the true casualty count of the Fourth in Otto's Cornfield, including those who later died of wounds was thirty-seven dead, seventy-five wounded, and three captured. Furthermore, nineteen men are listed as having "deserted in the face of the enemy." Going into the battle with 247 men, the regiment lost well over half of its strength, percentage wise the most ever lost by a Rhode Island unit in any battle of any war.[11]

If the casualty figures can be so different for just the Seventh Rhode Island, I knew that they would increase as well for the other regiments Rhode Island sent to the war. To begin my research, I drew up a plan to visit every town hall in Rhode Island, in addition to combining with a search through historic cemeteries. I gave myself very limited parameters. The notation of death entered into the ledger by the clerk had to clearly indicate that the man died as a direct result of his Civil War service. In the occupation field, the man would be listed as a "soldier," "volunteer" or "in U.S. Service." Under the heading of death, the notation had to clearly indicate that the man died of wounds or disease he encountered in the army. For example, I encountered in the Cranston records a recently discharged soldier who was run over by a railroad car shortly after returning home; this would not qualify as a Civil War death. In the graveyard search, the inscription on the headstone had to clearly indicate a Civil War death, such as the often encountered "Died of disease contracted in the service of his country" or "Died of wounds received in the Battle of...."

Although the Rhode Island General Assembly had required city and town clerks to record births, marriages, and deaths at the local level beginning in 1853, and had even sent books to the clerk offices for this purpose, by the 1860s, the system was still woefully inaccurate. Many such vital records continued to only be recorded in family Bibles. Some clerks such as those in Providence, Scituate, Coventry, and Warwick maintained meticulous records from the time, recording the deaths of men who were residents of the town, but died out of state while on military service, as well as those who died of wounds or disease at home. Indeed, the city clerk in Providence even took the time to record the street and address of where the deceased died. In addition, when a soldier died, he listed their unit. Surprisingly towns such as Burrillville, Glocester, Little Compton, and Westerly, who lost soldiers in the Civil War, and whose death records can be found elsewhere recorded no soldiers between 1861 and 1865 in their town vital records.[12]

The quest to determine the number of Rhode Islanders who died in the Civil War, specifically those who came home and died of wounds or illness took me to every clerk's office in Rhode Island. During the course of my research into these records, to date, I found that the clerks had recorded more than 300 soldiers in their records who died in the war; the vast majority of whom died at home of wounds or illness contracted in the service, not in camp or on the battlefield. A good example is Samuel Towne of Battery C, First Rhode Island Light Artillery. He died in North Providence on February 13, 1863, of dysentery he brought home from the army.[13]

Alpheus Salisbury was a married, thirty-year-old weaver from Scituate who served in Company K, Seventh Rhode Island Volunteers. Salisbury was shot in the neck in the Seventh's assault up Marye's Heights at the Battle of Fredericksburg. He was discharged from the service for disability on February 2, 1863, and sent home to Scituate. According to a published medical report filed by local doctor William H. Bowen who treated Salisbury:

> The most prominent symptoms were great pain in the head, frequent vomitings, constipation, and a kind of stupor. The wound in the head had not healed, and on probing it pus and blood were discharged. He learned that several pieces of bone had been taken away since the injury was inflicted. On July 1, he saw the patient, in consultation with another physician. Pain in the head and vomiting still continued, and there was more perfect unconsciousness. The next morning there was paralysis of the side opposite the wound in the head, with one pupil contracted while the other was dilated, and he was perfectly comatose. He thinks that the wound was the primary and the original cause of death.[14]

Private Salisbury died on July 2, 1863, as a direct result of his injuries sustained at Fredericksburg some seven months earlier; he was buried in the Clayville Cemetery. Federal pension clerks agreed with Dr. Bowen's findings and granted his wife a pension based on the fact that he died of his injuries sustained in government service. Despite the government's findings, the name of Alpheus Salisbury is not recorded on the Soldiers' and Sailors' Monument in Providence.[15]

Some Rhode Island families lost two of their sons in the service of the Union. Among those who lost two was the Pearce family of Richmond.

William and Harvey Pearce enlisted in Battery B, First Rhode Island Light Artillery in March 1862. William quickly fell ill on the Virginia Peninsula and was discharged for disability and sent home on June 30, 1862; Harvey struggled on until March 20, 1863, when he too was discharged for disability. Both men returned to Richmond where, according to inscriptions on both headstones, they "died of disease contracted in the U.S. Service during the Great Rebellion." The two Pearce brothers are buried side by side at Wood River Cemetery in Hope Valley, the only indication they died in the service is the inscription upon their now fading headstones. Neither name is inscribed on the monument in Providence, or in the local town records.[16]

Private Davis Crandall served in the Fourth Rhode Island Volunteers. He was the first Hopkinton soldier to die in the war, falling at New Bern in March 1862.

The Seventh Squadron of Rhode Island Cavalry is one of the state's more interesting Civil War units. Composed of one company raised from students from Dartmouth and Norwich, and one from men from northern Rhode Island, the squadron spent an uneventful three months of service in the Shenandoah Valley in the summer of 1862. Indeed, the small battalion's only glory came in the last days of their enlistment when they participated in a wild breakout from the Harpers Ferry garrison. According to the army records, only one squadron member, Arthur Coombs of Thetford, Vermont, a student from Norwich died of typhoid when the squadron was stationed near Winchester, Virginia. Another Seventh Squadron casualty was Henry C. Colwell of Glocester. He died of typhoid on November 3, 1862, in Chepachet, a month after returning home from the front. Colwell's name is not on the Soldiers' and Sailors' Monument, nor is that of Private Coombs.[17]

Ira E. Cole was seventeen and a farmer from Foster when he enlisted in Company E of the Third Rhode Island Heavy Artillery in the summer of 1861. Assigned to artillery duty in Georgia, Florida, and South Carolina, the Third, like the vast majority of Civil War regiments lost far more men to illness than to the enemy's guns. Private Cole survived his three-year enlistment unscathed. He returned to Foster in the summer of 1864 a sick man however. On August 31, 1865, according to the town clerk's notations, Cole died of "chronic dysentery contracted in camp" at his home in Foster. Like the majority of the men chronicled in this study, his name was not listed as a Civil War death by state authorities.[18]

This type of headstone, found in cemeteries throughout Rhode Island is typical for soldiers who died in the war. This example, located in Greenwood Cemetery in Coventry is for Reuben A. Whitman of the Seventh Rhode Island Volunteers. Like many markers, this stone is a cenotaph, as Private Whitman remains buried at City Point National Cemetery in Virginia.

Perhaps the most interesting find in the search has been a remarkable discovery regarding Private Ira Cornell of Coventry, who served in Company K of the Seventh Rhode Island Volunteers. Cornell was a farmer from Coventry who enlisted on August 14, 1862. A day later, his son Ira Cornell, Jr., also enlisted. The senior Cornell was wounded at Fredericksburg. According to the official army records, he "deserted at Cincinnati, O. April 1, 1863." His son, Ira Cornell junior was discharged for disability on October 14, 1864, and died of tuberculosis contracted in the army on April 29, 1867, in Coventry.[19]

When I conducted my initial survey of compiling a roster of the Seventh Rhode Island, I listed the senior Cornell as did the official records, as having deserted. In the back of my mind however, was why a father would desert the army, leaving his teenage son alone in the service. One day while researching in the Coventry Town Hall, I made a startling discovery. The town clerk in Coventry kept meticulous records of all volunteers who died in the army from the town. As I was busy looking through the register of deaths in Coventry, I saw the name of Ira Cornell. In the margin, the clerk had annotated, "Drowned in the Ohio River in the attempt of crossing it in the line of his duty." This record makes sense, for on that date the steamer *Kentucky*, transferred the Seventh Rhode Island across the Ohio River from Cincinnati to Covington, Kentucky. I have found no reference to the death in any letters from Seventh Rhode Island soldiers recording this, nor is it recorded in the official history of the regiment. Despite this, the Coventry records are highly accurate, and the clerk would have received first-hand information from a fellow soldier or a relative about the death. In addition, there is a cenotaph in Pine Grove Cemetery in Coventry for Cornell that gives a date of death of April 1, 1863. In my records of the Seventh Rhode Island I have changed my entry to reflect that Ira Cornell died in the service of his country and did not desert the flag. The Civil War was not kind to the Cornell family. In 1867, Ira Cornell, Jr., also died, of disease brought back to Coventry as a direct result of his wartime service.[20]

Will the exact number of Rhode Island soldiers who died as a result of battle injuries or of disease contracted in the service ever be known? The answer is never. Men immediately left the state after mustering out, some never returned, many never had their deaths recorded in the vital records, and today lie buried in an unmarked grave.

The best available data supports that **2,217** Rhode Island soldiers and sailors died as a direct result of their Civil War service, which severely contradicts the previous numbers as being too low.

Perhaps Thomas Williams

Many Rhode Islanders remain buried in National Cemeteries in the South. Private Oliver Wood of Foster served in Company K of the Seventh Rhode Island was killed in action June 3, 1864, and is interred at Cold Harbor National Cemetery.

ERECTED TO COMMEMORATE
THE NOBLE DEEDS OF THE
VOLUNTEER SOLDIERS AND SAILORS
OF WESTERLY AND VICINITY
IN MAINTAINING THE UNION
1861 ——— 1865

Till the mountains are worn out and the rivers forget to flow
shall their names be kept fresh with reverent honors which
are inscribed upon the book of "National Remembrance"
Henry Ward Beecher.

Every Rhode Island community honored their Civil War dead in a different way. This plaque hangs in the Westerly Public Library, which once housed the Budlong Post of the Grand Army of the Republic.

Bicknell summed it up best in his massive *The History of the State of Rhode Island and Providence Plantations* when describing the Civil War registers from the smallest state. "This report gives the name, date of enrollment, dates of mustering in and mustering out, promotions, transfers, or all soldiers and sailors from Rhode Island in the Civil War. Totals are not given and no record as to the nationality, birth, or birth-place of any of the whole number. In most cases the Rhode Island residence is noted. From these data, it is almost impossible to determine how many men Rhode Island contributed to the War. It can safely be stated that the State furnished the full quota of men and supplies that she was called to render."[21]

2

Methodology

The following roster of the Rhode Island soldiers and sailors who died in the Civil War is the result of nearly twenty years of research. Each man has been identified through a variety of resources to be listed in this study. First and foremost, the official state roster of deceased soldiers and sailors, published in the 1871 proceedings at the dedication of the Soldiers' and Sailors' Monument in Providence provided a base block to build this study.

Secondly, the *Revised Register of Rhode Island Volunteers,* in addition to the numerous regimental histories were also used to identify men. Most importantly, as stated in the introduction, this author has visited every town hall, cemetery, and archive in Rhode Island. This "boots on the ground" research identified scores of men not listed in the published resources. Town clerk records and information recorded on the gravestones provided much of this information. Furthermore, when available, the service and pension records at the National Archives provided details regarding some of these men. In addition, the letters and diaries of some men were consulted.

Although some information might not be supported by what is listed in the "official records," this roster represents the most complete and accurate set of data of the officers and men from Rhode Island who died in the Civil War. Furthermore, when known, the burial location of the veteran has been identified. To identify burial locations, each man was run through three data-bases, namely www.findagrave.com, the Rhode Island Historical Cemetery Database, as well as Civil War veteran burial locations of the Sons of Union Veterans of the Civil War. Furthermore, the Veterans Affairs National Cemetery database was also utilized. No doubt, many of these men will forever rest in a National Cemetery under a stone marked "Unknown." A cenotaph is a memorial marker in a cemetery in Rhode Island, the soldier's body remains buried in the South.

Each man is identified, followed by his rank and company in the afore-mentioned regiment. The residence is the residence stated on the man's enlistment form when known. The United States Army and United States Navy kept very poor records regarding the men who served on the Regular establishment. It is nearly impossible to determine the residence, and in some cases the fate of individual men who served in the Regulars. The information is provided as far as known.

Each battery of the First Rhode Island Light Artillery had an authorized strength of 150 officers and men. However, disease and battle casualties often reduced the batteries to fewer than 100 men. As such, the artillery officers would draft men from nearby infantry regiments to man the guns and horses of each battery. When these infantrymen were killed or wounded, they were listed on the official casualty returns for each battery, however, they were not a member of the battery. For this study, only men who were permanent members of the First Rhode Island Light Artillery and died of battle wounds, disease, or in accidents will be included.

Regarding the service record of each man. For the sake of brevity, only the wound or illness that directly contributed to the man's death is recorded on these pages. For additional information, the reader is referred to the *Revised Register of Rhode Island Volunteers*.

It is important to note the men who died of disease or wounds after they were mustered out or discharged from the service due to disability and are not listed elsewhere as officially dying in the service; these men died as a direct result of their military service and are recorded here as such. Most abbreviations used are self-explanatory with the one exception being Art for Artificer, which may warrant a definition as well. An artificer was a trained mechanic, such as a wheelwright, harness maker, or blacksmith that repaired equipment in an artillery unit.

In regards to the residence of the soldier, the residence is that claimed upon the enlistment form, or when not listed, where the soldier last knowingly resided. In the case of Woonsocket, it should be noted for the record that Woonsocket did not officially exist as a separate town until 1867. In 1862, the village of Woonsocket consisted of a large industrial area comprising both the towns of Smithfield on the west bank of the Blackstone River, and Cumberland on the east side. It is nearly impossible to determine which side of the river a soldier may have resided on. As many soldiers claimed the then unincorporated village of Woonsocket as their home, it is listed in this roster as a separate place of residence then Cumberland and Smithfield.

Furthermore, in 1861, the village of Fall River was still a part of the Town of Tiverton, Rhode Island. In 1862, Fall River became a city in Massachusetts, and Rhode Island gained the land that became East Providence. In addition, Smithfield was a much larger town at the time, and included what is now

Woonsocket, North Smithfield, Lincoln, Central Falls, and the present Smithfield. Narragansett was still a part of South Kingstown, and West Warwick did not exist as a separate entity until 1913. Other Rhode Island boundaries have changed over time as well; readers are advised to consult the wonderful book *Rhode Island Boundaries: 1636–1936* by John Hutchins Cady.

It is important to also note that many men came to Rhode Island, especially when enlistment bounties were high. These men, who resided out of state, served and died in a Rhode Island unit and will be listed here. A number of Rhode Islanders served in other state regiments, but were listed as residents of Rhode Island at the outbreak of the Civil War. They are listed on the Soldiers' and Sailors' Monument in Providence as residents of Rhode Island. As such, they are recorded in this volume as Rhode Islanders who died in the Civil War. Only these men are listed, not the soldiers from states outside of Rhode Island who ended up being buried in Rhode Island.

This register is the result of years of research and *countless* hours of study and revision. It will stand the test of time as the most complete and accurate record of Rhode Islanders who died during the Civil War. The men who served did their duty to free the slave and preserve the Republic. I hope I have done their memory justice in preserving an accurate record of their names and deeds for posterity.

3

Generals and Staff

Burges, Tristam, Jr. Col. Residence, Providence. Aide de camp to Maj. Gen. George B. McClellan. Mortally wounded in action at Williamsburg, VA, May 5, 1862. Died of wounds at Providence, RI, May 23, 1863. Interred at North Burial Ground, Providence, RI.

Ives, Robert Hale. 1st Lt. Residence, Providence. Aide de camp to Brig. Gen. I.P. Rodman. Mortally wounded in action at Antietam, MD, Sept. 17, 1862. Died of wounds at Hagerstown, MD, Sept. 27, 1862. Interred at North Burial Ground, Providence, RI.

Manchester, Joseph S. Capt. U.S. Vols. Residence, Bristol. Originally served as Sgt. Maj. and 1st Lt. Co. B, 7th R.I. Vols. Left arm severed at Fredericksburg, VA, Dec. 13, 1862. Promoted to Captain and Commissary of Subsistence, U.S. Vols. Awarded brevet majority for "gallant and meritorious services." Died of tuberculosis contracted in the service at Bristol, RI, May 4, 1872. Interred at Juniper Hill Cemetery, Bristol, RI.

Rodman, Isaac Peace. Brig. Gen. Residence, South Kingstown. Mortally wounded in action, shot in chest at Antietam, MD, Sept. 17, 1862. Died of wounds at Sharpsburg, MD, Sept. 30, 1862. Interred at Rodman Lot, South Kingstown Cemetery 30, South Kingstown, RI.

Stevens, Isaac Ingalls. Maj. Gen. Residence, Newport. Killed in action at Chantilly, VA, Sept. 1, 1862. Interred at Island Cemetery, Newport, RI.

Brigadier General Isaac Peace Rodman of South Kingstown is the highest-ranking native Rhode Islander to die in the Civil War; he was mortally wounded at Antietam.

18

Thurston, Alfred Henry. Maj. Residence, Newport. Medical Director Twelfth Corps and Grant Hospital, NY. Died of disease contracted in the service Aug. 2, 1865, at Newport, RI. Interred at Island Cemetery, Newport, RI.

Young, Henry Harrison. Lt. Col. Residence, Providence. Originally served as major, 2nd Rhode Island Volunteers. In 1864 joined the staff of Maj. Gen. Phillip Sheridan and acted as chief of scouts in the Shenandoah Valley. Mustered out of volunteer service and retained on staff of Gen. Sheridan. Sent to Texas to assist in Reconstruction duties. Killed in action "late 1866 while crossing the Rio Grande" by a band of ex Confederates while supporting campaign against Emperor Max-imillian. Body never recovered. In 1911, a statue "The Scout" was erected in Young's memory as a cenotaph at Burnside Park in Providence, RI.

Although born in Massachusetts, Major General Isaac Ingalls Stevens was a resident of Newport. He was killed at Chantilly, Virginia, on September 1, 1862.

4

First Rhode Island
Detached Militia

Ackley, William H. Pvt. Co. K. Residence, Providence. Died of exhaustion at Camp Sprague, Washington, D.C., July 24, 1861.

Arnold, John R. Corp. Co. D. Residence, Providence. Died of typhoid at Providence, RI, July 30, 1861. Interred at Swan Point Cemetery, Providence, RI.

Bolton, Thomas. Pvt. Co. B. Residence, Providence. Died of "congestion of the brain" at Washington, D.C., July 18, 1861.

Burdick, Albert H. Pvt. Co. I. Residence, Westerly. Killed in action at Bull Run, VA, July 21, 1861.

Comstock, Jesse. Pvt. Co. D. Residence, Providence. Killed in action at Bull Run, VA, July 21, 1861. Cenotaph at North Burial Ground, Providence, RI.

Crane, Robert M. Pvt. Co. F. Residence, Newport. Killed in action at Bull Run, VA, July 21, 1861.

Danforth, Samuel C. Pvt. Co. I. Residence, Providence. Killed in action at Bull Run, VA, July 21, 1861.

Davis, Henry C. Pvt. Co. K. Residence, Woonsocket. Died of typhoid at Washington, D.C., June 16, 1861. Interred at St. James Cemetery, Woonsocket, RI. The first Rhode Islander to die in the Civil War.

Deblois, Silas D. Pvt. Co. F. Residence, Newport. Died of disease contracted in the service at Newport, RI. Unknown date, c. 1862.

Dexter, Frederic. Pvt. Co. E. Residence, Cumberland. Died of typhoid at Cumberland, RI, Aug. 10, 1861. Interred at Swan Point Cemetery, Providence, RI.

Dougherty, James. Pvt. Co. H. Residence, Providence. Killed in action at Bull Run, VA, July 21, 1861.

Downs, Paul. Pvt. Co. G. Residence, Providence. Killed in action at Bull Run, VA, July 21, 1861.

Falvey, John. Pvt. Co. H. Residence, Providence. Captured at Bull Run, VA, July 21, 1861. Died as a prisoner of war at Richmond, VA, July 28, 1861.

Flagg, George W. Pvt. Co. D. Residence, Providence. Mortally wounded in action at Bull Run, VA, July 21, 1861. Died of wounds at Gordonsville, VA, Aug. 3, 1861. Cenotaph at North Burial Ground, Providence, RI.

Foster, Samuel. Corp. Co. D. Residence, Providence. Killed in action at Bull Run, VA, July 21, 1861. Cenotaph at Swan Point Cemetery, Providence, RI.

Goddard, Benjamin F. Pvt. Co. C. Residence, Newport. Died of disease contracted in the service at Newport, RI, Feb. 25, 1863. Interred at Common Burying Ground, Newport, RI.

Harrington, Thomas J. Pvt. Co. F. Residence, Newport. Killed in action at Bull Run, VA, July 21, 1861.

Harrop, Joseph. Pvt. Co. K. Residence, Woonsocket. Killed in action at Bull Run, VA, July 21, 1861.

Hawkins, Warren D. Pvt. Co. A. Residence, Providence. Killed in action at Bull Run, VA, July 21, 1861. Cenotaph at Riverside Cemetery, Pawtucket, RI.

King, Theodore Wheaton. Pvt. Co. F. Residence, Newport. Mortally wounded in action at Bull Run, VA, July 21, 1861. Captured. Released and died of wounds at Philadelphia, PA, Jan. 28, 1862. Interred at Island Cemetery, Newport, RI.

Knowles, Frank H. Pvt. Co. D. Residence, Providence. Died of "ulcer of the stomach" contracted in the service Oct. 30, 1864, at Providence, RI. Interred at Swan Point Cemetery, Providence, RI.

Luther, Henry H. Pvt. Co. A. Residence, Providence. Killed in action at Bull Run, VA, July 21, 1861.

Melville, Hugh. Pvt. Co. K. Residence, Woonsocket. Killed in action at Bull Run, VA, July 21, 1861.

Peckham, James H. Sgt. Co. A. Residence, Providence. Died of disease at Washington, D.C., July 24, 1861. Interred at North Burial Ground, Providence, RI.

Peckham, John P. Pvt. Co. F. Residence, Newport. Killed in action at Bull Run, VA, July 21, 1861. Cenotaph at Island Cemetery, Newport, RI.

The son of a wealthy Newport doctor, Private Theodore Wheaton King of Company F, First Rhode Island Detached Militia was severely wounded and captured at Bull Run. Released from prison, he died on his way home to Newport.

Penno, Albert. Pvt. Co. D. Residence, Providence. Mortally wounded in action at Bull Run, VA, July 21, 1861. Died of wounds at Manassas, VA, Aug. 4, 1861.

Prescott, Henry A. 2nd Lt. Co. D. Residence, Providence. Killed in action at Bull Run, VA, July 21, 1861. Cenotaph at Swan Point Cemetery, Providence, RI.

Quirk, Matthew. Pvt. Co. K. Residence, Woonsocket. Killed in action at Bull Run, VA, July 21, 1861.

Randall, Augustus S. Sgt. Co. B. Residence, Johnston. Died of tuberculosis contacted in the service at Johnston, RI, April 24, 1865. Interred at Woodlawn Cemetery, Johnston, RI.

Remington, Henry H. Pvt. Co. I. Residence, East Greenwich. Died of typhoid contracted in the service at East Greenwich, RI, Aug. 28, 1861.

Rhodes, Christopher. Pvt. Co. G. Residence, Warwick. Died of disease contracted in the service at Warwick, RI, July 28, 1862. Interred at Pawtuxet Burial Yard, Warwick, RI.

Second Lieutenant Henry A. Prescott of Providence was shot early in the fighting at Bull Run and his remains were never recovered. The first Grand Army of the Republic Post was named in his memory.

Schoker, Herman. Pvt. Co. G. Residence, Providence. Killed in action at Bull Run, VA, July 21, 1861.

Smith, Benedict F. Corp. Co. F. Residence, Newport. Died of disease contracted in the service at Newport, RI, Sept. 19, 1861. Interred at Island Cemetery, Newport, RI.

Tallman, Peleg G. Pvt. Co. D. Residence, Providence. Died of tuberculosis contracted in the service at Cranston, RI, Mar. 21, 1862.

Tillinghast, Henry Lyman. Pvt. Co. A. Residence, Providence. Died of disease contracted in the service at Providence, RI, Feb. 26, 1862. Interred at Swan Point Cemetery, Providence, RI.

White, Andrew J. Pvt. Co. A. Residence, Providence. Mortally wounded in action at Bull Run, VA, July 21, 1861. Captured and died as a prisoner of war at Richmond, VA, Aug. 4, 1861. Cenotaph at North Burial Ground, Providence, RI.

5

Second Rhode Island Volunteers

Aldrich, Robert C. Pvt. Co. C. Residence, Scituate. Died of tuberculosis contracted in the service at Buenos Aires, Argentina, Jan. 5, 1867. Cenotaph at Smithville Cemetery, Scituate, RI.

Aldrich, Wilson W. Pvt. Co. C. Residence, Scituate. Mortally wounded in action at the Wilderness, VA, May 6, 1864. Died of wounds at Washington, D.C., July 7, 1864. Interred at North Burial Ground, Providence, RI.

Alger, Matthew. Pvt. Co. C. Residence, Providence. Mortally wounded in action, shot in foot at Salem's Church, VA, May 3, 1863. Died of wounds at Washington, D.C., May 14, 1863. Interred at North Burial Ground, Providence, RI.

Allen, George M. Pvt. Co. B. Residence, Providence. Died of disease at New York, NY, Sept. 4, 1862. Interred at Cypress Hills National Cemetery, Brooklyn, NY. Grave 391.

Andrews, Asa. Pvt. Co. H. Residence, Providence. Mortally wounded in action at Fredericksburg, Dec. 13, 1862. Died of wounds at Portsmouth Grove Hospital, Portsmouth, RI, Mar. 31, 1863. Interred at Rockland Cemetery, Scituate, RI.

Andrews, John T. Pvt. Co. H. Residence, Warwick. Died of disease contracted in the service at Warwick, RI, Oct. 31, 1867. Interred at Greenwood Cemetery, Coventry, RI.

Angell, Marshall W. Pvt. Co. B. Residence, Scituate. Died of typhoid contracted in the service at Scituate, RI, July 22, 1863. Interred at Smithville Cemetery, Scituate, RI.

Armstrong, James. Pvt. Co. A. Residence, Providence. Mortally wounded in action at Seven Pines, VA, June 25, 1862. Died of wounds at Washington, D.C., July 6, 1862. Interred at Soldier's Home National Cemetery, Washington, D.C. Grave 3496.

Arnold, Leander. Pvt. Co. I. Residence, Woonsocket. Mortally wounded in action at Salem's Church, VA, May 3, 1863. Died of wounds at Falmouth, VA, May 6, 1863. Interred at Westfield Cemetery, Killingly, CT.

Arnold, William. Pvt. Co. B. Residence, Jamestown. Died of disease at New York, NY, July 8, 1864. Interred at Cypress Hills National Cemetery, Brooklyn, NY. Grave 1297.

Atwood, George B. Pvt. Co. B. Residence, Providence. Captured at Bull Run, VA, July 21, 1861. Released. Drowned on passage to New York, NY, aboard *Cossack,* May 29, 1862.

Bagley, Charles E. Sgt. Co. H. Residence, South Kingstown. Killed in action at Bull Run, VA, July 21, 1861.

Bailey, John. Pvt. Co. G. Residence, Providence. Died of disease at New Haven, CT, Feb. 20, 1865. Interred at St. Mary's Cemetery, West Warwick, RI.

Ball, Albert. Pvt. Co. I. Residence, Woonsocket. Died of "disease contracted in the U.S. Service" at Woonsocket, RI, Jan. 20, 1867. Interred at Oak Hill Cemetery, Woonsocket, RI.

Ballou, Sullivan. Maj. Residence, Woonsocket. Mortally wounded in action, legs blown off, at Bull Run, July 21, 1861. Died of wounds at Manassas, VA, July 28, 1861. Interred at Swan Point Cemetery, Providence, RI.

Barker, Thomas H. Corp. Co. I. Residence, Providence. Died of typhoid at New York, NY, July 29, 1862. Interred at Locust Grove Cemetery, Providence, RI.

Bartlett, Reuben. Pvt. Co. D. Residence, North Providence. Killed in action at Bull Run, VA, July 21, 1861.

Barton, Joseph A. Pvt. Co. A. Residence, Bristol. Mortally wounded in action, right arm amputated, at Opequon, VA, Sept. 19, 1864. Died of wounds at Philadelphia, PA, Sept. 27, 1864.

Bates, Clark E. 2nd Lt. Co. I. Residence, Warwick. Mortally wounded in action at Salem's Church, VA, May 3, 1863. Died of wounds at Washington, D.C., July 18, 1863. Interred at Nicholas Bates Lot, Exeter Cemetery 113, Exeter, RI.

Bently, William P. Pvt. Co. A. Residence, Warwick. Killed in action at Seven Pines, VA, June 25, 1862.

Bisher, James. Pvt. Co. C. Residence, Providence. Died of disease at Andersonville Prison, GA, July 29, 1864. Interred at Andersonville National Cemetery.

Blair, John. Corp. Co. C. Residence, Providence. Killed in action at the Wilderness, VA, May 5, 1864.

Blake, Ebenezer J. 1st Sgt. Co. K. Residence, Providence. Died of pneumonia contracted in the service at Providence, RI, Feb. 17, 1865. Interred at Locust Grove Cemetery, Providence, RI.

Blanchard, Henry T. Sgt. Co. K. Residence, Providence. Killed in action at the Wilderness, VA, May 6, 1864. Interred at Swan Point Cemetery, Providence, RI.

Bolles, Lucius S. Asst. Surgeon. Residence, Providence. "A man of delicate constitution, he was hardly fitted to endure the hardships of military service." Died of disease contracted in the service Aug. 15, 1873, at Philadelphia, PA. Interred at Swan Point Cemetery, Providence, RI.

Brady, Francis. Pvt. Co. B. Residence, Providence. Killed in action at the Wilderness, VA, May 6, 1864.

Brayton, Gardner. Pvt. Co. G. Residence, Portsmouth. Died of typhoid at Washington, D.C., Aug. 19, 1861. Interred at Pleasant View Cemetery, Tiverton, RI.

Brennan, John J. Pvt. Co. C. Residence, Providence. Killed in action at Salem's Church, VA, May 3, 1863.

Burke, John. Pvt. Co. A. Residence, Providence. Mortally wounded in action at Sailor's Creek, VA, April 6, 1864. Died of wounds at Annapolis, MD, April 30, 1865. Interred at Annapolis National Cemetery, Annapolis, MD. Grave 640.

Burns, William B. Pvt. Co. G. Residence, Bristol. Died of disease at Philadelphia, PA, Mar. 1, 1863.

Bush, Henry F. Corp. Co. G. Residence, Bristol. Mortally wounded in action at the Wilderness, VA, May 5, 1864. Died of wounds at Bristol, RI, Sept. 15, 1866. Interred at North Burial Ground, Bristol, RI.

Butler, James D. Pvt. Co. H. Residence, Providence. Died of typhoid at Washington, D.C., June 3, 1865. Interred at Arlington National Cemetery, Arlington, VA. Grave 10818.

Calligan, James. Pvt. Co. A. Residence, Providence. Died of disease at Andersonville Prison, GA, July 22, 1864. Interred at Andersonville National Cemetery.

Card, Peleg W. Pvt. Co. H. Residence, Coventry. Killed in action at Bull Run, VA, July 21, 1861. Cenotaph at Pine Grove Cemetery, Coventry, RI.

Carpenter, Thomas O.H. Corp. Co. C. Residence, Providence. Killed in action at Bull Run, VA, July 21, 1861.

Carr, Thomas H. 1st Lt. Co. H. Residence, Providence. Died of disease at Providence, RI, Jan. 2, 1863. Interred at North Burial Ground, Providence, RI.

Carroll, Patrick. Corp. Co. C. Residence, Smithfield. Mortally wounded in action at Sailor's Creek, VA, April 6, 1865. Died of wounds at Annapolis, MD, April 16, 1865.

Chamberlain, Bradford. 1st Sgt. Co. I. Residence, Glocester. Killed in action at Spotsylvania Court House, VA, May 12, 1864. Interred at Fredericksburg National Cemetery, Fredericksburg, VA. Grave 503. Cenotaph in Coman Lot, Glocester Cemetery 48, Glocester, RI.

Clark, James. Pvt. Co. C. Residence, Providence. Died of disease near Mine Run, VA, Nov. 20, 1863.

Clark, John. Pvt. Co. E. Residence, North Providence. Killed in action at the Wilderness, VA, May 6, 1864.

Cobb, Isaac N. Pvt. Co. G. Residence, Bristol. Mortally wounded in action at Bull Run, VA, July 21, 1861. Captured. Died of wounds at Richmond, VA, Aug. 12, 1861. Cenotaph at North Burial Ground, Providence, RI.

Cole, Alfred C. Pvt. Residence, Providence. Killed in action at Cold Harbor, VA, June 5, 1864. Interred at Cold Harbor National Cemetery, Mechanicsville, VA. Grave 259.

Cole, Henry J. Sgt. Co. G. Residence, Bristol. Killed in action at Seven Pines, VA, June 25, 1862. Interred at South Burial Ground, Warren, RI.

Cooper, Thomas. Pvt. Co. F. Residence, Pawtucket. Died of a "skull fracture" at Williamsport, MD, Oct. 27, 1862.

Coyle, James H. Sgt. Co. A. Residence, Coventry. Mortally wounded in action at Sailor's Creek, VA, April 6, 1865. Died of wounds at Washington, D.C., May 2, 1865. Interred at St. Mary's Cemetery, West Warwick, RI.

Crocker, Charles E. Pvt. Co. A. Residence, Providence. Captured Nov. 6, 1863. Died of disease at Andersonville Prison, GA, Sept. 26, 1864. Interred at Andersonville National Cemetery, GA. Grave 9814.

Crocker, Joel F. Sgt. Co. G. Residence, Woonsocket. Died of disease contracted in the service at Woonsocket, RI, July 19, 1866. Interred at Oak Grove Cemetery, Woonsocket, RI.

Davis, Albert F. Corp. Co. I. Residence, Glocester. Died of typhoid at Chester, PA, Aug. 20, 1862. Interred at Acotes Hill Cemetery, Glocester, RI.

Davis, Henry M. Pvt. Co. B. Residence, Scituate. Died of typhoid at Falmouth, VA, April 6, 1863.

Dean, John E. Pvt. Co. D. Residence, Providence. Killed in action at Spotsylvania Court House, VA, May 12, 1864. Cenotaph at Grove Cemetery, Belfast, ME.

Degnan, Thomas. Pvt. Co. B. Residence, Johnston. Died of disease at New York, NY, June 15, 1864. Interred at St. Patrick's Cemetery, Providence, RI.

Dewhurst, James W. Pvt. Co. E. Residence, Providence. Killed in action at Sailor's Creek, VA, April 6, 1865.

Donovan, John. Pvt. Co. I. Residence, Providence. Killed in action at Salem's Church, VA, May 3, 1863.

Dugan, James. Pvt. Co. D. Residence, Providence. Killed in action at Spotsylvania Court House, VA, May 12, 1864. Interred at St. Francis Cemetery, South Kingstown, RI.

Durfee, Nathan S. Pvt. Co. C. Residence, Glocester. Died of disease contracted in the service at Glocester, RI, Oct. 6, 1866. Interred at Acotes Hill Cemetery, Glocester, RI.

Earle, John. Pvt. Co. H. Residence, Providence. Died of disease at New Haven, CT, Mar. 6, 1865.

Ehlert, Ludwig. Pvt. Co. G. Residence, Providence. Killed in action at the Wilderness, VA, May 5, 1864.

Fales, Thomas H.B. Corp. Co. K. Residence, Providence. Killed in action at Salem's Church, VA, May 3, 1863.

Farrell, John. Pvt. Co. F. Residence, Providence. Mortally wounded in action, right leg amputated, at Spotsylvania Court House, VA, May 12, 1864. Died of wounds at Washington, D.C., June 6, 1864.

Fay, Michael. Pvt. Co. G. Residence, Providence. Died of disease at Downsville, MD, Sept. 27, 1862. Interred at Antietam National Cemetery, Sharpsburg, MD. Rhode Island Section. Grave 2840.

Feaghey, John. Pvt. Co. G. Residence, Providence. Died at Andersonville Prison, GA, Aug. 4, 1864. Interred at Andersonville National Cemetery.

Ford, John. Corp. Co. I. Residence, Woonsocket. Killed in action at Bull Run, VA, July 21, 1861.

Franklin, Augustus B. Pvt. Co. F. Residence, Swansea, MA. Died of disease contracted in the service at Swansea, MA, Dec. 15, 1864. Interred at Thomas Cemetery, Swansea, MA.

Galligan, James. Pvt. Co. F. Residence, Providence. Mortally wounded in action at Salem's Church, VA, May 3, 1863. Captured and Paroled. Died of wounds at Annapolis, MD, May 16, 1863.

Gibson, Daniel. Pvt. Co. F. Residence, Providence. Died of typhoid at Arlington, VA, June 30, 1865. Interred at Arlington National Cemetery, Arlington, VA. Section 13, Grave 12223.

Glancy, James T. Corp. Co. F. Residence, Providence. Mortally wounded in action at Petersburg, VA, April 2, 1865. Died of wounds at Petersburg, VA, April 3, 1865. Interred at Poplar Grove National Cemetery, Petersburg, VA. Grave 1423.

Gleason, Charles W. Capt. Co. G. Residence, Coventry. Killed in action at Sailor's Creek, VA, April 6, 1865. Interred at Greenwood Cemetery, Coventry, RI.

Goldsmith, Tobias A. Corp. Co. B. Residence, Providence. Killed in action at Salem's Church, VA, May 3, 1863.

Grant, Richard M. Pvt. Co. C. Residence, Providence. Killed in action at the Wilderness, VA, May 5, 1864.

Graves, Samuel W. Pvt. Co. K. Residence, Warwick. Killed in action at Spotsylvania Court House, VA, May 12, 1864. Interred at Brayton Cemetery, Warwick, RI.

Greene, Daniel. Pvt. Co. H. Residence, Warwick. Captured at Spotsylvania

Court House, VA, May 21, 1864. Died of dysentery at Andersonville Prison, GA, Sept. 28, 1864. Interred at Andersonville National Cemetery. Grave 9978.

Greene, Francis C. Corp. Co. H. Residence, Warwick. Died of tuberculosis contracted in the service at Warwick, RI, Dec. 27, 1865. Interred at Swan Point Cemetery, Providence, RI.

Greene, George W. Pvt. Co. I. Residence, Glocester. Killed in action at Spotsylvania Court House, VA, May 18, 1864.

Greene, Henry A. 1st Sgt. Co. I. Residence, Woonsocket. Killed in action at Salem's Church, VA, May 3, 1863. Interred at Oak Hill Cemetery, Woonsocket, RI.

Greene, Richard. Pvt. Co. B. Residence, Johnston. Died of disease at Andersonville Prison, GA, Sept. 10, 1864. Interred at Andersonville National Cemetery. Grave 8308.

Greene, William. Pvt. Co. B. Residence, Scituate. Mortally wounded in action at Spotsylvania Court House, VA, May 12, 1864. Died of wounds at Washington, D.C., May 27, 1864. Interred at Arlington National Cemetery, Arlington, VA. Section 27. Grave 257.

Grey, Willis P. Pvt. Co. E. Residence, Providence. Died of typhoid at City Point, VA, April 27, 1865. Interred at City Point National Cemetery, Hopewell, VA. Section E. Grave 561.

Grinnell, John G. Pvt. Co. B. Residence, South Kingstown. Mortally wounded in action at Opequon, VA, Sept. 19, 1864. Died of wounds at Winchester, VA, Oct. 5, 1864. Interred at Winchester National Cemetery, Winchester, VA. Grave 3588.

Haile, Charles. Corp. Co. G. Residence, Bristol. Killed in action at the Wilderness, VA, May 5, 1864.

Hall, Bernard M. Principal Mus. Residence, South Kingstown. Died of tuberculosis contracted in the service at Cranston, RI, Dec. 8, 1865. Interred at Hall-Carpenter Lot, North Kingstown Cemetery 18, North Kingstown, RI.

Hall, John C. Sgt. Co. F. Residence, Smithfield. Died of typhoid at Falmouth, VA, Mar. 16, 1863. Interred at Fredericksburg National Cemetery, Fredericksburg, VA. Grave 5386.

Heavey, Patrick. Pvt. Co. H. Residence, Providence. Died of disease at Warrenton, VA, Dec. 6, 1863.

Hennessey, Thomas. Pvt. Co. H. Residence, East Greenwich. Died of typhoid at Washington, D.C., Feb. 5, 1862.

Hines, Albert. Pvt. Co. G. Residence, North Kingstown. Killed in action at Spotsylvania Court House, VA, May 12, 1864.

Holland, Stephen. Corp. Co. E. Residence, South Kingstown. Killed in action at Bull Run, VA, July 21, 1861. Cenotaph at Holland Lot, South Kingstown Cemetery 60, South Kingstown, RI.

Hunt, Job. Pvt. Co. E. Residence, North Kingstown. Died of disease at Hagerstown, MD, Nov. 1, 1862.

Hunt, John W. Corp. Co. K. Residence, East Greenwich. Died of disease at Falmouth, VA, April 11, 1863. Interred at Hunt Cemetery, North Kingstown Cemetery 10, North Kingstown, RI.

Hunter, Albert B. Pvt. Co. B. Died of typhoid at Harrison's Landing, VA, Aug. 8, 1862. Interred at Glendale National Cemetery, Beaver Dam Creek, VA. Grave 84.

Hutchinson, George B. Corp. Co. I. Residence, Smithfield. Died of disease contracted in the service at Pawtucket, RI, Aug. 15, 1862. Interred at Slatersville Cemetery, North Smithfield, RI.

Ingraham, George S. Pvt. Co. G. Residence, Bristol. Died of disease contracted in the service at Bristol, RI, Dec. 15, 1869. Interred at North Burial Ground, Bristol, RI.

Island, Patrick. Pvt. Co. K. Residence, Smithfield. Died of typhoid at Washington, D.C., May 21, 1862. Interred at Soldier's Home National Cemetery, Washington, D.C. Section B, Grave 2098.

Jacques, Henry L. Pvt. Co. E. Residence, South Kingstown. Mortally wounded in action at Bull Run, VA, July 21, 1861. Captured. Died of wounds at Richmond, VA, Aug. 12, 1861.

Jeanneret, Numa. Pvt. Co. B. Residence, Providence. Died of disease at Andersonville, GA, Sept. 20, 1864. Interred at Andersonville National Cemetery.

Johnson, James G. Pvt. Co. H. Residence, Coventry. Died of disease at Point Lookout, MD, Aug. 13, 1862. Interred at Arlington National Cemetery, Arlington, VA.

Jordan, James B. Pvt. Co. A. Residence, Warwick. Killed in action at Seven Pines, VA, June 25, 1862.

Jordan, William. Pvt. Co. D. Residence, Providence. Died of disease at

Like many Rhode Island soldiers, Private Patrick Island of Smithfield, who served in Company K of the Second Rhode Island, died of typhoid.

Baltimore, MD, Feb. 10, 1865. Interred at Loudoun Park National Cemetery, Baltimore, MD. Section A, Grave 1086.

Keating, Frank. Sgt. Co. G. Residence, Bristol. Killed in action at the Wilderness, VA, May 6, 1864. Cenotaph at North Burial Ground, Bristol, RI.

Kelley, James. Pvt. Co. C. Residence, Providence. Mortally wounded in action at Salem's Church, VA, May 3, 1863. Died of wounds at Washington, D.C., May 9, 1863.

Kelley, Thomas J. Corp. Co. I. Residence, Woonsocket. Killed in action at Bull Run, VA, July 21, 1861.

Kent, Caleb B. Sgt. Co. C. Residence, Providence. Mortally wounded in action near Funkstown, MD, July 12, 1863. Died of wounds at Frederick, MD, July 25, 1863. Interred at Antietam National Cemetery, Sharpsburg, MD. Rhode Island Section, Grave 2884.

King, James A. Sgt. Co. C. Residence, Warwick. Died of tuberculosis at Philadelphia, PA, May 15, 1865. Interred at Philadelphia National Cemetery, Philadelphia, PA. Section D, Grave 45.

Laney, John. Pvt. Co. F. Residence, Providence. Died of disease contracted in the service at Providence, RI, May 31, 1865. Interred at North Burial Ground, Providence, RI.

Lawless, James. 1st Lt. Co. C. Residence, Providence. Died of disease contracted in the service at Providence, RI, Dec. 15, 1865. Interred at St. Patrick's Cemetery, Providence, RI.

Lawton, Ambrose W. Pvt. Co. A. Residence, Warwick. Killed in action at Spotsylvania Court House, VA, May 12, 1864. Interred at Natick Cemetery, West Warwick, RI.

Lawton, Henry C. Pvt. Co. A. Residence, Scituate. Died of disease at Falmouth, VA, April 7, 1863.

Lawton, John T. Pvt. Co. A. Residence, Scituate. Died of typhoid at Harpers Ferry, WV, Nov. 12, 1863.

Leach, Leander W. Pvt. Co. E. Residence, Cranston. Died of disease contracted in the service Dec. 25, 1865 at Cranston, RI. Interred at Nathan Thornton Lot, Cranston Cemetery 24, Cranston, RI.

Lewis, James E. Pvt. Co. H. Residence, Providence. Killed in action at the Wilderness, VA, May 6, 1864.

Lewis, Thomas. Pvt. Co. C. Residence, Smithfield. Mortally wounded in action at Opequon, VA, Sept. 19, 1864. Died of wounds at Winchester, VA, Sept. 20, 1864.

Littlefield, William D. Pvt. Co. B. Residence, Scituate. Killed in action at Salem's Church, VA, May 3, 1863. Interred at Fredericksburg National Cemetery, Fredericksburg, VA. Grave 1465. Cenotaph at Glenford Cemetery, Scituate, RI.

Luther, Jeremiah. Pvt. Co. G. Residence, Bristol. Died of disease near Yorktown, VA, April 18, 1862. Interred at North Burial Ground, Bristol, RI.

Malcom, Hugh. Pvt. Co. A. Residence, Cranston. Killed in a railroad accident en route to Washington, D.C., Sept. 13, 1862.

Marland, Henry. Pvt. Co. G. Residence, Bristol. Killed in action at the Wilderness, VA, May 5, 1864. Interred at North Burial Ground, Bristol, RI.

Mansell, James. Corp. Co. E. Residence, Johnston. Killed in action at Sailor's Creek, VA, April 6, 1865.

Marsden, George. Pvt. Co. A. Residence, Providence. Killed in action at Spotsylvania Court House, VA, May 12, 1864.

Martin, James. Pvt. Co. I. Residence, Cumberland. Mortally wounded in action at Spotsylvania Court House, VA, May 12, 1864. Died of wounds at field hospital near Spotsylvania, VA, May 15, 1864. Interred at Brayton Cemetery, Warwick, RI.

Martin, Michael. Corp. Co. D. Died of tuberculosis contracted in the service at Providence, RI, Feb. 20, 1866. Interred at North Burial Ground, Providence, RI.

Matteson, Harrison G. Pvt. Co. A. Residence, Scituate. Killed in action at Spotsylvania Court House, VA, May 12, 1864. Interred at Matteson Lot, Coventry Cemetery 45, Coventry, RI.

Matteson, Stillman T. Corp. Co. A. Residence, Scituate. Died of typhoid at New York, NY, June 30, 1862. Interred at Matteson Lot, Coventry Cemetery 45, Coventry, RI.

Maxfield, George H. Pvt. Co. E. Residence, Bristol. Killed in action at the Wilderness, VA, May 5, 1864.

McCabe, James. Pvt. Co. C. Residence, Providence. Died of typhoid at Brandy Station, VA, Nov. 12, 1863. Interred at St. Patrick's Cemetery, Providence, RI.

McCabe, John. Pvt. Co. F. Residence, Providence. Killed in action at Sailor's Creek, VA, April 6, 1865.

McCann, William. Pvt. Co. K. Residence, Newport. Killed in action at Bull Run, VA, July 21, 1861.

McCoole, Patrick. Pvt. Co. B. Residence, Providence. Killed in action at Salem's Church, VA, May 3, 1863.

McElroy, John. Pvt. Co. D. Residence, Providence. Killed in action at Sailor's Creek, VA, April 6, 1865. Interred at Poplar Grove National Cemetery, Petersburg, VA. Grave 5264.

McGregor, John. Pvt. Co. G. Residence, Providence. Died of dysentery contracted in the service at Providence, RI, Mar. 1, 1863.

McIntyre, Joseph. Capt. Co. E. Residence, Providence. Killed in action at the Wilderness, VA, May 5, 1864. Interred at Swan Point Cemetery, Providence, RI.

McKay, Thomas. Pvt. Co. F. Residence, Providence. Died of disease at Andersonville Prison, GA, Aug. 31, 1864. Interred at Andersonville National Cemetery. Grave 7393.

McLane, Andrew. Pvt. Co. C. Residence, Scituate. Killed in action at Salem's Church, VA, May 3, 1863.

Medbury, William H. Pvt. Co. B. Residence, Foster. Captured at Harrison's Landing, VA, July 2, 1862. Died of scurvy as a prisoner of war at Richmond, VA, Aug. 23, 1862. Interred at Glenford Cemetery, Scituate, RI.

Mills, Alexander. Corp. Co. E. Residence, Warwick. Killed in action at Petersburg, VA, April 2, 1865.

Miner, Christopher. Pvt. Co. A. Residence, Warwick. Died of typhoid at Washington, D.C., Nov. 17, 1862. Interred at Soldier's Home National Cemetery, Washington, D.C.

Moon, Sanford E. Sgt. Co. A. Residence, Warwick. Killed in action at Salem's Church, VA, May 3, 1863.

Morse, Edward T. Pvt. Co. K. Residence, Providence. Killed in action at Bull Run, VA, July 21, 1861.

Mowry, Charles F. Pvt. Co. F. Residence, Cranston. Died of typhoid at Washington, D.C., June 13, 1865. Interred at North Burial Ground, Providence, RI.

Mowry, Daniel. Pvt. Co. K. Residence, Providence. Died of typhoid at Washington, D.C., Dec. 18, 1862.

Mullen, Patrick J. Pvt. Co. K. Residence, Providence. Killed in action at Bull Run, VA, July 21, 1861.

Murphy, Patrick J. Pvt. Co. C. Residence, Scituate. Killed in action at the Wilderness, VA, May 5, 1864.

Newman, Daniel A. Pvt. Co. K. Died of typhoid at Yorktown, VA, May 14, 1862. Interred at Yorktown National Cemetery, Yorktown, VA. Grave 1563.

Newman, Simeon A. 1st Sgt. Co. G. Residence, Bristol. Died of disease at Washington, D.C., Mar. 18, 1862. Interred at North Burial Ground, Providence, RI.

Nichols, James C. 1st Sgt. Co. B. Residence, Scituate. Killed in action at Salem's Church, VA, May 3, 1863.

Nichols, William H. Pvt. Co. E. Residence, South Kingstown. Killed in action at Bull Run, VA, July 21, 1861.

Nicholson, John C. Pvt. Co. K. Residence, Newport. Killed in action at Bull Run, VA, July 21, 1861.

Peck, Noah A. Sgt. Co. D. Residence, Barrington. Mortally wounded in action, leg amputated, at Salem's Church, VA, May 3, 1863. Died of wounds Washington, D.C., June 2, 1863. Interred at Prince's Hill Burial Ground, Barrington, RI.

Perry, Samuel T. Corp. Co. K. Residence, South Kingstown. Killed in action at Spotsylvania Court House, VA, May 12, 1864. Interred at Quaker Cemetery, South Kingstown, RI.

Perry, William H. 1st Lt. Co. F. Residence, Pawtucket. Killed in action at Sailor's Creek, VA, April 6, 1865. Interred in Unknown Grave, Poplar Grove National Cemetery, Petersburg, VA.

Phillips, Joseph A. Pvt. Co. I. Residence, Smithfield. Killed in action at Spotsylvania Court House, VA, May 18, 1864.

Pickett, Michael. Pvt. Co. C. Residence, Providence. Died of tuberculosis contracted in the service at Providence, RI, Oct. 25, 1863.

Powers, Charles. Pvt. Co. C. Residence, Providence. Killed in action at Gettysburg, PA, July 3, 1863. Interred at Gettysburg National Cemetery, Gettysburg, PA. Rhode Island Section.

Railton, William. Pvt. Co. E. Residence, Providence. Mortally wounded in action at Sailor's Creek, VA, April 6, 1865. Died of wounds at Washington, D.C., July 6, 1865.

Randall, Isaac C. Pvt. Co. A. Residence, Providence. Died of typhoid at Providence, RI, Mar. 18, 1865. Interred at North Burial Ground, Providence, RI.

Randall, William H. Pvt. Co. K. Residence, Providence. Killed in action at Seven Pines, VA, June 25, 1862. Interred at Seven Pines National Cemetery, Fair Oaks, VA. Grave 1521. Cenotaph at North Burial Ground, Providence, RI.

Records, William H. Pvt. Co. E. Residence, Scituate. Died of typhoid at Falmouth, VA, Mar. 28, 1863. Interred at Fredericksburg National Cemetery, Fredericksburg, VA. Grave 5390.

Reynolds, William E. Pvt. Co. D. Residence, Providence. Died of typhoid

First Sergeant James C. Nichols of Scituate was killed in action at Salem's Church on May 3, 1863. His body was never recovered. After the war, the veterans of Scituate and Foster named the local Grand Army of the Republic Hall in his honor.

at Yorktown, VA, May 11, 1862. Interred at Swan Point Cemetery, Providence, RI.

Rice, Joel E. Corp. Co. A. Residence, Warwick. Killed in action at Salem's Church, VA, May 3, 1863. Cenotaph at Locust Grove Cemetery, Providence, RI.

Rice, John. Corp. Co. G. Residence, Providence. Killed in action at the Wilderness, VA, May 12, 1864.

Riley, John. Pvt. Co. K. Residence, Cumberland. Killed in action at Bull Run, VA, July 21, 1861.

Rodman, Isaac C. Pvt. Co. E. Residence, South Kingstown. Mortally wounded in action at Bull Run, VA, July 21, 1861. Captured. Died of wounds at Richmond, VA, Sept. 26, 1861. Cenotaph at First Cemetery, Hopkinton, RI.

Ronan, Francis T. Corp. Co. F. Residence, Pawtucket. Killed in action at Bull Run, VA, July 21, 1861.

Russell, Samuel. Pvt. Co. F. Residence, Providence. Died of typhoid at Fairfax, VA, June 19, 1865. Interred at Alexandria National Cemetery, Alexandria, VA. Grave 3044.

Salisbury, Ferdinand A. Pvt. Co. F. Residence, Pawtucket. Died of disease contracted in the service at Pawtucket, RI, Jan. 28, 1868. Interred at Mineral Spring Cemetery, Pawtucket, RI.

Salisbury, Smith. Pvt. Co. F. Residence, Pawtucket. Died of disease contracted in the service at Pawtucket, RI, May 25, 1867. Interred at Mineral Spring Cemetery, Pawtucket, RI.

Seamans, James. 1st Sgt. Co. E. Residence, Providence. Killed in action at Sailor's Creek, VA, April 6, 1865.

Shane, Robert. Pvt. Co. K. Residence, Newport. Killed in action at Seven Pines, VA, June 25, 1862.

Shaw, John P. Capt. Co. K. Residence, Providence. Killed in action at Spotsylvania Court House, VA, May 12, 1864. Interred at North Burial Ground, Providence, RI.

Shaw, Leander R. Pvt. Co. D. Residence, Providence. Killed in action at Bull Run, VA, July 21, 1861. Cenotaph at North Burial Ground, Providence, RI.

Shaw, Stephen A. Corp. Co. F. Residence, Providence. Died of typhoid at

Captain John P. Shaw of Providence commanded Company K, Second Rhode Island Volunteers. He was killed in action May 12, 1864, at Spotsylvania Court House, Virginia. Library of Congress.

Baltimore, MD, May 1, 1865. Interred at Loudoun Park National Cemetery, Baltimore, MD. Section A, Grave 1009. Cenotaph at Swan Point Cemetery, Providence, RI.

Sheldon, Walter M. Pvt. Co. K. Residence, Providence. Killed in action at Bull Run, VA, July 21, 1861. Cenotaph at Swan Point Cemetery, Providence, RI.

Sherman, Benjamin W. Pvt. Co. H. Residence, Coventry. Killed in action at the Wilderness, VA, May 6, 1864.

Sherman, Edwin K. Capt. Co. K. Residence, Providence. Died of typhoid at New York, NY, July 15, 1862. Interred at Swan Point Cemetery, Providence, RI.

Simmons, Edward A. Pvt. Co. G. Residence, Smithfield. Killed in action at Salem's Church, VA, May 3, 1863. Interred at Knight Hill Cemetery, Scituate, RI.

Slocum, Henry. Pvt. Co. G. Residence, Warwick. Died of disease at New Haven, CT, Feb. 4, 1865.

Slocum, John H. Pvt. Co. E. Residence, Richmond. Killed in action at Spotsylvania Court House, VA, May 12, 1864. Cenotaph at Wood River Cemetery, Richmond, RI.

Slocum, John Stanton. Col. Residence, Providence. Mortally wounded in action, shot in head, at Bull Run, VA, July 21, 1861. Died of wounds at Manassas, VA, July 23, 1861. Interred at Swan Point Cemetery, Providence, RI.

Smith, Anson G. Pvt. Co. K. Residence, Newport. Killed in action at Cold Harbor, VA, June 3, 1864. Interred at Cold Harbor National Cemetery, Mechanicsville, VA. Grave 620.

Smith, Esek B. Corp. Co. E. Residence, South Kingstown. Mortally wounded in action at Bull Run, VA, July 21, 1861. Captured. Died of wounds at Richmond, VA, Aug. 6, 1861. Cenotaph at Oak Dell Cemetery, South Kingstown, RI.

Smith, George H. Pvt. Co. D. Residence, Providence. Mor-

Colonel John Stanton Slocum was mortally wounded at Bull Run and died two days later. His last words, "now show them what Rhode Island can do," became a rallying call for Rhode Islanders throughout the war.

tally wounded in action at Cold Harbor, VA, June 3, 1864. Died of wounds at Washington, D.C., June 10, 1864. Interred at Locust Grove Cemetery, Providence, RI.

Smith, James. Pvt. Co. G. Residence, Providence. Killed in action at Petersburg, VA, April 2, 1865. Interred at Poplar Grove National Cemetery, Petersburg, VA. Grave 32.

Smith, Samuel J. Capt. Co. I. Residence, Woonsocket. Killed in action at Bull Run, VA, July 21, 1861. Cenotaph at Swan Point Cemetery, Providence, RI.

Smith, Thorndike J. Adjutant. Residence, Glocester. Mortally wounded in action at Petersburg, VA, June 18, 1864. Died of wounds at Webster, MA, June 18, 1869. Interred at Latham Lot, Smithfield Cemetery 41, Smithfield, RI.

Spencer, John. Pvt. Co. A. Residence, Warwick. Died of typhoid at New York, NY, June 28, 1862. Interred at Spencer Lot, East Greenwich Cemetery 9, East Greenwich, RI.

Spencer, Richard A. Pvt. Co. H. Residence, East Greenwich. Died of meningitis at New Haven, CT, Feb. 19, 1865. Interred at Spencer Lot, East Greenwich Cemetery 9, East Greenwich, RI.

Stanley, James E. Sgt. Co. E. Residence, Providence. Mortally wounded in action at Salem's Church, VA, May 3, 1863. Died of wounds at Washington, D.C., May 22, 1863. Interred at Mineral Spring Cemetery, Pawtucket, RI.

Steere, James F. Pvt. Co. C. Residence, Smithfield. Died of disease at Washington, D.C., May 5, 1862.

Stetson, Albert. Pvt. Co. D. Residence, Providence. Killed in action at Bull Run, VA, July 21, 1861.

Stone, Albert H. Pvt. Co. I. Residence, Scituate. Died of typhoid at Portsmouth Grove Hospital, Portsmouth, RI, July 15, 1862. Interred at Glenford Cemetery, Scituate, RI.

Strange, Henry A. Pvt. Co. F. Residence, Pawtucket. Died of typhoid at Petersburg, VA, Feb. 24, 1865. Interred at North Burial Ground, Providence, RI.

Sullivan, Timothy. Pvt. Co. G. Residence, Providence. Died of disease at City Point, VA, April 23, 1865. Interred at City Point National Cemetery, Hopewell, VA. Grave 114.

Swain, Frederick W. Pvt. Co. D. Residence, Providence. Mortally wounded in action at the Wilderness, VA, May 6, 1864. Died of wounds at Washington, D.C., May 15, 1864.

Sweet, Samuel P. Pvt. Co. H. Residence, Coventry. Died of typhoid at Washington, D.C., Sept. 6, 1861. Interred at Manchester Cemetery, Coventry, RI.

Taft, Henry L. Sgt. Co. C. Residence, Smithfield. Mortally wounded in action at Salem's Church, VA, May 3, 1863. Died of wounds at Washington, D.C., May 11, 1863. Interred at North Burial Ground, Providence, RI.

Tanner, Job. Corp. Co. B. Residence, Providence. Mortally wounded in action at the Wilderness, VA, May 6, 1864. Died of wounds at Washington, D.C., July 14, 1864. Interred at Arlington National Cemetery, Arlington, VA. Section 13, Grave 6335.

Tarbox, Benjamin. Pvt. Co. G. Residence, East Greenwich. Died of disease at New Haven, CT, Mar. 3, 1865. Interred at Rodman Vaughn Lot, East Greenwich Cemetery 94, East Greenwich, RI.

Tayer, Henry C. Pvt. Co. I. Residence, Smithfield. Died of tuberculosis contracted in the service at Smithfield, RI, Nov. 18, 1863. Interred at Mineral Spring Cemetery, Pawtucket, RI.

Taylor, James. Sgt. Co. K. Residence, Newport. Killed in action at Spotsylvania Court House, VA, May 12, 1864.

Taylor, John H. Pvt. Co. C. Residence, Providence. Died of typhoid at Warwick Court House, VA, April 17, 1862. Interred at Yorktown National Cemetery, Yorktown, VA. Grave 138. Cenotaph at Moshassuck Cemetery, Central Falls, RI.

Thurber, Darius N. Pvt. Co. G. Residence, Providence. Died of disease at Brandy Station, VA, April 30, 1864. Interred at Locust Grove Cemetery, Providence, RI.

Tibbetts, Henry C. Pvt. Co. D. Residence, Providence. Killed in action at Cold Harbor, VA, June 5, 1864. Interred at Cold Harbor National Cemetery, Mechanicsville, VA. Grave 118.

Tourgee, Alonzo. Pvt. Co. A. Residence, Warwick. Killed in action at Spotsylvania Court House, VA, May 8, 1864. Interred at Fredericksburg National Cemetery, Fredericksburg, VA. Grave 4775. Cenotaph at Brayton Cemetery, Warwick, RI.

Tower, Levi. Capt. Co. F. Residence, Providence. Killed in action at Bull Run, VA, July 21, 1861. Interred at Mineral Spring Cemetery, Pawtucket, RI.

Toye, Robert. Corp. Co. G. Residence, Bristol. Killed in action at Salem's Church, VA, May 3, 1863. Interred at North Burial Ground, Bristol, RI.

Tucker, Charles W. Pvt. Co. G. Residence, Providence. Died of disease at New Haven, CT, Feb. 1, 1865. Interred at Evergreen Cemetery, New Haven, CT.

Tupper, Charles R. Pvt. Co. F. Residence, Providence. Mortally wounded in action at Sailor's Creek, VA, April 6, 1865. Died of wounds April 9, 1865.

Vallett, Edward D. Corp. Co. D. Residence, Johnston. Died of typhoid at Petersburg, VA, Jan. 12, 1865. Interred at Poplar Grove National Cemetery, Petersburg, VA. Grave 1446.

Captain Levi Tower of Pawtucket was killed at Bull Run, commanding Company F, Second Rhode Island Volunteers.

Vanderheider, William. Pvt. Co. C. Residence, Providence. Died of typhoid at Washington, D.C., Nov. 23, 1863.

Vatelacerci, Joseph. Pvt. Co. A. Residence, Providence. Died of disease at Washington, D.C., Dec. 27, 1864.

Visser, Paul. Sgt. Co. E. Residence, South Kingstown. Killed in action at the Wilderness, VA, May 6, 1864.

Vose, Charles H. Pvt. Co. I. Residence, Providence. Died of epilepsy at Brandy Station, VA, Dec. 12, 1863.

Wade, James A. Pvt. Co. B. Residence, Providence. Mortally wounded in action at Sailor's Creek, VA, April 6, 1865. Died of wounds at Burkeville, VA, April 8, 1865.

Warner, William D. Pvt. Co. A. Residence, Warwick. Died of tuberculosis contracted in the service at Providence, RI, Sept. 25, 1863. Interred at Locust Grove Cemetery, Providence, RI.

Warren, Wallace F. Pvt. Co. E. Residence, Bristol. Killed in action at the Wilderness, VA, May 5, 1864.

Webb, William C. Sgt. Co. D. Residence, Barrington. Killed in action at the Wilderness, VA, May 6, 1864. Interred at Prince's Hill Burial Ground, Barrington, RI.

Whipple, Ethan. Pvt. Co. B. Residence, Providence. Mortally wounded in action, shot in leg and was amputated, at Petersburg, VA, Mar. 27, 1865. Died of wounds at Washington, D.C., April 5, 1865. Interred at North Burial Ground, Providence, RI.

Wight, Samuel. Sgt. Co. I. Residence, Scituate. Mortally wounded in action at Salem's Church, VA, May 3, 1863. Died of wounds at Washington, D.C., May 15, 1863. Interred at Joseph Thurston Lot, Johnston Cemetery 13, Johnston, RI.

Wilcox, Caleb. Pvt. Co. B. Residence, Providence. Died of disease at Washington, D.C., June 8, 1865.

Wilcox, George W. Pvt. Co. I. Residence, Woonsocket. Killed in an accidental explosion of a shell near Prospect Hill, VA, Mar. 12, 1862.

Wilson, John A. Pvt. Co. H. Residence, Cranston. Killed in action at Cold Harbor, VA, June 1, 1864. Interred at Cold Harbor National Cemetery, Mechanicsville, VA. Grave 567.

Wilson, Lewis B. Corp. Co. A. Residence, Warwick. Killed in action at the Wilderness, VA, May 5, 1864. Cenotaph at Oak Grove Cemetery, Pawtucket, RI.

Winsor, Pitts Smith. Pvt. Co. I. Residence, Scituate. Mortally wounded in action at Salem's Church, VA, May 3, 1863. Died of wounds at Washington, D.C., May 23, 1863. Interred at Smithville Cemetery, Scituate, RI.

6

Third Rhode Island Heavy Artillery

Adams, Samuel. Pvt. Co. D. Residence, Scituate. Died of disease contracted in the service at Scituate, RI, Dec. 4, 1864. Interred at Rockland Cemetery, Scituate, RI.

Alby, Charles. Pvt. Co. M. Residence, Mendon, MA. Killed in action at Morris Island, SC, Aug. 30, 1863.

Angell, Henry S. Corp. Co. L. Residence, Scituate. Died of yellow fever at Hilton Head, SC, Dec. 13, 1862. Interred at Beaufort National Cemetery, Beaufort, SC. Grave 1540.

Arnold, Daniel Lyman. Pvt. Co. B. Residence, Smithfield. Mortally wounded in action at Secessionville, SC, June 16, 1862. Died of wounds at James Island, SC, June 24, 1862. Interred at Swan Point Cemetery, Providence, RI.

Aylesworth, Isaiah. Pvt. Co. A. Residence, Providence. Died of disease contracted in the service at Providence, RI, Aug. 26, 1866. Interred at Locust Grove Cemetery, Providence, RI.

Barber, James D. Residence, Warwick. Died of apoplexy at Morris Island, SC, Jan. 10, 1864. Interred at Natick Cemetery, West Warwick, RI.

Bartholomew, Erastus S. 2nd Lt. Co. E. Residence, Woonsocket. Mortally wounded in action at Secessionville, SC, June 16, 1862. Died of wounds at James Island, SC, June 17, 1862. Interred at Wyoming Cemetery, Wyoming, NY.

Blair, William. Pvt. Co. I. Residence, Fitchburg, MA. Died of disease at Hilton Head, SC, Aug. 25, 1862. Interred at Beaufort National Cemetery, Beaufort, SC. Grave 1580.

Bogman, J. Nelson. Corp. Co. M. Residence, Brookline, MA. Killed in action at Pocotaligo, SC, Oct. 25, 1862. Interred at Swan Point Cemetery, Providence, RI.

Brayton, Benjamin F. Pvt. Co. C. Residence, Tiverton. Died of typhoid at Hilton Head, SC, July 14, 1862. Interred at Beaufort National Cemetery, Beaufort, SC. Grave 1579.

Briggs, Daniel B. Pvt. Co. M. Residence, Foster. Died of typhoid at Hilton Head, SC, May 19, 1862. Interred at Beaufort National Cemetery, Beaufort, SC. Grave 1581.

Brophy, William. Pvt. Co. I. Residence, Providence. Mortally wounded in action at Secessionville, SC, June 16, 1862. Died of wounds at James Island, SC, June 17, 1862.

Brown, George. Pvt. Co. A. Residence, Johnston. Died of typhoid at Hilton Head, SC, May 15, 1862. Interred at Hilton Head National Cemetery, Beaufort, SC. Grave 2488.

Brown, Nathaniel W. Col. Residence, Providence. Died of yellow fever at Hilton Head, SC, Oct. 30, 1862. Interred at North Burial Ground, Providence, RI.

Brown, William L. Pvt. Co. A. Residence, Huntington, MA. Died of tuberculosis contracted in the service at Huntington, MA, April 7, 1864. Interred at Norwich Bridge Cemetery, Huntington, MA.

Bullock, John S. Pvt. Co. D. Residence, Bristol. Died of disease at Hilton Head, SC. Jan. 19, 1862. Interred at Beaufort National Cemetery, Beaufort, SC. Grave 1577.

Burdick, Franklin E. Pvt. Co. A. Residence, Hopkinton. Died of disease at Hilton Head, SC, May 10, 1862.

Burke, Patrick. Pvt. Co. I. Residence, Providence. Died of disease at Hilton Head, SC, Aug. 28, 1862. Interred at Beaufort National Cemetery, Beaufort, SC. Grave 1586.

Left: Second Lieutenant Erastus S. Bartholomew of Woonsocket was killed at the Battle of Secessionville on June 16, 1862. Right: Colonel Nathaniel W. Brown of Providence died of yellow fever at Hilton Head, South Carolina.

Burns, Michael. Pvt. Co. F. Residence, Warwick. Died of typhoid at Beaufort, SC, July 17, 1863.

Burroughs, William. Pvt. Co. F. Residence, Warwick. Mortally wounded in action at Secessionville, SC, June 16, 1862. Died of wounds at Hilton Head, SC, Aug. 10, 1862. Interred at Beaufort National Cemetery, Beaufort, SC. Grave 1599.

Callahan, James. Pvt. Co A. Residence, Providence. Killed in action at Secessionville, SC, June 16, 1862.

Campbell, Thomas. Pvt. Co. H. Residence, Pawtucket. Killed in action at Fort Pulaski, GA, April 11, 1862.

Carpenter, George. 1st Lt. Co. D. Residence, East Providence. Died of disease at Hilton Head, SC, June 28, 1862.

Carpenter, John J., Jr. Sgt. Co. A. Residence, Providence. Died of disease at Port Royal, SC, Sept. 22, 1862.

Carroll, Frank. Pvt. Co. K. Residence, Providence. Mortally wounded in action at Secessionville, SC, June 16, 1862. Died of wounds at Hilton Head, SC, June 29, 1862. Interred at Beaufort National Cemetery, Beaufort, SC. Grave 1596.

Carroll, Henry. Pvt. Co. I. Residence, Tiverton. Died of disease at Hilton Head, SC, Nov. 30, 1861. Interred at Beaufort National Cemetery, Beaufort, SC. Grave 1583.

Case, Nathaniel M. Pvt. Co. B. Residence, South Kingstown. Killed in action at Morris Island, SC, Oct. 19, 1864.

Cavanaugh, John. Mus. Co. A Residence, Providence. Died of disease at Hilton Head, SC, April 11, 1862.

Chace, Benjamin. Pvt. Co. D. Residence, Cumberland. Died of heart disease at Hilton Head, SC, Mar. 25, 1862. Interred at Oak Grove Cemetery, Fall River, MA.

Chaffee, Willard. Pvt. Co. E. Residence, Rehoboth, MA. Killed in action at Secessionville, SC, June 16, 1862.

Cody, William. Corp. Co. K. Residence, Pawtucket. Killed in action at Secessionville, SC, June 16, 1862.

Cole, Ira E. Pvt. Co. E. Residence, Foster. Died of dysentery contracted in the service at Foster, RI, Aug. 31, 1865. Interred at Horace Cole Lot, Foster Cemetery 24, Foster, RI.

Conboy, Henry. Pvt. Co. H. Residence, Cumberland. Died of disease at Hilton Head, SC, July 22, 1862. Interred at St. Charles Cemetery, Blackstone, MA.

Connolly, Peter. Pvt. Co. F. Residence, Providence. Killed in action at James Island, SC, July 3, 1864.

Crosby, Daniel. Pvt. Co. B. Residence, Cumberland. Drowned at Hilton Head, SC, July 20, 1864.

Crosby, Elisha H. Pvt. Co. B. Residence, Cumberland. Killed in an accidental explosion at Fort Welles, SC, Aug. 4, 1864. Interred at Beaufort National Cemetery, Beaufort, SC. Grave 1831.

Crowley, James. Pvt. Co. E. Residence, Warwick. Died of disease at sea, aboard the *Argo,* Aug. 19, 1864.

Damon, George D. Corp. Co. H. Residence, Providence. Died of dysentery contracted in the service at Providence, RI, April 5, 1865. Interred at Laurel Hill Cemetery, Fitchburg, MA.

Davis, William. Pvt. Co. B. Residence, Smithfield. Mortally wounded in action at Secessionville, SC, June 16, 1862. Died of wounds at Hilton Head, SC, July 25, 1862. Interred at Beaufort National Cemetery, Beaufort, SC. Grave 1384.

Dexter, George R. Pvt. Co. C. Residence, Scituate. Died "at sea" Dec. 15, 1862. Cenotaph at Dexter Lot, Scituate Cemetery 8, Scituate, RI.

Diggle, Daniel. Pvt. Co. A. Residence, Easton, PA. Died of dysentery at Port Royal, SC, Nov. 20, 1862. Interred at Beaufort National Cemetery, Beaufort, SC. Grave 1581.

Doherty, Thomas. Pvt. Co. B. Residence, Woonsocket. Killed in action at Secessionville, SC, June 16, 1862.

Dunbar, Edward. Pvt. Co. H. Residence, East Providence. Killed in action at Secessionville, SC, June 16, 1862.

Dunn, John. Pvt. Co. A. Residence, Providence. Died of disease at Beaufort, SC, Dec. 1, 1864. Interred at Beaufort National Cemetery, Beaufort, SC. Grave 1568.

Eagan, Robert. Pvt. Co. C. Residence, Providence. Died of heart disease at Petersburg, VA, Feb. 9, 1865. Interred at St. Francis Cemetery, Pawtucket, RI.

Eddy, Warren. Pvt. Co. H. Residence, Scituate. Killed in action at Morris Island, SC, Aug. 18, 1862.

Edwards, George H. Pvt. Co. A. Residence, Glocester. Died of disease contracted in the service at Glocester, RI, Sept. 4, 1865. Interred at Acotes Hill Cemetery, Glocester, RI.

Elwell, Noel. Pvt. Co. D. Residence, Waldo, ME. Died of disease at Hilton Head, SC, June 15, 1862. Interred at Beaufort National Cemetery, Beaufort, SC. Grave 1600.

Esten, Joel. Pvt. Co. F. Residence, Burrillville. Died of disease contracted in the service at Burrillville, RI, Sept. 2, 1864. Interred at Joseph Esten Lot, Burrillville Cemetery 31, Burrillville, RI.

Fallon, John. Pvt. Co. A. Residence, Warwick. Killed in action aboard the *George Washington* in naval engagement off Charleston, SC, April 9, 1863.

Farrar, William. Pvt. Co. B. Residence, Smithfield. Died of disease at Hilton Head, SC, Oct. 11, 1863.

Farrell, Lawrence. Pvt. Co. B. Residence, Providence. Killed in an accidental cannon discharge at Fort Welles, SC, Aug. 16, 1864. Interred at Beaufort National Cemetery, Beaufort, SC. Grave 1558.

Fenney, Michael. Pvt. Co. H. Residence, Providence. Killed in action at Secessionville, SC, June 16, 1862.

Fish, Joseph H. Sgt. Co. M. Residence, Tiverton. Killed in action at Morris Island, SC, Aug. 23, 1863. Interred at Beaufort National Cemetery, Beaufort, SC. Grave 1638.

Fiske, Emery. Pvt. Co. D. Residence, Cumberland. Killed in an accidental cannon explosion at Charleston, SC, May 24, 1865. Interred at Beaufort National Cemetery, Beaufort, SC. Grave1548.

Fuller, Martin V.B. Pvt. Co. D. Residence, Pawtucket. Died of disease Feb. 10, 1864 at New York, NY. Interred at Oak Grove Cemetery, Pawtucket, RI.

Gannon, Patrick. Pvt. Co. E. Residence, Providence. Killed in action at Secessionville, SC, June 16, 1862.

Gibbons, Michael I. Pvt. Co. B. Residence, Providence. Killed in an accidental shell explosion at Fort Pulaski, GA, April 14, 1862.

Gilligan, Patrick H. Sgt. Co. F. Residence, Pawtucket. Killed in action at Secessionville, SC, June 16, 1862.

Gleason, William H. Pvt. Co. D. Residence, North Providence. Died of tuberculosis at North Providence, RI, Jan. 31, 1863. Interred at North Burial Ground, Providence, RI.

Golden, Daniel. Pvt. Co. G. Residence, Providence. Struck by lightning and killed at Hilton Head, SC, Feb. 8, 1862.

Goodwin, George F. Pvt. Co. M. Residence, Providence. Died of typhoid at Hilton Head, SC, July 24, 1862.

Gorton, John A. Pvt. Co. B. Residence, Cumberland. Killed in an accidental shell explosion at Fort Pulaski, GA, April 14, 1862. Interred at Beaufort National Cemetery, Beaufort, SC. Grave 1554.

Greene, George W. 1st Lt. Co. B. Residence, Woonsocket. Mortally wounded in action April 14, 1862 at Fort Pulaski, GA. "Received a wound in his face from a fragment of the copper primer of the gun he was working. Thinking little of the injury, as he was always fearless and intent on duty, he did not report it to the surgeon. His wound, for some cause- perhaps from the copper and mercurial powder that long remained in his face- finally became most serious, and though he faithfully served his three years, produced great suffering, and led to his death." Died of wounds Jan. 18, 1879, at Woonsocket, RI. Interred at Oak Hill Cemetery, Woonsocket, RI.

Greenhalgh, William J. Pvt. Co. A. Residence, North Providence. Killed in action aboard the *George Washington* in naval engagement off Charleston, SC, April 9, 1863.

Grimes, James. Pvt. Co. K. Residence, Providence. Died of disease at Fort Pulaski, GA, Mar. 5, 1864. Interred at Beaufort National Cemetery, Beaufort, SC. Grave 2169.

Gunter, Daniel. Pvt. Co. A. Residence, Providence. Died of disease at Hilton Head, SC, Oct. 29, 1864.

Hackett, Edward. Pvt. Co. G. Residence, Warwick. Died of "brain fever" at Daufuskie Island, SC, April 21, 1862.

Harrington, David T. Pvt. Co. A. Residence, Warwick. Died of disease at Hilton Head, SC, April 20, 1862. Interred at Hopkins Hollow Cemetery, Coventry, RI.

Harris, James. Pvt. Co. C. Residence, Providence. Severely wounded and captured at Olustee, FL, Feb. 20, 1864. Died of wounds at Providence, RI, June 10, 1865. Interred at Grace Church Cemetery, Providence, RI.

Havens, James D. Pvt. Co. B. Residence, Smithfield. Died of tuberculosis at Morris Island, SC, Nov. 10, 1863. Interred at Mineral Spring Cemetery, Pawtucket, RI.

Hazard, Albert. Pvt. Co. B, 3rd R.I. Residence, Coventry. Died of disease contracted in the service at Coventry, RI, Sept. 10, 1863. Interred at Greenwood Cemetery, Coventry, RI.

Heeney, Martin. Sgt. Co. I. Residence, Providence. Killed in action at Secessionville, SC, June 16, 1862.

Hicks, George W. Pvt. Co. E. Residence, Tiverton. Died of disease at Hilton Head, SC, Aug. 11, 1862.

Hill, George J. Sgt. Co. B. Residence, Cumberland. Killed in an accidental shell explosion at Fort Pulaski, GA, April 14, 1862. Interred at Beaufort National Cemetery, Beaufort, SC. Grave 1570.

Holbrook, Henry. 1st Lt. Co. M. Residence, Worcester, MA. Killed in action at Morris Island, SC, Aug. 21, 1863.

Hollohan, James. Pvt. Co. H. Residence, Providence. Killed in action at Secessionville, SC, June 16, 1862.

Horton, Edwin R. M. Pvt. Co. A. Residence, Rehoboth, MA. Died of typhoid at Hilton Head, SC, Jan. 17, 1862. Interred at Cole Brook Cemetery, Rehoboth, MA.

Howe, Martin S. Pvt. Co. M. Residence, Providence. Died of disease at Morris Island, SC, Nov. 21, 1863.

Hughes, Joseph. Pvt. Co. H. Residence, South Kingstown. Mortally wounded in action at Morris Island, SC, Feb. 2, 1864. Died of wounds at Hilton Head, SC, Feb. 14, 1864.

Hughes, Thomas. Pvt. Co. F, 3rd R. I. Residence, Pawtucket. Died of disease contracted in the service at Pawtucket, RI, Dec. 11, 1867. Interred at St. Mary's Cemetery, Pawtucket, RI.

Hyde, John. Pvt. Co. A. Residence, Providence. Killed in action aboard the *George Washington* in naval engagement off Charleston, SC, April 9, 1863.

Ide, Almon D. Pvt. Co. A. Residence, Foster. Died of disease at Annapolis, MD, Mar. 22, 1865. Interred at Hopkins-Ide Lot. Foster Cemetery, 26, Foster, RI.

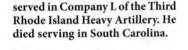

Edward A. Joslin of Smithfield served in Company L of the Third Rhode Island Heavy Artillery. He died serving in South Carolina.

Jaquith, George W. Pvt. Co. B. Residence, Cumberland. Died of disease at New York, NY, Aug. 18, 1862. Interred at Cypress Hills National Cemetery, Brooklyn, NY.

Jefferson, George C. Pvt. Co. D. Residence, Douglas, MA. Died of disease at New York, NY, Oct. 28, 1863. Interred at Cypress Hills National Cemetery, Brooklyn, NY. Grave 913.

Joslin, Edward A. Pvt. Co. L. Residence, Smithfield. Died of disease at Hilton Head, SC, Oct. 10, 1864. Interred at Beaufort National Cemetery, Beaufort, SC. Grave 1559.

Kallaher, Patrick. Pvt. Co. I. Residence, Providence. Died of dysentery at Hilton Head, SC, Jan. 18, 1864.

Keene, Edwin W. 1st Lt. Co. B. Residence, Providence. Died of tuberculosis contracted in the service at Providence, RI, July 1, 1865. Interred at North Burial Ground, Providence, RI.

Kelly, James. Pvt. Co. F. Residence, Warwick. Died of typhoid at Hilton Head, SC, Aug. 4, 1863. Interred at Beaufort National Cemetery, Beaufort, SC. Grave 1596.

Ketchum, Alfred S. Pvt. Co. K. Residence, Huntington, NY. Died of disease at Hilton Head, SC, Jan. 10, 1862. Interred at Beaufort National Cemetery, Beaufort, SC. Grave 1588.

Lake, George W. Pvt. Co. M. Residence, Tiverton. Died of disease at Philadelphia, PA, July 20, 1864. Interred at Philadelphia National Cemetery, Philadelphia, PA. Section D, Grave 222.

Lambe, John. Pvt. Co. E. Residence, North Providence. Died of disease at Hilton Head, SC, Sept. 10, 1862.

Leonard, Abial L. Pvt. Co. H. Residence, Providence. Died of disease at Providence, RI, Sept. 1, 1862. Interred at North Burial Ground, Providence, RI.

Luther, Joseph T. Pvt. Co. B. Residence, Providence. Killed in an accidental shell explosion at Fort Pulaski, GA, April 14, 1862. Interred at Beaufort National Cemetery, Beaufort, SC. Grave 1533.

Mace, George W. Pvt. Co. M. Residence, Natick, MA. Died of typhoid at Hilton Head, SC, Aug. 10, 1862. Interred at Beaufort National Cemetery, Beaufort, SC. Grave 1576.

Malone, Dennis. Pvt. Co. F. Residence, Providence. Accidentally killed in an explosion at Hilton Head, SC, Sept. 30, 1864. Interred at Beaufort National Cemetery, Beaufort, SC. Grave 1539.

Manton, Walter B. 2nd Lt. Co. L. Residence, Providence. Died of yellow fever at Hilton Head, SC, Oct. 25, 1862. Interred at Swan Point Cemetery, Providence, RI.

McCool, John. Pvt. Co. G. Residence, Providence. Killed in an accidental cannon explosion at Morris Island, SC, Sept. 30, 1864. Interred at Beaufort National Cemetery, Beaufort, SC. Grave 1545.

McGahan, James. Pvt. Co. D. Residence, Blackstone, MA. Killed in action at Morris Island, SC, Mar. 9, 1864. Interred at Beaufort National Cemetery, Beaufort, SC. Grave 1564.

McKenna, John. Pvt. Co. K. Residence, Providence. Died of disease as a prisoner of war at Andersonville Prison, GA, Nov. 10, 1864. Interred at Andersonville National Cemetery, GA. Grave 8305.

McKenzie, Alexander R. Pvt. Co. A. Residence, Providence. Discharged for disability Aug. 5, 1862. Died of disease contracted in the service at Providence, RI, c. 1863. Interred at North Burial Ground, Providence, RI.

McQuillin, Francis. Pvt. Co. A. Residence, Pawtucket. Died of dysentery at Hilton Head, SC, Aug. 5, 1865.

Megan, Michael. Pvt. Co. G. Residence, Providence. Died of disease at Hilton Head, SC, April 8, 1862.

Metcalf, Frederick. 1st Lt. Co. B. Resi-

Only seventeen years old, First Lieutenant Frederick Metcalf served in Company B of the Third Rhode Island Heavy Artillery. He died of yellow fever.

dence, Providence. Died of yellow fever at Hilton Head, SC, Aug. 28, 1864. Interred at Beaufort National Cemetery, Beaufort, SC. Grave 190.

Miner, Thomas. Pvt. Co. K. Residence, Cranston. Killed in action at Secessionville, SC, June 16, 1862.

Monroe, Charles H. Pvt. Co. E. Residence, Providence. Died of heart disease at Hilton Head, SC, Dec. 30, 1861. Interred at Beaufort National Cemetery, Beaufort, SC. Grave 1594.

Moon, Horatio N. Pvt. Co. A. Residence, Smithfield. Died of disease at Hilton Head, SC, June 3, 1862.

Morgan, Charles. Pvt. Co. B. Residence, Northbridge, MA. Severely injured in an accidental cannon explosion at Fort Pulaski, GA, April 14, 1862. Died of injuries May 26, 1862. Interred at Beaufort National Cemetery, Beaufort, SC. Grave 1552.

Mowry, Manton B. Pvt. Co. B. Residence, Webster, MA. Died of disease at Hilton Head, SC, July 5, 1863.

Murray, Bernard. Pvt. Co. I. Residence, Tiverton. Died of disease at Hilton Head, SC, Nov. 6, 1862. Interred at Beaufort National Cemetery, Beaufort, SC. Grave 1595.

Nailan, Peter. Pvt. Co. H. Residence, Newport. Mortally wounded in action at Secessionville, SC, June 16, 1862. Died of wounds at Hilton Head SC, July 27, 1862. Interred at Beaufort National Cemetery, Beaufort, SC. Grave 1584.

Nickerson, John. Pvt. Co. D. Residence, Yarmouth, MA. Killed in action at Morris Island, SC, Nov. 20, 1863. Interred at Beaufort National Cemetery, Beaufort, SC. Grave 1567.

O'Donnell, James. Pvt. Co. F. Residence, Smithfield. Killed in action at Secessionville, SC, June 16, 1862.

O'Sullivan, James. Pvt. Co. A. Residence, Tiverton. Died of disease at Hilton Head, SC, July 26, 1865. Interred at Beaufort National Cemetery, Beaufort, SC. Grave 1557.

Peck, Foster S. Corp. Co. H. Residence, North Providence. Killed in action at Morris Island, SC, Oct. 12, 1863. Interred at Beaufort National Cemetery, Beaufort, SC. Grave 1551.

Perry, Altheus S. Sgt. Co. G. Residence, East Providence. Died of disease at Providence, RI, Mar. 27, 1863. Interred at North Burial Ground, Providence, RI.

Potter, Israel A. Pvt. Co. B. Residence, Cranston. Captured at Kiawah Island, SC, Dec. 4, 1863. Died as a prisoner of war Mar. 17, 1865.

Prew, Mitchell. Pvt. Co. A. Residence, North Providence. Killed in action at Gainesville, FL, Aug. 17, 1864.

Rice, George. Pvt. Co. A. Residence, Cumberland. Killed in action at Devaux Neck, SC, Dec. 27, 1864.

Rounds, Charles H. Pvt. Co. A. Residence, Providence. Died of disease at Hilton Head, SC, May 22, 1862. Interred at North Burial Ground, Providence, RI.

Ryan, James. Pvt. Co. L. Residence, Providence. Died of disease at Hilton Head SC, Dec. 24, 1862. Interred at Beaufort National Cemetery, Beaufort, SC. Grave 1560.

Ryan, Thomas. Pvt. Co. D. Residence, Providence. Died in an accidental explosion of a cannon at Charleston, SC, May 2, 1865. Interred at Cumberland Cemetery 6, Cumberland, RI.

Saunders, Asa B. Pvt. Co. A. Residence, Providence. Died of disease at Hilton Head, SC, Aug. 30, 1864. Interred at Wilder Burial Ground, Glocester Cemetery 10, Glocester, RI.

Sayles, Benjamin L. Pvt. Co. E. Residence, Smithfield. Killed in action at Secessionville, SC, June 16, 1862.

Smith, David. Pvt. Co. F. Residence, North Bridgewater, MA. Died of disease at Morris Island, SC, July 26, 1863.

Smith, George W. Pvt. Co. A. Residence, Tiverton. Mortally wounded in action aboard the *George Washington* in naval engagement off Charleston, SC, April 9, 1863. Died of wounds at Hilton Head, SC, April 12, 1863. Interred at Beaufort National Cemetery, Beaufort, SC. Grave 1536.

Smith, Lyman R. Pvt. Co. A. Residence, Providence. Killed in action aboard the *George Washington* in naval engagement off Charleston, SC, April 9, 1863.

Stalker, Charles D. Corp. Co. A. Residence, Providence. Died of disease as a prisoner of war at Florence, SC, Feb. 1, 1865. Interred at Florence National Cemetery, Florence, SC. Mass Grave.

Stewart, Silas H. Pvt. Co. G. Residence, Warwick. Died of disease at Fort Pulaski, GA, July 30, 1862.

Stowe, Walter. Pvt. Co. D. Residence, Providence. Died of disease at Beaufort, SC, Oct. 23, 1863.

Stuart, John E. Pvt. Co. B. Residence, Pawtucket. Killed in an accidental cannon explosion at Hilton Head, SC, Aug. 4, 1864.

Sweet, Samuel S. Residence, Glocester. Pvt. Co. E. Died of disease at Hilton Head, SC, Aug. 24, 1862. Interred at Beaufort National Cemetery, Beaufort, SC. Grave 1593.

Taft, Francis H. Pvt. Co. K. Residence, Providence. Mortally wounded in action at Secessionville, SC, June 16, 1862. Died of wounds at New York, NY, July 27, 1862. Interred at North Burial Ground, Providence, RI.

Tanner, Thomas B. Pvt. Co. D. Residence, Hopkinton. Killed in action at Morris Island, SC, Aug. 9, 1863. Interred at Beaufort National Cemetery, Beaufort, SC. Grave 1601.

Templeton, Isaac. Pvt. Co. L. Residence, Antrim, NH. Died of malaria at Hilton Head, SC, Nov. 3, 1862. Interred at Beaufort National Cemetery, Beaufort, SC. Grave 1585.

Tence, George. Pvt. Co. H. Residence, Bristol. Died of a hernia contracted in the service at Bristol, RI, June 25, 1863. Interred at North Burial Ground, Bristol, RI.

Thornton, Martin G. Pvt. Co. H. Residence, Smithfield. Died of disease at Hilton Head, SC, Sept. 26, 1863. Interred at Beaufort National Cemetery, Beaufort, SC. Grave 1542.

Tillinghast, William C. Pvt. Co. D. Residence, Richmond. Killed in action at Morris Island, SC, July 25, 1863. Interred at Wood River Cemetery, Richmond, RI.

Trumbull, Thomas W. Pvt. Co. E. Residence, Providence. Died of typhoid "at sea" Nov. 4, 1861.

Valleley, Edward J. Pvt. Co. A. Residence, New Shoreham. Mortally wounded in action aboard the *George Washington* in naval engagement off Charleston, SC, April 9, 1863. Died of wounds at Hilton Head, SC, April 15, 1863. Interred at Beaufort National Cemetery, Beaufort, SC. Grave 1565.

Warfield, Henry H. Pvt. Co. C. Residence, Newport. Died in a cannon accident while drilling at New York, NY, Oct. 8, 1861. Interred at Oak Grove Cemetery, Fall River, MA.

Warner, John B. Pvt. Co. A. Residence, Burrillville. Died of disease at Burrillville, RI, Mar. 27, 1864. Interred at Hope Cemetery, Worcester, MA.

Weeden, Charles W. Corp. Co. E. Residence, Pawtucket. Died of typhoid contracted in the service at Pawtucket, RI, Nov. 28, 1861. Interred at Swan Point Cemetery, Providence, RI.

Wells, Stephen B. Pvt. Co. F. Residence, East Greenwich. Killed in action at Secessionville, SC, June 16, 1862.

Welsh, Henry. Pvt. Co. H. Residence, Providence. Died of disease at Hilton Head, SC, Nov. 9, 1862. Interred at Beaufort National Cemetery, Beaufort, SC. Grave 1587.

Woodmancey, James A. Pvt. Co. A. Residence, Richmond. Died of "disease contracted in the service" at Richmond, RI, July 26, 1868. Interred at Wood River Cemetery, Richmond, RI.

Worden, William H. Pvt. Co. C. Residence, Hopkinton. Died of typhoid "at sea" Nov. 1, 1861.

Wright, Reuben. Pvt. Co. A. Residence, Providence. Died of disease at Pocotaligo, SC, Feb. 6, 1865.

7

Fourth Rhode Island Volunteers

Abbott, Abial. J.W. Pvt. Co. H. Residence, Warwick. Mortally wounded in action, shot in leg, at Antietam, MD, Sept. 17, 1862. Died of wounds near Keedysville, MD, Oct. 7, 1862. Interred at Antietam National Cemetery, Sharpsburg, MD. Rhode Island Section, Grave 2836.

Anthony, William J. Pvt. Co. H. Residence, Newport. Died of typhoid at Washington, D.C., Dec. 18, 1862. Interred at Island Cemetery, Newport, RI.

Austin, Jacob V. Pvt. Co. H. Residence, North Kingstown. Died of diph-theria at Portsmouth, VA, Sept. 1, 1863. Interred at Hampton National Cemetery, Hampton, VA. Section A, Grave 3670.

Baker, Charles C. Pvt. Co. H. Residence, North Kingstown. Killed in action at New Bern, NC, Mar. 14, 1862. Interred at Elm Grove Cemetery, North Kingstown, RI.

Bane, William H. Pvt. Co. B. Residence, Charlestown. Died of typhoid at Alexandria, VA, Jan. 4, 1862. Interred at Wood River Cemetery, Richmond, RI.

Bates, Albert E. Pvt. Co. B. Residence, Charlestown. Died of typhoid at Philadelphia, PA, Jan. 1, 1863. Interred at Philadelphia National Cemetery, Philadelphia, PA. Section B. Grave 211.

Bills, Samuel D. Pvt. Co. C. Res-

Private Charles C. Baker of North Kingstown served in Company H of the Fourth Rhode Island. He was killed in action March 14, 1862, at New Bern, North Carolina. His remains were brought home and interred at Elm Grove Cemetery in Wickford.

idence, Providence. Died of typhoid at Washington, D.C., Aug. 6, 1864. Interred at Arlington National Cemetery, Arlington, VA. Section 13, Grave 7726.

Bliven, David H. Pvt. Co. H. Residence, Exeter. Died of disease contracted in the service at Exeter, RI, Aug. 9, 1864. Interred at Wood River Cemetery, Richmond, RI.

Bloomer, Thomas. Wag. Co. H. Residence, North Kingstown. Died of typhoid at Alexandria, VA, Oct. 11, 1864. Interred at Arlington National Cemetery, Arlington, VA. Section 13, Grave 13310.

Boss, Daniel A. Wag. Co. G. Residence, Newport. Interred at New Bern National Cemetery, New Bern, NC. Grave 1873.Cenotaph at Common Burying Ground, Newport, RI.

Briggs, Charles H. Pvt. Co. I. Residence, Uxbridge, MA. Died of typhoid at Carolina City, NC, April 24, 1862. Interred at New Bern National Cemetery, New Bern, NC. Section 11, Grave 1874.

Brown, Daniel. Pvt. Co. A. Residence, Concord, NH. Died of typhoid at New Bern, NC, May 3, 1863.

Brownell, Wilson D. Pvt. Co. H. Residence, Portsmouth. Died of typhoid at Portsmouth, RI, Feb. 22, 1864. Interred at Portsmouth Village Cemetery, Portsmouth, RI.

Buffum, George R. 2nd Lt. Co. D. Residence, Burrillville. Mortally wounded in action, shot in chest, at Antietam, MD, Sept. 17, 1862. Died of wounds at Sharpsburg, MD, Oct. 21, 1862. Interred at Antietam National Cemetery, Sharpsburg, MD. Officer's Section.

Bumpus, Sullivan L. Pvt. Co. A. Residence, Rochester, MA. Killed in action at Antietam, MD, Sept. 17, 1862. Interred at Woodside Cemetery, Plymouth, MA.

Burdick, Benjamin F. Corp. Co. D. Residence, Hopkinton. Killed in action at Antietam, MD, Sept. 17, 1862. Interred at Antietam National Cemetery, Sharpsburg, MD. Rhode Island Section, Grave 2928. Cenotaph at Rockville Cemetery, Hopkinton, RI.

Burdick, Stephen H. Pvt. Co. B. Residence, South Kingstown. Mortally wounded in action, shot in groin, at Antietam, MD, Sept. 17, 1862. Died of wounds Sept. 27, 1862, at Sharpsburg, MD. Interred at Antietam National Cemetery, Sharpsburg, MD. Rhode Island Section, Grave 2822.

Burns, Timothy. Pvt. Co. B. Residence, Providence. Died of typhoid at Beaufort, NC June 17, 1862.

Cameron, David H. Pvt. Co. C. Residence, Coventry. Mortally wounded in action at New Bern, NC, Mar. 14, 1862. Died of wounds at New Bern, NC, April 6, 1862. Interred at New Bern National Cemetery, New Bern, NC. Section 11, Grave 1865.

Card, Jonathan. Mus. Co. B. Residence, South Kingstown. Died of typhoid at Roanoke, NC, Mar. 1, 1862. Interred at New Bern National Cemetery, New Bern, NC. Section 11, Grave 1880. Cenotaph at Pine Grove Cemetery, Coventry, RI.

Carr, William H. Pvt. Co. G. Residence, Newport. Died of typhoid June 14, 1862, at Beaufort, NC.

Chaill, Watt. Pvt. Co. K. Residence, Providence. Drowned Aug. 1, 1862, in the Potomac River.

Chapman, Henry. Pvt. Co. A. Residence, Providence. Died of pneumonia Jan. 15, 1862, at Annapolis, MD.

Chase, John W. Pvt. Co. G. Residence, Newport. Died of typhoid April 26, 1862, at Carolina City, NC. Interred at New Bern National Cemetery, New Bern, NC. Section 11, Grave 1876.

Church, George H. Sgt. Co. H. Residence, North Kingstown. Killed in action at New Bern, NC, Mar. 14, 1862. Interred at Elm Grove Cemetery, North Kingstown, RI.

Church, Isaac M. Capt. Co. G. Residence, South Kingstown. Promoted from 1st Lt. Co. E, 2nd R.I. Vols. Oct. 8, 1862. Formerly prisoner of war, captured at Bull Run, July 21, 1861. Discharged for disability Dec. 27, 1862. "His health was impaired by his captivity, and he never fully recovered his former strength." Died of illness contracted in the service Oct. 27, 1874, at North Kingstown, RI. Interred at Riverside Cemetery, South Kingstown, RI.

Clarke, John T. Pvt. Co. D. Residence, Newport. Killed in action at New Bern, NC, Mar. 14, 1862. Interred at Common Burying Ground, Newport, RI.

Collum, George. Pvt. Co. A. Residence, Middletown. Killed in action, at the Crater, Petersburg, VA, July 30, 1864.

Costigan, Cornelius. Pvt. Co. E. Residence, Cumberland. Killed in action at Antietam, MD, Sept. 17, 1862.

Crandall, Davis. Pvt. Co. D. Residence, Hopkinton. Killed in action at New Bern, NC, Mar. 14, 1862. Interred at Rockville Cemetery, Hopkinton, RI.

Curtis, Joseph B. Lt. Col. Residence,

Riding his horse into action at Fredericksburg, Lieutenant Colonel Joseph B. Curtis was the Fourth's only fatality on December 13, 1862. Library of Congress.

Providence. Killed in action at Fredericksburg, VA, Dec. 13, 1862. Interred at North Burial Ground, Providence, RI.

Curtis, Samuel. Pvt. Co. G. Residence, South Kingstown. Died of typhoid at Portsmouth, RI, Aug. 20, 1862. Interred at Riverside Cemetery, South Kingstown, RI.

Dailey, Daniel. Pvt. Co. C. Residence, Providence. Died of typhoid Aug. 18, 1862, at Roanoke, NC.

Davis, Clark E. Pvt. Co. E. Residence, Eaton, NH. Killed in action at the Crater, Petersburg, VA, July 30, 1864.

Davis, James. Pvt. Co. D. Residence, Smithfield. Killed in action at Hatcher's Run, VA, Aug. 19, 1864. Interred at Poplar Grove National Cemetery, Petersburg, VA. Grave 1421.

Denham, William S. Corp. Co. G. Residence, Newport. Died of typhoid at Carolina City, NC, April 18, 1862. Interred at New Bern National Cemetery, New Bern, NC. Section 11, Grave 1875.

Doran, Patrick. Pvt. Co. H. Residence, Providence. Died of dysentery contracted in the service, at Providence, RI. April 29, 1865. Interred at North Burial Ground, Providence, RI.

Dugan, Patrick. Pvt. Co. A. Residence, Providence. Died of typhoid at Fredericksburg, VA, Aug. 15, 1862.

Dunnegan, Henry. Pvt. Co. G. Residence, Newport. Killed in building collapse Nov. 28, 1863, at Portsmouth, VA. Interred at Hampton National Cemetery, Hampton, VA. Section B, Grave 4654.

Dyer, Byron W. Corp. Co. C. Residence, Cranston. Killed in action at the Crater, Petersburg, VA, July 30, 1864.

Edgers, Edward. Pvt. Co. A. Residence, Providence. Died of tuberculosis June 4, 1864, at Portsmouth, RI. Interred at Locust Grove Cemetery, Providence, RI.

Farley, James. H. 2nd Lt. Co. C. Residence, Scituate. Killed in action

Having previously served in both Battery A and Battery F, First Rhode Island Light Artillery, Second Lieutenant George W. Field served in Company B of the Fourth Rhode Island. He was shot through the heart and instantly killed at the Crater; his body was never recovered.

at Petersburg, VA, July 26, 1864. Interred at City Point National Cemetery, Hopewell, VA. Grave 2577.

Field, George W. 2nd Lt. Co. B. Residence, Providence. Killed in action at the Crater, Petersburg, VA, July 30, 1864. Cenotaph at Swan Point Cemetery, Providence, RI.

Fish, Henry. Pvt. Co. G. Residence, Newport. Killed in action at Antietam, MD, Sept. 17, 1862. Interred at Antietam National Cemetery, Sharpsburg, MD. Rhode Island Section, Grave 2824. Cenotaph at Oakland Cemetery, Cranston, RI.

Fish, Stephen F. Pvt. Co. I. Residence, Bristol. Died of disease contracted in the service June 4, 1866, at Bristol, RI. Interred at Portsmouth Cemetery, Portsmouth, RI.

Fitzgerald, John. Pvt. Co. F. Residence, Providence. Died of typhoid at New Bern, NC, May 9, 1862.

Frisby, Silas. Pvt. Co. F. Residence, Cumberland. Mortally wounded in action at New Bern, NC, Mar. 14, 1862. Died of wounds at New Bern, NC April 3, 1862. Interred at New Bern National Cemetery, New Bern, NC. Section 11, Grave 1864.

Gallagher, Patrick. Pvt. Co. A. Residence, Providence. Accidentally killed at Point Lookout, MD, May 7, 1864.

Gardiner, Gustavus B. Sgt. Co. G. Residence, Newport. Killed in action at Antietam, MD, Sept. 17, 1862. Interred at Island Cemetery, Newport, RI.

Gardiner, William H. Pvt. Co. A. Residence, Providence. Died of tuberculosis contracted in the service at Providence, RI, Dec. 24, 1862. Interred at Grace Church Cemetery, Providence, RI.

Gavitt, Edwin D. Pvt. Co. D. Residence, Hopkinton. Mortally wounded in action at New Bern, NC, Mar. 14, 1862. Died of wounds at New York, NY, June 16, 1862. Interred at Oak Grove Cemetery, Hopkinton, RI.

Gilfoil, Patrick. Pvt. Co. A. Residence, Providence. Mortally wounded in action and captured at the Crater, Petersburg, VA, July 30, 1864. Released. Died of wounds at Annapolis, MD, Mar. 3, 1865. Interred at Annapolis National Cemetery, Annapolis, MD. Section N, Grave 120.

Gladding, Henry F. Corp. Co. K. Residence, Bristol. Died of dysentery May 7, 1864, at Portsmouth, RI. Interred at North Burial Ground, Bristol, RI.

Gorton, Charles A. 1st Sgt. Co. K. Residence, Warwick. Mortally wounded in action at the Crater, Petersburg, VA, July 30, 1864. Died of wounds as a prisoner of war at Salisbury, NC, Dec. 6, 1864. Interred in mass grave at Salisbury National Cemetery, Salisbury, NC.

Gorton, Henry W. Pvt. Co. C. Residence, Coventry. Died of tuberculosis

Dec. 14, 1862, at Falmouth, VA. Interred at Gorton Lot, Coventry Cemetery 83, Coventry, RI.

Griffin, William. Pvt. Co. A. Residence, North Bridgewater, MA. Died Nov. 2, 1864, of typhoid contracted in the service at North Bridgewater, MA. Interred at North Bridgewater, MA.

Grimwood, James. Corp. Co. A. Residence, Providence. Killed in action May 3, 1863, near Suffolk, VA.

Guild, Charles E. 1st Sgt. Co. D. Residence, Glocester. Mortally wounded in action at Antietam, MD, Sept. 17, 1862. Died of wounds at Sharpsburg, MD Sept. 25, 1862. Interred at Acotes Hill Cemetery, Glocester, RI.

Hardman, Robert. Pvt. Co. C. Residence, Newport. Died of typhoid Feb. 24, 1863, at Washington, D.C. Interred at Island Cemetery, Newport, RI.

Hardy, John. Pvt. Co. D. Residence, Tiverton. Killed in action at Antietam, MD, Sept. 17, 1862. Interred at Antietam National Cemetery, Sharpsburg, MD. Rhode Island Section, Grave 2827.

Harrington, Jeremiah. Pvt. Co. F. Residence, Ellsworth, ME. Died of typhoid at Roanoke, NC Feb. 16, 1862. Interred at New Bern National Cemetery, New Bern, NC. Section 11, Grave 1869.

Harris, Andrew F. Corp. Co. D. Residence, Burrillville. Died Nov. 3, 1863, of disease contracted in the service at Burrillville, RI. Interred at Acotes Hill Cemetery, Glocester, RI.

Harvey, Samuel. Corp. Co. B. Residence, Hopkinton. Killed in action at Antietam, MD, Sept. 17, 1862. Interred at Antietam National Cemetery, Sharpsburg, MD. Rhode Island Section, Grave 2842.

Hawkins, Robert H. Pvt. Co. G. Residence, East Greenwich. Died of disease contracted in the service Aug. 18, 1864 at East Greenwich, RI. Interred at First Cemetery, East Greenwich, RI.

Hayden, Robert. Corp. Co. F. Residence, Providence. Died of typhoid June 12, 1862, at Washington, D.C.

Hayes, John. Corp. Co. I. Residence, Tiverton. Killed in action at Antietam, MD, Sept. 17, 1862.

Healy, Thaddeus C. Pvt. Co. E. Residence, Charlestown. Died of diphtheria at Suffolk, VA, Aug. 23, 1863. Interred at Hampton National Cemetery, Hampton, VA. Section B, Grave 4664.

Hendrick, Benjamin W. Pvt. Co. C. Residence, Providence. Died of disease contracted in the service at Rehoboth, MA, Mar. 25, 1866. Interred at Jonathan Wheeler Cemetery, Rehoboth, MA.

Henry, John. Pvt. Co. E. Residence, Woonsocket. Killed in action at Petersburg, VA, July 27, 1864. Interred at City Point National Cemetery, Hopewell, VA. Grave 1976.

Hogan, Bernard. Pvt. Co. E. Residence, Woonsocket. Died of small pox Feb. 26, 1864, at Portsmouth, VA. Interred at Hampton National Cemetery, Hampton, VA. Section B, Grave 4662.

Hopkins, Adin B. Pvt. Co. I. Residence, Blackstone, MA. Killed in action at New Bern, NC, Mar. 14, 1862. Interred at Oak Grove Cemetery, Pawtucket, RI.

Hopkins, Allen. Pvt. Co. B. Residence, Glocester. Killed in action at Antietam, MD, Sept. 17, 1862. Interred at Smithville Cemetery, Scituate, RI.

Hopkins, Henry V. Corp. Co. I. Residence, Pawtucket. Mortally wounded in action at Antietam, MD, Sept. 17, 1862. Died of wounds at Sharpsburg, MD, Oct. 26, 1862. Interred at Oak Grove Cemetery, Pawtucket, RI.

Hopkins, William S. Pvt. Co. H. Residence, East Greenwich. Died of typhoid at Carolina City, NC, April 12, 1862. Interred at New Bern National Cemetery, New Bern, NC. Section 11, Grave 1878.

Horton, Jerome B. Pvt. Co. K. Residence, Burrillville. Died of typhoid at New Bern, NC, April 29, 1862.

Jefferson, James W. Pvt. Co. B. Residence, Boston, MA. Died of typhoid Feb. 6, 1863, at Falmouth, VA.

Jenness, Nelson. Pvt. Co. D. Residence, Burrillville. Mortally wounded in action at the Crater, Petersburg, VA, July 30, 1864. Died of wounds as a prisoner of war at Richmond, VA, Sept. 7, 1864. Cenotaph at Hillcrest Cemetery, Hollis, ME.

Johnson, Elijah. Pvt. Co. B. Residence, East Greenwich. Killed in action at Antietam, MD, Sept. 17, 1862. Interred at Elijah Johnson Lot, South Kingstown Cemetery 59, South Kingstown, RI.

Johnson, John F. Pvt. Co. F. Residence, Warwick. Died of disease contracted in the service, August 22, 1863, at Warwick, RI. Interred at Large Maple Root Cemetery, Coventry, RI.

Johnson, Philip. Pvt. Co. A. Residence, Providence. Killed in action at New Bern, NC, Mar. 14, 1862.

Kelley, George W. Pvt. Co. F. Residence, Coventry. Died of typhoid Dec. 20, 1862, at Falmouth, VA. Interred at Walker-Kelley Cemetery, Coventry Cemetery 14, Coventry, RI.

Kentworthy, Robert. Pvt. Co. B. Residence, Cumberland. Killed in action at New Bern, NC, Mar. 14, 1862.

Knight, Brayton. Regimental QM. Residence, Warwick. Died of disease contracted in the service at Warwick, RI, June 15, 1865. Interred at Stephen Knight Lot, Cranston Cemetery 91, Cranston, RI.

Knowles, John K. 2nd Lt. Co. A. Residence, South Kingstown. Killed in action at the Crater, Petersburg, VA, July 30, 1864. Cenotaph at James Knowles Lot, South Kingstown Cemetery 32, South Kingstown, RI.

Lake, Thomas O. Pvt. Co. G. Residence, Newport. Mortally wounded in action at Petersburg, VA, July 23, 1864. Died of wounds at Washington, D.C., Aug. 1, 1864. Interred at Island Cemetery, Newport, RI.

Landers, James H. Pvt. Co. G. Residence, Newport. Killed in action Sept. 30, 1864, at Poplar Spring Church, VA. Interred at Island Cemetery, Newport, RI.

Langworthy, Thomas A. Sgt. Co. A. Residence, North Kingstown. Killed in action at the Crater, Petersburg, VA, July 30, 1864. Cenotaph at First Cemetery, Hopkinton, RI.

Leddy, John. Pvt. Co. G. Residence, Newport. Mortally wounded in action at Poplar Spring Church, VA, Sept. 30, 1864. Died of wounds at Washington, D.C., Oct. 18, 1864. Interred at Arlington National Cemetery, Arlington, VA. Section 13, Grave 8320.

Livesey, Theodore. Pvt. Co. K. Residence, Providence. Killed in action at Antietam, MD, Sept. 17, 1862. Interred at Grace Church Cemetery, Providence, RI.

Lynch, Edward A. Pvt. Co. I. Residence, Providence. Killed in action at Antietam, MD, Sept. 17, 1862.

Lyons, Thomas. Pvt. Co. A. Residence, East Greenwich. Died of typhoid at Falmouth, VA, Dec. 19, 1862.

Manchester, Thomas. Pvt. Co. F. Residence, Tiverton. Died of typhoid Nov. 23, 1862, at Sharpsburg, MD. Interred at Antietam National Cemetery, Sharpsburg, MD. Rhode Island Section, Grave 2839.

Martin, George. Pvt. Co. C. Residence, Johnston. Killed in action at Petersburg, VA, July 24, 1864. Interred at City Point National Cemetery, Hopewell, VA. Grave 2663.

Matthewson, John A. Pvt. Co. D. Residence, Coventry. Killed in action at Antietam, MD, Sept. 17, 1862.

McCabe, Michael. Pvt. Co. D. Residence, Burrillville. Killed in action at Antietam, MD, Sept. 17, 1862.

McCandless, Robert. Pvt. Co. I. Residence, Pawtucket. Killed in action at Antietam, MD, Sept. 17, 1862.

McDonald, Edward. Pvt. Co. B. Residence, Coventry. Detached on staff of Gen. O.O. Howard. Died of disease July 7, 1864, at Nashville, TN. Interred at Nashville National Cemetery, Nashville, TN. Section H, Grave 10069. Cenotaph at Pine Grove Cemetery, Coventry, RI.

McFarland, John N. Pvt. Co. A. Residence, Cranston. Died of tuberculosis at Cranston, RI, Feb. 13, 1862.

McGowen, William. Pvt. Co. C. Residence, Providence. Killed in action at Antietam, MD, Sept. 17, 1862. Interred at Antietam National Cemetery, Sharpsburg, MD. Rhode Island Section, Grave 2831.

McKee, Andrew. Pvt. Co. D. Residence, Warwick. Died in railroad accident Oct. 21, 1862, near Harpers Ferry, WV. Interred at North Burial Ground, Providence, RI.

McNamee, Miles M. Pvt. Co. C. Residence, Providence. Died of typhoid Jan. 1, 1863, at Washington, D.C.

McNeal, Patrick. Pvt. Co. B. Residence, Johnston. Killed in action at Antietam, MD, Sept. 17, 1862. Interred at Antietam National Cemetery, Sharpsburg, MD. Rhode Island Section, Grave 2832.

Miller, William A. Pvt. Co. C. Residence, Bristol. Died of dysentery Mar. 30, 1862, at Roanoke, NC. Interred at North Burial Ground, Bristol, RI.

Moon, Josiah. Pvt. Co. B. Residence, Coventry. Killed in action at Antietam, MD, Sept. 17, 1862. Interred at Antietam National Cemetery, Sharpsburg, MD. Rhode Island Section, Grave 2829.

Moore, Andrew S. Pvt. Co. K. Residence, Camden, ME. Died of tuberculosis Nov. 29, 1863, at Portsmouth, RI.

Moore, Joseph B. Pvt. Co. I. Residence, Smithfield. Mortally wounded in action at Antietam, MD, Sept. 17, 1862. Died of wounds at Alexandria, VA, Jan. 10, 1863.

Munn, Henry. Pvt. Co. F. Residence, Hull, MA. Trans. to Veterans Reserve Corps Sept. 7, 1863. Died of disease Feb. 3, 1865, at Elmira, NY. Interred at Woodlawn National Cemetery, Elmira, NY. Grave 66.

Murphy, Cornelius. Pvt. Co. I. Residence, Providence. Died of dysentery at Providence, RI, Sept. 23, 1864. Interred at North Burial Ground, Providence, RI.

Murphy, John. Pvt. Co. C. Residence, Providence. Died of typhoid at Roanoke, NC, Feb. 20, 1862. Interred at New Bern National Cemetery, New Bern, NC. Section 11, Grave 1911.

Myrick, Cromwell P. Sgt. Co. B. Residence, Coventry. Mortally wounded in action in front of Petersburg, VA, July 17, 1864. Died of wounds at City Point, VA, July 19, 1864. Interred at City Point National Cemetery, Hopewell, VA. Grave 1623. Cenotaph in Manchester Cemetery, Coventry, RI.

Myrick, Samuel. Pvt. Co. B. Residence, Coventry. Killed in action at New Bern, NC, Mar. 14, 1862. Interred at Greenwood Cemetery, Coventry, RI.

O'Donnell, Patrick. Pvt. Co. F. Residence, Providence. Died of tuberculosis June 14, 1863, at Providence, RI. Interred at St. Patrick's Cemetery, Providence, RI.

Oliver, Joseph. Pvt. Co. B. Residence, Providence. Killed in action at Antietam, MD, Sept. 17, 1862.

Olney, William C. 2nd Lt. Co. G. Residence, Providence. Died of disease contracted in the service June 20, 1867, at Providence, RI. Interred at North Burial Ground, Providence, RI.

O'Mara, Thomas. Pvt. Co. A. Residence, North Bridgewater, MA. Killed in action at Elizabeth City, NC, Feb. 16, 1862.

Peabody, Frank D. Pvt. Co. G. Residence, Newport. Died of disease contracted in the service Sept. 13, 1863 at Newport, RI. Interred at Island Cemetery, Newport, RI.

Peabody, Frederick J. Sgt. Co. G. Killed in action at Poplar Spring Church, VA, Sept. 30, 1864. Interred at Common Burying Ground, Newport, RI.

Perkins, Austin A. Corp. Co. B. Residence, Richmond. Killed in action at Antietam, MD, Sept. 17, 1862.

Pike, Ephraim. Pvt. Co. F. Residence, Warwick. Killed in action at Antietam, MD, Sept. 17, 1862. Interred at Greenwood Cemetery, Coventry, RI.

Randall, James H. Pvt. Co. B. Residence, Providence. Died of small pox Mar. 12, 1864 at Portsmouth, VA. Interred at Hampton National Cemetery, Section B, Grave 4662. Cenotaph at Intervale Cemetery, North Providence, RI.

Rathbun, Larkin W. Pvt. Co. A. Residence, Exeter. Died of typhoid at Washington, D.C., Mar. 21, 1862. Interred at Soldiers Home National Cemetery, Washington, D.C. Section H, Grave 4552.

Ready, John. Pvt. Co. B. Residence, Providence. Died of dysentery at Hatteras, NC, Jan. 25, 1862.

Remington, Andrew J. Pvt. Co. I. Residence, Scituate. Died of small pox at Washington, D.C., Mar. 5, 1862. Interred at Soldier's Home National Cemetery, Washington, D.C. Section G, Grave 826.

Reynolds, Albert F. Pvt. Co. H. Residence, Providence. Died of tuberculosis Dec. 3, 1862, at Portsmouth, RI. Interred at North Burial Ground, Providence, RI.

Roberts, Henry. Pvt. Co. B. Residence, Providence. Killed in action at Antietam, MD, Sept. 17, 1862. Interred in unknown grave, Antietam National Cemetery, Sharpsburg, MD.

Roe, Jacob. Pvt. Co. B. Residence, Johnston. Killed in action at Antietam, MD, Sept. 17, 1862.

Rose, Thomas G. Pvt. Co. H. Residence, North Kingstown. Died of dysentery at North Kingstown, RI, Aug. 9, 1864. Interred at Elm Grove Cemetery, North Kingstown, RI.

Sanford, Alexander. Sgt. Co. H. Residence, North Kingstown. Died of typhoid Dec. 10, 1861, at Washington, D.C. Interred at Elm Grove Cemetery, North Kingstown, RI.

Saunders, Henry Freeman. Pvt. Co. D. Residence, Hopkinton. Mortally wounded in action at Antietam, MD, Sept. 17, 1862. Died of wounds at Sharpsburg, MD, Oct. 25, 1862. Interred at Oak Grove Cemetery, Hopkinton, RI.

Shakshaft, George. Pvt. Co. A. Residence, Coventry. Mortally wounded in action, shot in chest, at the Crater, Petersburg, VA, July 30, 1864. Died of wounds at New York, NY, Aug. 18, 1864. Interred at St. Mary's Cemetery, West Warwick, RI.

Sheridan, Patrick. Pvt. Co. C. Residence, Providence. Killed in action at New Bern, NC, Mar. 14, 1862.

Sherman, Edward. Pvt. Co. I. Residence, Newport. Died of typhoid at Falmouth, VA, Dec. 6, 1862.

Simmons, Lloyd. Pvt. Co. H. Residence, North Kingstown. Died of typhoid at Providence, RI, June 25, 1862. Interred at Swan Point Cemetery, Providence, RI

Smalley, George L. Asst. Surg. Residence, Coventry. Died of disease contracted in the service at Providence, RI, Nov. 23, 1862. Interred at Mt. Wollaston Cemetery, Quincy, MA.

Smith, John. Pvt. Co. F. Residence, Newport. Died of disease contracted in the service Nov. 30, 1864, at Newport, RI. Interred at Island Cemetery, Newport, RI.

Smith, Thomas E. Pvt. Co. C. Residence, Newburyport, MA. Killed in action at the Crater, Petersburg, VA, July 30, 1864.

Stacey, Michael E. Pvt. Co. C. Residence, Providence. Killed in action at Antietam, MD, Sept. 17, 1862. Interred at Antietam National Cemetery, Sharpsburg, MD. Rhode Island Section, Grave 2826.

Stafford, William H. Pvt. Co. G. Residence, Cranston. Died of dysentery at Cranston, RI, May 23, 1864. Interred at Greenwood Cemetery, Coventry, RI.

Staples, Albert H. Pvt. Co. D. Residence, Smithfield. Died of typhoid at Alexandria, VA, Jan. 6, 1862. Interred at Alexandria National Cemetery, Alexandria, VA. Grave 1145.

Steere, Willard. Pvt. Co. D. Residence, Burrillville. Mortally wounded in action at New Bern, NC, Mar. 14, 1862. Died of wounds at New Bern, NC, Mar. 29, 1862. Interred at Baker Cemetery, Douglas, MA.

Street, Edwin. Pvt. Co. E. Residence, Smithfield. Killed in action at New Bern, NC, Mar. 14, 1862.

Tanner, Thomas B. Corp. Co. G. Residence, Newport. Served as Regimental Color Bearer. Killed in action at Antietam, MD, Sept. 17, 1862. Interred at Island Cemetery, Newport, RI.

Tew, Richard T. Pvt. Co. G. Residence, Newport. Died of diphtheria Aug. 3, 1863 at Suffolk, VA. Interred at Hampton National Cemetery, Hampton, VA. Section B, Grave 4658.

Tew, William C. Pvt. Co. A. Residence, Newport. Drowned Apr. 13, 1864, in Long Island Sound while returning from veteran furlough. Interred at Island Cemetery, Newport, RI.

Thayer, Henry R. Corp. Co. D. Residence, Burrillville. Died of typhoid Jan. 2, 1862, at Washington, D.C. Interred at Pascoag Cemetery, Burrillville, RI.

Thomas, George S. Corp. Co. H. Residence, North Kingstown. Promoted from Pvt. Killed in action at the Crater, Petersburg, VA, July 30, 1864. Cenotaph at Elm Grove Cemetery, North Kingstown, RI.

Thornton, Augustus F. Pvt. Co. B. Residence, Dedham, MA. Killed in action at the Crater, Petersburg, VA, July 30, 1864.

Tillinghast, Charles. Capt. Co. H. Residence, Providence. Killed in action at New Bern, NC, Mar. 14, 1862. Interred at Swan Point Cemetery, Providence, RI.

Tillinghast, William W. Pvt. Co. C. Residence, East Greenwich. Wounded in action at New Bern, NC, Mar. 14, 1862. Discharged for disability Oct. 29, 1862, at Providence, RI. "Died of war wounds" at East Greenwich, RI, Aug. 27, 1866. Interred at Elm Grove Cemetery, North Kingstown, RI.

Corporal George S. Thomas of Wickford was killed at the Battle of the Crater.

Tompkins, Daniel. Pvt. Co. K. Residence, Providence. Died of disease contracted in the service Sept. 10, 1863. Interred at Oak Grove Cemetery, Fall River, MA.

Tourgee, John F. Pvt. Co. H. Residence, North Kingstown. Died of dysentery at Washington, D.C., Nov. 23, 1862. Interred at Elm Grove Cemetery, North Kingstown, RI.

Tourtellott, Reuben. Pvt. Co. D. Residence, Burrillville. Died of typhoid at Washington, D.C., Oct. 31, 1861. Interred at Soldier's Home National Cemetery, Washington, D.C. Section G, Grave 3763. Cenotaph at Pascoag Cemetery, Burrillville, RI.

Tripp, Alden. Pvt. Co. C. Residence, Tiverton. Killed in action at the Crater, Petersburg, VA, July 30, 1864.

Tyler, Archibald. Pvt. Co. D. Residence, Coventry. Died of typhoid at Falmouth, VA, Jan. 26, 1863. Interred in unmarked grave at Fredericksburg National Cemetery, Fredericksburg, VA. Cenotaph at Knotty Oak Cemetery, Coventry, RI.

Tyler, Edwin. Pvt. Co. E. Residence, Smithfield. Mortally wounded in action, shot in wrist and leg, at Antietam, MD, Sept. 17, 1862. Died of wounds at Sharpsburg, MD Oct. 13, 1862. Interred at Antietam National Cemetery, Sharpsburg, MD. Rhode Island Section, Grave 2837. Cenotaph at Slatersville Cemetery, North Smithfield, RI.

Walker, James. Pvt. Co. G. Residence, Middletown. Mortally wounded in action, shot in stomach, at Antietam, MD, Sept. 17, 1862. Died of wounds at Baltimore, MD, Dec. 11, 1862. Interred at Common Burying Ground, Newport, RI.

Weaver, Benoni. Pvt. Co. K. Residence, Middletown. Killed in action at Antietam, MD, Sept. 17, 1862. Interred at Antietam National Cemetery, Sharpsburg, MD. Rhode Island Section, Grave 2825. Cenotaph at Island Cemetery, Newport, RI.

Wilcox, Willard P. Corp. Co. B. Residence, Coventry. Killed in action at Antietam, MD, Sept. 17, 1862. Interred at Antietam National Cemetery, Sharpsburg, MD. Rhode Island Section, Grave 2821.

Williams, Archelus A. Pvt. Co. B. Residence, Providence. Died of "heart disease" contracted in the service at Providence, RI, February 6, 1866. Interred at North Burial Ground, Providence, RI.

Williams, Robert. Mus. Co. G. Residence, Newport. Died of typhoid at Beaufort, NC, April 19, 1862. Interred at Common Burying Ground, Newport, RI.

Wood, George M. Pvt. Co. F. Residence, Deerfield, MA. Mortally wounded in action, shot in foot, at Antietam, MD, Sept. 17, 1862. Died of wounds at Frederick, MD, Oct. 22, 1862. Interred at Antietam National Cemetery, Sharpsburg, MD. Rhode Island Section, Grave 2841.

8

Fifth Rhode Island
Heavy Artillery

Allen, John M. Wag. Co. C. Residence, Newport. Died of yellow fever at New Bern, NC, Oct. 10, 1864. Interred at Common Burying Ground, Newport, RI.

Ballou, Dennis H. Pvt. Co. A. Residence, Smithfield. Died of scurvy as a prisoner of war at Charleston, SC, Oct. 16, 1864.

Bane, Frederick. Pvt. Co. A. Residence, Providence. Died of disease at Andersonville Prison, GA, Aug. 2, 1864. Interred at Andersonville National Cemetery, GA. Grave 4576.

Barnes, Samuel. Pvt. Co. E. Residence, Barrington. Died of typhoid at New Bern, NC, June 13, 1862. Interred at Prince's Hill Burial Ground, Barrington, RI.

Beers, Charles E. 2nd Lt. Co. G. Residence, Providence. Died of anemia at Providence, RI, Feb. 12, 1864. Interred at Oak Grove Cemetery, Fall River, MA.

Boss, Edward F. Pvt. Co. A. Residence, Newport. Mortally wounded in action at New Bern, NC, Mar. 14, 1862. Died of wounds at New Bern, NC, Mar. 16, 1862. Interred at North Burial Ground, Providence, RI.

Bourne, Isaac D. Pvt. Co. E. Residence, Falmouth, MA. Died of typhoid at New Bern, NC, Mar. 24, 1862. Interred at Sagamore Cemetery, Bourne, MA.

Brady, James. Pvt. Co. A. Residence, Providence. Died of dysentery at Annapolis, MD, Dec. 13, 1864. Interred at Annapolis National Cemetery, Annapolis, MD. Grave 809.

Brown, John. Pvt. Co. B. Residence, Providence. Drowned at New Bern, NC, Aug. 13, 1863. Interred at New Bern National Cemetery, New Bern, NC. Grave 1940.

Bugbee, Leander W. Pvt. Co. F. Residence, Providence. Died of congestive fever at New Bern, NC, Oct. 16, 1864. Interred at North Woodstock Cemetery, Woodstock, CT.

Calder, Charles. Pvt. Co. D. Residence, Johnston. Died of dysentery contracted in the service at Johnston, RI, July 18, 1865. Interred at Pocasset Cemetery, Cranston, RI.

Callahan, Patrick. Pvt. Co. D. Residence, Cumberland. Drowned at New Bern, NC, Mar. 24, 1865.

Campbell, David. Pvt. Co. A. Residence, Warren. Died of typhoid at Beaufort, NC, Sept. 16, 1862. Interred at New Bern National Cemetery, New Bern, NC. Grave 1867.

Caswell, William F. Pvt. Co. A. Residence, Newport. Died of disease Dec. 12, 1862 at Newport, RI. Interred at Common Burying Ground, Newport, RI.

Chace, Charles F. Pvt. Co. A. Residence, Warren. Died of typhoid at Warren, RI, Jan. 19, 1864. Interred at South Burial Ground, Warren, RI.

Chase, Francis R. Pvt. Co. E. Residence, Swansea, MA. Died of disease at New Bern, NC, Aug. 23, 1863. Interred at New Bern National Cemetery, New Bern, NC. Grave 1938.

Clark, Charles C. Pvt. Co. C. Residence, Providence. Died of disease at New Bern, NC, June 4, 1863. Interred at New Bern National Cemetery, New Bern, NC. Grave 1932.

Collins, Thomas. Pvt. Co. A. Residence, Warwick. Died of disease at Andersonville Prison, GA, Aug. 16, 1864. Interred at Andersonville National Cemetery, GA. Grave 5908.

Colvin, Edward O. Corp. Co. A. Residence, Blackstone, MA. Died of disease at Andersonville Prison, GA, Sept. 6, 1864. Interred at Andersonville National Cemetery, GA. Grave 7966. Cenotaph at East Blackstone Quaker Cemetery, Blackstone, MA.

Cooney, Thomas. Pvt. Co. E. Residence, Smithfield. Killed in a railroad accident at New Bern, NC, Jan. 24, 1863. Interred at New Bern National Cemetery, New Bern, NC. Grave 1967

Copeland, Charles. Pvt. Co. A. Residence, Hadley, MA. Died of disease at New Bern, NC, Oct. 27, 1862. Interred at New Bern National Cemetery, New Bern, NC. Grave 1969.

Curtis, Charles F. Pvt. Co. A. Residence, Providence. Executed at Andersonville Prison, GA, as one of The Raiders, July 11, 1864. Interred at Andersonville National Cemetery, GA.

Dailey, John. Pvt. Co. C. Residence, Providence. Executed for desertion at New Bern, NC, Aug. 14, 1864.

Dean, George B. Pvt. Co. C. Residence, Tiverton. Died of typhoid at Newport, NC, April 4, 1862. Interred at New Bern National Cemetery, New Bern, NC. Grave 1901.

Delaney, Charles H. Pvt. Co. A. Residence, New York, NY. Died of disease at Florence Prison, SC, Feb. 22, 1865. Interred at Florence National Cemetery, Florence, SC. Mass Grave.

Doolittle, George L. Pvt. Co. A. Residence, Providence. Died of disease at Andersonville Prison, GA, Aug. 6, 1864. Interred at Andersonville National Cemetery, GA. Grave 4927.

Doyle, James. Pvt. Co. A. Residence, Johnston. Died of disease at Andersonville Prison, GA, Aug. 14, 1864. Interred at Andersonville National Cemetery, GA. Grave 5670.

Dunlap, George. Sgt. Co. E. Residence, South Kingstown. Died of disease at Andersonville Prison, GA, Nov. 11, 1864. Interred at Andersonville National Cemetery, GA.

Eaton, Amos. Pvt. Co. A. Residence, Attleboro, MA. Died of disease at Andersonville Prison, GA, Oct. 1, 1864. Interred at Andersonville National Cemetery, GA. Grave 10203.

Eddy, Charles H. Corp. Co. E. Residence, Swansea, MA. Died of malaria at New Bern, NC, Oct. 18, 1863. Interred at Mason-Horton Cemetery, Swansea, MA.

Eddy, James M. Pvt. Co. A. Residence, Providence. Died of dysentery at Annapolis, MD, Dec. 30, 1864. Interred at Uriah Eddy Lot, Cranston Cemetery 25, Cranston, RI.

Eddy, Samuel R. Sgt. Co. A. Residence, Warwick Died of disease at Andersonville Prison, GA, Nov. 19, 1864. Interred at Uriah Eddy Lot, Cranston Cemetery 25, Cranston, RI.

Farrell, Patrick. Pvt. Co. A. Residence, Providence. Died "at sea" Nov. 1, 1864.

Fee, Arthur. Pvt. Co. A. Residence, Johnston. Died of disease at Andersonville Prison, GA, Aug. 31, 1864. Interred at Andersonville National Cemetery, GA. Grave 7356.

Fielding, Philip. Pvt. Co. C. Residence, Providence. Died of disease at New Bern, NC, Sept. 10, 1864.

Flood, John. Pvt. Co. B. Residence Johnston. Died of tuberculosis at New York, NY, Nov. 28, 1864.

Frazier, Robert. Pvt. Co. C. Residence, Tiverton. Died of disease at New Bern, NC, Oct. 19, 1862. Interred at New Bern National Cemetery, New Bern, NC. Grave 1937.

Gallagher, John M. Corp. Co. C. Residence, Exeter. Died of erysipelas at New Bern, NC, May 21, 1864. Interred at New Bern National Cemetery, New Bern, NC. Grave 1937.

Gardner, Thaddeus. Pvt. Co. D. Residence, Providence. Died of disease at New Bern, NC, Oct. 9, 1863. Interred at New Bern National Cemetery, New Bern, NC. Grave 1968.

Garvey, William. Pvt. Co. A. Residence, Providence. Died of disease at Andersonville Prison, GA, Aug. 13, 1864. Interred at Andersonville National Cemetery, GA. Grave 5562.

Gladding, Munro H. Regimental QM. Residence, Providence. Died of disease at Beaufort, NC, Nov. 2, 1862. Interred at North Burial Ground, Providence, RI.

Gleason, Nathan. Sgt. Co. H. Residence, Warwick. Died of dysentery at Warwick, RI, Feb. 8, 1865. Interred at Greenwood Cemetery, Coventry, RI.

Regimental Quartermaster Munro H. Gladding died of disease at Beaufort, North Carolina. Like many officers, his body was returned to Providence and interred at North Burial Ground.

Goudy, John. Pvt. Co. A. Residence, Providence. Died of disease at Andersonville Prison, GA, June 12, 1864. Interred at Andersonville National Cemetery, GA. Grave 1866.

Gould, Edwin A. Pvt. Co. F. Residence, Providence. Died of jaundice at New Bern, NC, Dec. 10, 1862. Interred at North Burial Ground, Providence, RI.

Green, John. Pvt. Co. C. Residence, Providence. Died of yellow fever at New Bern, NC, Oct. 14, 1864.

Greenup, Isaac W. Pvt. Residence, Cumberland. Died of disease at New Haven, CT, Dec. 24, 1864. Interred at Oak Hill Cemetery, Woonsocket, RI.

Gregg, James. Capt. Co. A. Residence, Providence. Died of heart disease contracted in the service at Providence, RI, April 1, 1864. Interred at Grace Church Cemetery, Providence, RI.

Grimwood, Samuel H. Corp. Co. E. Residence, Providence. Died of typhoid

Captain James Gregg commanded Company A of the Fifth Rhode Island Heavy Artillery and died of heart disease at his home in Providence on April 1, 1864.

at New Bern, NC, May 22, 1862. Interred at New Bern National Cemetery, New Bern, NC. Grave 1869. Cenotaph at North Burial Ground, Providence, RI.

Haines, Pasco. Mus. Co. F. Residence, Providence. Died of yellow fever at New Bern, NC, Oct. 20, 1864.

Hall, Thomas. Pvt. Co. E. Residence, Providence. Died of dysentery at Providence, RI, May 24, 1863. Interred at North Burial Ground, Providence, RI.

Hall, William Ware. 1st Lt. Co. B. Residence, Providence. Died of tuberculosis contracted in the service at Providence, RI, Aug. 9, 1864. Interred at Swan Point Cemetery, Providence, RI.

Hampstead, John. Pvt. Co. A. Residence, Providence. Died of disease at Andersonville Prison, GA, Aug. 1, 1864. Interred at Andersonville National Cemetery, GA.

Hanley, Thomas. Sgt. Co. A. Residence, Providence. Died of disease at Andersonville Prison, GA, Nov. 15, 1864. Interred at Andersonville National Cemetery, GA. Grave 12016.

Hart, Michael. Pvt. Co. F. Residence, Providence. Died of malaria at New Bern, NC, Nov. 10, 1863. Interred at New Bern National Cemetery, New Bern, NC. Grave 1966.

Haskell, Abner, Jr. Pvt. Co. D. Residence, Cumberland. Died of yellow fever at New Bern, NC, Oct. 10, 1864. Interred at Prospect Hill Cemetery, Uxbridge, MA.

Hawkins, Daniel F. Mus. Co. A. Residence, Newport. Died of disease at Andersonville Prison, GA, Nov. 5, 1864. Interred at Andersonville National Cemetery, GA. Grave 11843.

Henry, Lewis. Pvt. Co. F. Residence, Providence. Died of yellow fever at New Bern, NC, Oct. 13, 1864.

Hill, Smith. Pvt. Co. E. Residence, Glocester. Died of typhoid at New Bern, NC, May 19, 1865. Interred at Acotes Hill Cemetery, Glocester, RI.

Hopkins, George W. Pvt. Co. B. Residence, Foster. Mortally wounded in action at New Bern, NC, Mar. 14, 1862. Died of wounds at New Bern, NC, Mar. 15, 1862. Interred at Hopkins-Ide Lot, Foster Cemetery 26, Foster, RI.

Hornby, John. Pvt. Co. A. Residence, Johnston. Died of disease at Andersonville Prison, GA, Nov. 15, 1864. Interred at Andersonville National Cemetery, GA.

Hubbard, Henry E. Sgt. Co. F. Residence, Johnston. Died of tuberculosis contracted in the service at Providence, RI, June 29, 1866. Interred at North Burial Ground, Providence, RI.

Ives, Daniel. Pvt. Co. G. Residence, Providence. Died of disease at New Bern, NC, May 26, 1863. Interred at New Bern National Cemetery, New Bern, NC. Grave 1899.

Johnson, Andrew J. Pvt. Co. A. Residence, Providence. Died of disease at Andersonville Prison, GA, July 8, 1864. Interred at Andersonville National Cemetery, GA. Grave 3049.

Johnson, Charles. Pvt. Co. G. Residence, Portland, ME. Died of tuberculosis at Philadelphia, PA, Mar. 7, 1865. Interred at Philadelphia National Cemetery, Philadelphia, PA.

Johnson, Daniel. Pvt. Co. A. Residence, Warwick. Died of tuberculosis contracted in the service at Coventry, RI, Mar. 1, 1863. Interred at Brayton Cemetery, Warwick, RI.

Kellehan, Cornelius. Pvt. Co. A. Residence, Providence. Died of disease at Andersonville Prison, GA, July 18, 1864. Interred at Andersonville National Cemetery, GA.

Kennedy, Michael. Sgt. Co. A. Residence, Providence. Died of disease as a prisoner of war at Charleston, SC, Oct. 4, 1864. Interred at Beaufort National Cemetery, Beaufort, SC. Grave 2499.

Lawton, Charles E. Regimental QM. Residence, Newport. Died of apoplexy at New Bern, NC, Dec. 26, 1864. Interred at Island Cemetery, Newport, RI.

Lawton, Thomas J. Pvt. Co. B. Died of typhoid at New Bern, NC Aug. 20, 1862. Interred at New Bern National Cemetery, New Bern, NC. Grave 1934.

Lee, Cornelius. Pvt. Co. A. Residence, Johnston. Died of disease at Andersonville Prison, GA, Aug. 25, 1864. Interred at Andersonville National Cemetery, GA. Grave 6798.

Leonard, Benjamin F. Pvt. Co. C. Residence, Glocester. Died of disease contracted in the service at Glocester, RI, Sept. 20, 1862. Interred at Acotes Hill Cemetery, Glocester, RI.

Lewis, Edward. Pvt. Co. A. Residence, Providence. Died of disease at Andersonville Prison, GA, July 29, 1864. Interred at Andersonville National Cemetery, GA. Grave 4215.

Lillibridge, William H. Corp. Co. A. Residence, Exeter. Died of disease at Andersonville Prison, GA, Aug. 16, 1864. Interred at Andersonville National Cemetery, GA. Grave 5827.

Liscomb, Byron D. Pvt. Co. B. Residence, Bristol. Died of "congestion of the brain" at New Bern, NC, Nov. 3, 1863. Interred at New Bern National Cemetery, New Bern, NC. Grave 2006.

Livingston, John. Mus. Co. A. Residence, Providence. Died of disease at Andersonville Prison, GA, Oct. 30, 1864. Interred at Andersonville National Cemetery, GA. Grave 11688.

Ludwig, Lorenzo V. Sgt. Co. B. Residence, Bristol. Died of typhoid at

New Bern, NC, April 24, 1862. Interred at New Bern National Cemetery, New Bern, NC. Grave 1877. Cenotaph at Howard Cemetery, Dansville, MI.

Mathewson, Joseph W. Pvt. Co. E. Residence, Providence. Died of typhoid at Providence RI, Mar. 26, 1863. Interred at North Burial Ground, Providence, RI.

McDonald, Donald. Pvt. Co. I. Residence, Smithfield. Died of typhoid at New Bern, NC, May 29, 1863. Interred at New Bern National Cemetery, New Bern, NC. Grave 1902.

McElroy, Patrick. Pvt. Co. I. Residence, Johnston. Died of heart disease at Hatteras NC, Oct. 29, 1863.

McLaughlin, James. Pvt. Co. A. Residence, Providence. Mortally wounded in action at New Bern, NC, Mar. 14, 1862. Died of wounds at New Bern, NC, Mar. 30, 1862.

Miller, John W. Pvt. Co. E. Residence, Killingly, CT. Died of disease at New Bern, NC, Aug. 22, 1863. Interred at New Bern National Cemetery, New Bern, NC. Grave 1939

Miller, John W. Pvt. Co. H. Residence, Providence. Died of yellow fever at New Bern, NC, Oct. 7, 1864.

Montgomery, George. Pvt. Co. A. Died of disease at Andersonville Prison, GA, Nov. 28, 1864. Interred at Andersonville National Cemetery, GA.

Murphy, Jeremiah. Pvt. Co. C. Residence, Tiverton. Died of disease at New Bern, NC, Oct. 1, 1863. Interred at New Bern National Cemetery, New Bern, NC.

Norris, Trustworthy. Pvt. Co. I. Residence, Smithfield. Died of typhoid at New Bern, NC, April 29, 1863. Interred at New Bern National Cemetery, New Bern, NC.

O'Leary, Patrick. Pvt. Co. A. Residence, Providence. Killed in action at New Bern, NC, Mar. 14, 1862.

O'Neil, Cornelius. Pvt. Co. A. Residence, Providence. Died of "disease contracted in the U.S. Service during the Great Rebellion," at Providence, RI. April 23, 1864. Interred at St. Patrick's Cemetery, Providence, RI.

O'Neil, James. Pvt. Co. E. Residence, New York, NY. Died of dysentery at Providence, RI, Dec. 18, 1864. Interred at North Burial Ground, Providence, RI.

Paull, Walter W. Corp. Co. F. Residence, Providence. Died of typhoid at New Bern, NC, July 22, 1863. Interred at New Bern National Cemetery, New Bern, NC. Grave 1941.

Peck, Edwin B. Pvt. Co. E. Residence, Barrington. Died of typhoid at Roanoke, NC, Feb. 9, 1862. Interred at Prince's Hill Burial Ground, Barrington, RI.

Peck, James E. Pvt. Co. A. Residence, Warren. Died of disease at New

Bern, NC, Nov. 27, 1862. Interred at New Bern National Cemetery, New Bern, NC. Grave 1993.

Perrigo, Charles. Sgt. Co. A. Residence, Providence. Mortally wounded in action at New Bern, NC, Mar. 14, 1862. Died of wounds at Providence, RI, April 20, 1862. Interred at Grace Church Cemetery, Providence, RI.

Pierce, Henry R. 1st Lt. Co. D. Residence, Woonsocket. Killed in action at New Bern, NC, Mar. 14, 1862. Interred at Oak Hill Cemetery, Woonsocket, RI.

Prouty, William W. Regimental QM. Residence, Newport. Died of an aneurism at New Bern, NC, Dec. 31, 1863. Interred at Island Cemetery, Newport, RI.

Redding, George. Wag. Co. F. Residence, Providence. Died of yellow fever at New Bern, NC, Oct. 3, 1864.

Riley, Michael. Corp. Co. A. Residence, Johnston. Died of disease at Andersonville Prison, GA, Sept. 20, 1864. Interred at Andersonville National Cemetery, GA. Grave 9413

Rourke, Patrick. Pvt. Co. C. Residence, Tiverton. Died of disease at New Bern, NC, Aug. 3, 1864. Interred at New Bern National Cemetery, New Bern, NC. 1870.

Rowlands, Thomas. Pvt. Co. H. Residence, Providence. Died of typhoid at Providence, RI, Jan. 3, 1863. Interred at North Burial Ground, Providence, RI.

Ryan, John. Pvt. Co. E. Residence, New York, NY. Died of disease at Annapolis, MD, Jan. 8, 1862.

Ryan, Patrick. Pvt. Co. I. Residence, Providence. Died of yellow fever at New Bern, NC, Oct. 3, 1864.

Ryan, Thomas. Pvt. Co. D. Residence, Cumberland. Killed in action at New Bern, NC, Mar. 14, 1862.

Ryan, William. Pvt. Co. G. Residence, Providence. Died of bronchitis at New Bern, NC, Jan. 24, 1865.

Sanders, Charles. Pvt. Co. A. Residence, Providence. Died of disease at Andersonville Prison, GA, Aug. 28, 1864. Interred at Andersonville National Cemetery, GA. Grave 7129.

Schmidt, Louis. Pvt. Co. H. Residence, Providence. Died of yellow fever at New Bern, NC, Sept. 30, 1864.

Seymour, Henry. Pvt. Co. A. Residence, Providence. Died of disease at Andersonville Prison, GA, Aug. 19, 1864. Interred at Andersonville National Cemetery, GA. 6187.

Sherman, Amos B. 1st Sgt. Co. C. Residence, Newport. Died of yellow fever at Newport, RI, Sept. 4, 1864. Interred at Island Cemetery, Newport, RI.

Shippy, Thomas. Pvt. Co. G. Residence, Foster. Mortally wounded in action at Whitehall, NC, Dec. 16, 1862. Died of wounds at New Bern, NC, Dec. 17, 1862.

Simmons, James. Pvt. Co. C. Residence, Providence. Executed for desertion at New Bern, NC, Aug. 18, 1864.

Simpson, Thomas. Pvt. Co. A. Residence, Newport. Died of disease contracted in the service at Newport, RI, April 13, 1862. Interred at Common Burying Ground, Newport, RI.

Sisson, Charles S. Pvt. Co. A. Residence, Warren. Died of disease at Andersonville Prison, GA, Aug. 19, 1864. Cenotaph at North Burial Ground, Bristol, RI.

Slocum, Charles A. Corp. Co. A. Residence, South Kingstown. Died of disease at Andersonville Prison, GA, Aug. 31, 1864. Interred at Andersonville National Cemetery, GA. Grave 6186.

Smith, George. Pvt. Co. G. Residence, Providence. Died of disease at New Bern, NC, Sept. 28, 1864.

Smith, Samuel. Pvt. Co. B. Residence, Providence. Died of typhoid at New Bern, NC, April 25, 1864. Interred at New Bern National Cemetery, New Bern, NC. Grave 1963.

Stewart, Charles. Pvt. Co. D. Residence, Providence. Drowned at New Bern, NC, Mar. 24, 1865. Interred at New Bern National Cemetery, New Bern, NC. Grave 1990.

Sullivan, Jerry. Pvt. Co. A. Residence, Smithfield. Died of disease at Andersonville Prison, GA, Aug. 21, 1864. Interred at Andersonville National Cemetery, GA. Grave 6351.

Thomas, John. Pvt. Co. A. Residence, Providence. Died of disease at Andersonville Prison, GA, Sept. 11, 1864. Interred at Andersonville National Cemetery, GA. Grave 8522.

Tracy, Christopher. Pvt. Co. G. Residence, Providence. Died of yellow fever at New Bern, NC, Sept. 29, 1864.

First Lieutenant George F. Turner died of yellow fever at New Bern, North Carolina. He was a resident of Newport.

Turner, George F. 1st Lt. Co. E. Residence, Newport. Died of yellow fever at New Bern, NC, Oct. 6, 1864. Interred at Island Cemetery, Newport, RI.

Vallett, William H. Pvt. Co. A. Residence, Glocester. Died of disease at Andersonville Prison, GA, Nov. 20, 1864. Interred at Andersonville National Cemetery, GA. Grave 12100.

Vaughn, Pardon B. Sgt. Co. G. Residence, Providence. Died of dysentery contracted in the service at Providence, RI, Aug. 25, 1865. Interred at Swan Point Cemetery, Providence, RI.

Wallace, William. Pvt. Co. A. Residence, Providence. Died of disease at Andersonville Prison, GA, July 11, 1864. Interred at Andersonville National Cemetery, GA. Grave 3173

Weed, Matthew. Pvt. Co. I. Residence, Philadelphia, PA. Died of yellow fever at New Bern, NC, Sept. 27, 1864.

White, Emery. Pvt. Co. G. Residence, Lisbon, CT. Died of disease at New Bern, NC, June 19, 1863. Interred at New Bern National Cemetery, New Bern, NC. Grave 1942.

Wickes, Franklin. Pvt. Co. A. Residence, Providence. Died of disease at Andersonville Prison, GA, Nov. 5, 1864. Interred at Oliver Wickes Lot, East Greenwich Cemetery 62, East Greenwich, RI.

Williams, John. Pvt. Co. G. Residence, Providence. Died of typhoid at New Bern, NC, July 30, 1864. Interred at New Bern National Cemetery, New Bern, NC. Grave 1964.

Wilson, Buchanan. Pvt. Co. G. Residence, Wrentham, MA. Died of malaria at New Bern, Oct. 26, 1864. Interred at New Bern National Cemetery, New Bern, NC. Grave 1963.

Wilson, Jerry. Pvt. Co. A. Residence, Providence. Died of disease at Andersonville Prison, GA, Sept. 4, 1864. Interred at Andersonville National Cemetery, GA. Grave 7831.

Wright, Thomas. Pvt. Co. F. Residence, Providence. Died of tuberculosis at New Bern, NC, Oct. 30, 1862. Interred at New Bern National Cemetery, New Bern, NC. Grave 1970.

9

Seventh Rhode Island
Volunteers

Adams, Sabine G. Pvt. Co. C. Residence, Glocester. Died of typhoid at Baltimore, MD, Jan. 20, 1863. Interred at Loudon Park National Cemetery. Baltimore, MD. Grave 1687.

Albro, Edmund B. Pvt. Co. H. Residence, East Greenwich. Died of typhoid at regimental hospital at Falmouth, VA, Dec. 30, 1862. Interred at First Cemetery, East Greenwich, RI.

Aldrich, Moses H. Corp. Co. C. Residence, Burrillville. Died of disease contracted in the service at Burrillville, RI, Dec. 17, 1865. Interred at Cooper Mowry Lot, Burrillville Cemetery 46, Burrillville, RI.

Alexander, Hartford. Pvt. Co. E. Residence, Cumberland. Killed in action at Bethesda Church, VA, June 3, 1864. Interred at Cold Harbor National Cemetery, Mechanicsville, VA. Grave 795.

Arnold, Benjamin F. Pvt. Co. B. Residence, Coventry. Drowned in New York Harbor, July 15, 1865. Interred at Elm Grove Cemetery, North Kingstown, RI.

Arnold, Job. Lt. Col. Residence, Providence. Died of malaria contracted in the service at Providence, RI, Dec. 28, 1869. Interred at North Burial Ground, Providence, RI.

Arnold, Reuben. Pvt. Co. H. Residence, East Greenwich. Killed in action at Fredericksburg, VA, Dec. 13, 1862. Cenotaph at Vaughn Arnold Lot, North Kingstown Cemetery 9, North Kingstown, RI.

Ashworth, William. Pvt. Co. K. Residence, Warwick. Died of typhoid in hospital at Lexington, KY, Jan. 30, 1864. Interred at St. Phillips Episcopal Cemetery, West Warwick, RI.

Austin, Benjamin K. Pvt. Co. A. Residence, Hopkinton. Killed in action at Spotsylvania Court House, VA, May 12, 1864. Interred at Fredericksburg National Cemetery, Fredericksburg, VA. Grave 4168.

Austin, Wanton G. Pvt. Co. G. Residence, South Kingstown. Died of

Lieutenant Colonel Job Arnold of Providence became severely ill during the 1863 Vicksburg Campaign and resigned from the service in May 1864. In December 1869, he died as a direct result of the disease he contracted in Mississippi.

Yazoo Fever onboard the *David Tatum*, Aug. 10, 1863. Cenotaph at Beriah B. Gardner Lot, South Kingstown Cemetery 13, South Kingstown, RI.

     Babbitt, Jacob. Maj. Residence, Bristol. Mortally wounded in action, shot in chest, at Fredericksburg, VA, Dec. 13, 1862. Died of wounds at Alexandria, VA, Dec. 23, 1862. Interred at Juniper Hill Cemetery, Bristol, RI.

     Bacon, James H. Pvt. Co. G. Residence, South Kingstown. Died of typhoid at Falmouth, VA, Jan. 24, 1863. Interred at Oak Dell Cemetery, South Kingstown, RI.

Ballou, George E. Pvt. Co. B. Residence, Burrillville. Died of typhoid at Lincoln Hospital, Washington, D.C., Jan. 27, 1865. Interred at Arlington National Cemetery. Section 13, Grave 9396.

Barber, Israel A. Pvt. Co. G. Residence, Hopkinton. Died of Yazoo Fever onboard *David Tatum*, Mississippi River, Aug. 5, 1863. Cenotaph at Usquepaugh Cemetery, South Kingstown, RI.

Barber, Jesse N. Pvt. Co. G. Residence, Hopkinton. Killed in action at Fredericksburg, VA, Dec. 13, 1862. Cenotaph at Wood River Cemetery, Richmond, RI.

Barker, Alexander. Pvt. Co. I. Residence, Newport. Died of disease contacted in the service at Newport, RI, Aug. 5, 1866. Interred at Common Burying Ground, Newport, RI.

Bateman, George. Pvt. Co. K. Residence, Providence. Died of Yazoo Fever at Covington, KY Aug. 20, 1863. Interred at Camp Nelson National Cemetery, Nicholasville, KY. Section G, Grave 2023.

Battey, Hiram Salisbury. Pvt. Co. K. Residence, Johnston. Detached to Battery E, Second U.S. Artillery. Died of dysentery at Marine Hospital, Cincinnati, OH, Aug. 16, 1863. Interred at Spring Grove National Cemetery, Cincinnati, OH. Grave 521. Cenotaph at Atwood Salisbury Lot, Scituate Cemetery 44, Scituate, RI.

Bentley, William. Pvt. Co. A.

A wealthy banker from Bristol, Major Jacob Babbitt was mortally wounded at Fredericksburg trying to save his men from a perilous position.

Hiram Salisbury Battey of Scituate served in Company K of the Seventh. Like so many members of the regiment, he died as a result of his service in Mississippi. Private Battey died of dysentery at Cincinnati, Ohio, on August 16, 1863.

Residence, North Stonington, CT. Killed in a boiler explosion accident at Nicholasville, KY, June 6, 1863.

Bishop, Charles H. Corp. Co. B. Residence, Providence. Killed in action at Fredericksburg, VA, Dec. 13, 1862. Served in Color Guard.

Bitgood, Joseph A. Pvt. Co. B. Residence, Providence. Died in hospital of typhoid at Washington, Jan. 4, 1863. Interred at Soldier's Home National Cemetery, Washington, D.C. Grave 5465.

Bolles, Albert A. 1st Lt. Co. F. Residence, Pawtucket. Mortally wounded in action, shot in throat, at Petersburg, VA, April 2, 1865. Died of wounds April 9, 1865, at Petersburg, VA. Interred at Mineral Spring Cemetery, Pawtucket, RI.

Bollig, John N. Pvt. Co. G. Residence, Providence. Died of disease contracted in the service at Providence, RI, Aug. 29, 1865. Interred at North Burial Ground, Providence, RI.

Boyle, Charles. Pvt. Co. E. Residence, Johnston. Mortally wounded in action at Fredericksburg, VA, Dec. 13, 1862. Died of wounds at Emory Hospital, Washington, D.C., Feb. 1, 1863. Interred at Oak Grove Cemetery, Pawtucket, RI.

Brayman, Henry. Pvt. Co. G. Residence, South Kingstown. Died of Yazoo Fever at Camp Nelson, KY, Sept. 14, 1863. Interred at Camp Nelson National Cemetery, Nicholasville, KY. Section D, Grave 1264.

Brickley, James. Pvt. Co. B. Residence, Woonsocket. Killed in action at Fredericksburg, VA, Dec. 13, 1862.

Bridgehouse, Timothy. Corp. Co. B. Residence, Providence. Died of typhoid at General Hospital, Camp Dennison, OH, Sept. 14, 1863. Served in Color Guard. Interred at Spring Grove National Cemetery Cincinatti, OH. Grave 1000.

Briggs, Benjamin G. Pvt. Co. H. Residence, Newport. Died of typhoid at Pleasant Valley, MD, Nov. 4, 1862.

Briggs, Nathan O. Pvt. Co. G. Residence, Glocester. Died of tuberculosis contracted in the service June 6, 1867, at Putnam, CT. Interred at Grove Street Cemetery, Putnam, CT.

Briggs, Rowland B. Corp. Co. F. Residence, Exeter. Died of typhoid at Mansion House Hospital, Alexandria, VA, Nov. 21, 1862. Interred at Wood River Cemetery, Richmond, RI.

Brown, Albert G. Pvt. Co. F. Residence, Exeter. Died of pneumonia at Newport News, VA, Feb. 27, 1863. Interred at Elm Grove Cemetery, North Kingstown, RI.

Brown, John F. Pvt. Co. F. Residence, Exeter. Died of typhoid at Mouth Pleasant Hospital, Washington, D.C., Oct. 5, 1862. Interred at Elm Grove Cemetery, North Kingstown, RI.

Brown, Samuel G. Corp. Co. H. Residence, East Greenwich. Died of dysentery at Camp Dennison, OH, Aug. 26, 1863. Interred at Spring Grove National Cemetery. Grave 908.

Brownell, William. Pvt. Co. C. Residence, Johnston. Died of disease contracted in the service Mar. 20, 1863 at Johnston, RI. Interred at Intervale Cemetery, North Providence, RI.

Browning, Orlando N. Pvt. Co. G. Residence, South Kingstown. Killed in action at Fredericksburg, VA, Dec. 13, 1862. Cenotaph at Browning Lot, South Kingstown Cemetery 63, South Kingstown, RI.

Bryden, Wilson C. Pvt. Co. K. Residence, Burrillville. Died of typhoid fever contracted in the service Dec. 29, 1862, at Webster, MA. Interred at Mount Zion Cemetery, Webster, MA.

Budlong, Benjamin. Corp. Co. C. Residence, Warwick. Mortally wounded in action at Fredericksburg, VA, Dec. 13, 1862. Died of wounds at Washington, D.C., Jan. 12, 1863. Interred at Greenwood Cemetery, Coventry, RI.

Burdick, Joseph Weeden. Pvt. Co. A. Residence, Hopkinton. Died of Yazoo Fever at Milldale, MS, July 19, 1863. Interred near Milldale, MS. Cenotaph in Rockville Cemetery, Hopkinton, RI.

Burdick, Welcome C. Pvt. Co. G. Residence, Hopkinton. Mortally wounded in action at Fredericksburg, VA, Dec. 13, 1862. Died of wounds at Douglass General Hospital, Washington, D.C., Dec. 26, 1862. Interred at Soldier's Home National Cemetery, Washington, D.C. Section D, Grave 5209. Cenotaph at River Bend Cemetery, Westerly, RI.

A popular member of Company A, Joseph Weeden Burdick died of Yazoo Fever in Mississippi. His family erected a cenotaph to his memory at Rockville Cemetery in Hopkinton; today he is interred in an unmarked grave near Milldale, Mississippi.

Burgess, Benjamin W. Pvt. Co. C. Residence, Glocester. Killed in action at Fredericksburg, VA, Dec. 13, 1862.

Burke, John. Pvt. Co. H. Residence, Smithfield. Died of dysentery at Big Black River, MS, July 12, 1863.

Cahoone, Sylvester. Pvt. Co. E. Residence, Exeter. Died of typhoid at Pleasant Valley, MD, Nov. 16, 1862.

Cameron, Uz. Pvt. Co. G Residence, South Kingstown. Drowned in the Mississippi River, June 9, 1863.

Caswell, Alfred A. Pvt. Co. B. Residence, Scituate. Died of dysentery in Regimental Hospital at Lexington, KY, Sept. 22, 1863. Interred at Lexington National Cemetery. Grave 467.

Chace, John H. Corp. Co. C. Residence, Providence. Died of dysentery contracted in the service at Providence, RI June 20, 1865. Interred at Swan Point Cemetery, Providence, RI.

Champlin, Charles E. Pvt. Co. G. Residence, South Kingstown. Died of dysentery at South Kingstown, RI July 21, 1863. Interred at Perryville Cemetery, South Kingstown, RI.

Chase, Artemas B. Pvt. Co. B. Residence, New Bedford, MA. Died of disease contracted in the service at New Bedford, Massachusetts, Dec. 15, 1865.

Chatter, Joseph. Pvt. Co. F. Residence, Exeter. Died of typhoid at Falmouth, VA, Dec. 3, 1862.

Cheever, John T. H. 2nd Lt. Co. I. Residence, Providence. Died of illness contracted in the service at Wrentham, MA, June 6, 1865. Interred at Gerould Cemetery, Wrentham, MA.

Clark, John Burr. Pvt. Co. A. Residence, Richmond. Mortally wounded in action, shot in back, at Fredericksburg, VA, Dec. 13, 1862. Died of wounds at Baltimore, MD, May 10, 1863. Interred at Union Cemetery, North Stonington, CT.

Clarke, Jonathan R. Pvt. Co. G. Residence, South Kingstown. Killed in action at Jackson, MS, July 13, 1863. Interred near Jackson, MS.

Clarke, Stephen A. Pvt. Co.

A farmer from Richmond, Stephen A. Clarke was killed in action at Poplar Spring Church, Virginia, on September 30, 1864. He served in Company K of the Seventh Rhode Island.

K. Residence, Hopkinton. Killed in action at Poplar Spring Church, VA, Sept. 30, 1864. Interred at Poplar Grove National Cemetery. Grave 3171. Cenotaph in Wood River Cemetery, Richmond, RI.

Cole, Darius I. 1st Lt. Co. B. Residence, Providence. Killed in action at Spotsylvania Court House, VA, May 13, 1864. Interred at Fredericksburg National Cemetery, Fredericksburg, VA. Grave 952.

Cole, Henry S. Pvt. Co. K. Residence, Foster. Killed in action at Fredericksburg, VA, Dec. 13, 1862. Cenotaph in Cole Lot, Foster Cemetery 52, Foster, RI.

Collins, Gideon Franklin. Pvt. Co. A. Residence, Hopkinton. Died of typhoid at Pleasant Valley, MD, Oct. 10, 1862.

Collins, William. Pvt. Co. I. Residence, Bristol. Detached temporarily to Battery D, 1st RI Light Artillery, Jan. 15, 1863. Died of dysentery in Asylum Hospital, Knoxville, TN, May 1, 1864. Interred at Knoxville National Cemetery, Knoxville, TN. Section D, Grave 758.

Colvin, Nathan D. Pvt. Co. C. Residence, Coventry. Died of typhoid at David's Island, NY Harbor, Sept. 26, 1864. Interred at Royal Colvin Lot, Coventry Cemetery 117, Coventry, RI.

Colwell, William. Wag. Co. A. Residence, Providence. Died of typhoid at Falmouth, VA, Jan. 14, 1863.

Coman, William A. Wag. Co. C. Residence, Glocester. Mortally wounded in action at Fredericksburg, VA, Dec. 13, 1862. Died of wounds at Falmouth, VA, Dec. 19, 1862. Interred at Fredericksburg National Cemetery, Fredericksburg, VA. Grave 4899. Cenotaph in Coman Lot, Glocester Cemetery 48, Glocester, RI.

Congdon, George W. 1st Sgt. Co. D. Residence, Pawtucket. Killed in action at Bethesda Church, VA, June 3, 1864. Interred at Cold Harbor National Cemetery, Mechanicsville, VA. Grave 806.

Corbin, Amasa N. Pvt. Co. K. Residence, Scituate. Died of typhoid at Falmouth, VA, Dec. 24, 1862. Interred at Clayville Cemetery, Foster, RI.

Corey, Charles H. Pvt. Co. K. Residence, North Providence. Died of dysentery at Camp Dennison, OH, Sept. 15, 1863. Interred at Spring Grove National Cemetery, Cincinnati, OH. Section 21, Grave 837.

Cornell, Ira. Pvt. Co. K. Residence, Coventry. Borne on the rolls of the Rhode Island Adjutant General as having deserted at Cincinnati, OH, April 1, 1863. According to the vital records of Coventry, RI, he died at Cincinnati, OH, April 1, 1863. "Drowned in the Ohio River in the attempt of crossing it in the line of duty." Carried on this roll as having drowned April 1, 1863, at Cincinnati, OH. Cenotaph in Pine Grove Cemetery, Coventry, RI.

Cornell, Ira, Jr. Pvt. Co. K. Residence, Coventry. Died of tuberculosis contracted in the service at Coventry, RI April 27, 1867. Interred at Pine Grove Cemetery, Coventry, RI.

Cornell, Martin. Pvt. Co. H. Residence, Warwick. Mortally wounded in action at Spotsylvania Court House, VA, May 14, 1864. Died of wounds at Annapolis, MD, June 1, 1864. Interred at Large Maple Root Cemetery, Coventry, RI.

Costello, George B. 1st Lt. Co. B. Residence, Providence. Died of tuberculosis contracted in the service at Providence, RI, July 21, 1868. Interred at North Burial Ground, Providence, RI.

Cox, William. Pvt. Co. B. Residence, Providence. Killed in action at Fredericksburg, VA, Dec. 13, 1862.

Crandall, Courtland E. Pvt. Co. G. Residence, South Kingstown. Died of typhoid contracted in the service at Norwich, CT, January 24, 1863.

Crane, Thomas. Pvt. Co. B. Residence, Woonsocket. Died of dysentery in General Hospital at Lexington, KY, Nov. 7, 1863. Interred at Lexington National Cemetery. Grave 471.

Dempster, John. Pvt. Co. E. Residence, Providence. Killed in action at Fredericksburg, VA, Dec. 13, 1862.

Devitt, John M. Corp. Co. F. Residence, Tiverton. Mortally wounded in action at Bethesda Church, VA, June 3, 1864. Died of wounds at Harewood General Hospital, Washington, D.C. July 8, 1864.

Donnelly, Patrick. Pvt. Co. D. Residence, Providence. Died of dysentery in hospital at Lexington, KY, June 30, 1863. Interred at St. Francis Cemetery, Pawtucket, RI.

Dorrance, John. Pvt. Co. C. Residence, Foster. Died of typhoid in Second Division, Ninth Army Corps Field Hospital, Windmill Point, at Aquia Creek, VA, Jan. 26, 1863. Interred at Benjamin Cahoone Lot, Coventry Cemetery 101, Coventry, RI.

Dow, Byron E. Pvt. Co. D. Residence, Providence. Died June 16, 1869, "of disease contracted in the U.S. service during the Great Rebellion." Interred at Locust Grove Cemetery, Providence, RI.

Durfee, Gilbert. Pvt. Co. C. Residence, Glocester. Killed in action at Poplar Spring Church, VA, Sept. 30, 1864. Interred at Smithville Cemetery, Scituate, RI.

Eddy, John S. Pvt. Co. G. Residence, Cranston. Killed in action at Cold Harbor, VA, June 8, 1864. Interred at Arlington National Cemetery. Section 27, Grave 473. Cenotaph at North Burial Ground, Providence, RI.

Eldridge, James E. Pvt. Co. C. Residence, Warwick. Died of typhoid at Washington, D.C., July 16, 1864.

Essex, Richard. Pvt. Co. E. Residence, West Greenwich. Died of dysentery at Lexington, KY, Sept. 23, 1863. Interred at Camp Nelson National Cemetery, Nicholasville, KY. Section D, Grave 1263.

Farrow, Enos. Pvt. Co. K. Residence, Foster. Died of typhoid at Washington, D.C., Dec. 3, 1862. Interred at Soldier's Home National Cemetery. Section H, Grave 3552.

Ferry, James. Pvt. Co. B. Residence, Woonsocket. Died of typhoid at Hampton, VA, Mar. 22, 1863. Interred at Chase Cemetery, Sutton, VA.

Field, George A. Pvt. Co. K. Residence, Scituate. Died of dysentery at general hospital, Lexington, KY, April 5, 1864. Interred at Isaac Field Lot, Scituate Cemetery 59, Scituate, RI.

Finley, William. Pvt. Co. G. Residence, South Kingstown. Died of dysentery at Covington, KY, Aug. 15, 1863. Interred at Covington National Cemetery. Section G, Grave 2014.

Flaherty, Michael. Sgt. Co. A. Residence, Providence. Killed in action at Bethesda Church, VA, June 3, 1864. Cenotaph in St. Patrick's Cemetery, Providence, RI.

Flanagan, Bernard. Pvt. Co. A. Residence, Providence. Died of Yazoo Fever at Cincinnati, OH, July 25, 1863.

Follett, Samuel O. Pvt. Co. H. Residence, East Greenwich. Mortally wounded in action at Spotsylvania Court House, VA, May 14, 1864. Died of wounds at Alexandria, VA, June 16, 1864. Interred at Alexandria National Cemetery. Grave 2166.

Franklin, Chester Lewis. Pvt. Co. F. Residence, Exeter. Mortally wounded in action at the North Anna River, VA, May 25, 1864. Died of wounds at Port Royal, VA, May 28, 1864. Interred at Greenwood Cemetery, Coventry, RI.

Franklin, Josephus. Pvt. Co. I. Residence, Bristol. Died of typhoid at Falmouth, VA, Nov. 29, 1862. Interred at North Burial Ground, Bristol, RI.

Gallagher, Owen. Pvt. Co. G. Residence, South Kingstown. Killed in action at Fredericksburg, VA, Dec. 13, 1862.

Gardiner, Charles W. Pvt. Co. G. Residence, South Kingstown. Died of typhoid at Marine Hospital, Cincinnati, OH, Aug. 24, 1863. Interred at Usquepaugh Cemetery, South Kingstown, RI.

Gardiner, George W. Pvt. Co. A. Residence, Hopkinton. Died of typhoid at Pleasant Valley, MD, Oct. 18, 1862. Interred at Pine Grove Cemetery, Hopkinton, RI.

Gardner, Francis W. Pvt. Co. I. Residence, Smithfield. Died of Yazoo Fever at Camp Nelson, KY, Aug. 28, 1863

Gladding, James H. Pvt. Co. I. Residence, Bristol. Mortally wounded in action, shot in arm, at Bethesda Church, VA, June 3, 1864. Died of wounds at Mount Pleasant Hospital, Washington, D.C., July 3, 1864. Interred at North Burial Ground, Bristol, RI.

Godfrey, Henry H. Pvt. Co. A. Residence, Hopkinton. Died of Yazoo Fever contracted in the service at Hopkinton, RI, September 7, 1863. Interred at Pine Grove Cemetery, Hopkinton, RI.

Gordon, Henry W. Pvt. Co. G. Residence, Coventry. Died of disease at Fort Schuyler Hospital, NY, Feb. 1, 1865.

Private Henry H. Godfrey died of Yazoo Fever shortly after returning to his Hopkinton home on September 7, 1863. He had served in Company A, Seventh Rhode Island Volunteers.

Gorton, Joel B. Pvt. Co. A. Residence, West Greenwich. Died of Yazoo Fever at Camp Nelson, KY, Sept. 11, 1863. Interred at Camp Nelson National Cemetery, Nicholasville, KY. Section D, Grave 1262.

Gorton, Richard, Jr. Pvt. Co. H. Residence, North Kingstown. Killed in action at Spotsylvania Court House, VA, May 18, 1864. Interred at Fredericksburg National Cemetery, Fredericksburg, VA. Grave 1165.

Gorton, Thomas. Pvt. Co. H. Residence, East Greenwich. Killed in action at Fredericksburg, VA, Dec. 13, 1862.

Grant, George S. Pvt. Co. E. Residence, Cumberland. Died of typhoid at Cumberland, RI, Jan. 16, 1863. Interred at Moshassuck Cemetery, Central Falls, RI.

Grant, Ira W. Pvt. Co. E. Residence, Cumberland. Killed in action at Bethesda Church, VA, June 3, 1864. Cenotaph at Moshassuck Cemetery, Central Falls, RI.

Greene, Charles B. Pvt. Co. A. Residence, Hopkinton. Died of typhoid at Frederick, MD Oct. 5, 1862. Interred at First Cemetery, Hopkinton, RI.

Greene, Jedediah. Pvt. Co. A. Residence, Hopkinton. Killed in action at Fredericksburg, VA, Dec. 13, 1862.

Greene, Robert B. Pvt. Co. G. Residence, South Kingstown. Mortally wounded in action at Fredericksburg, VA, Dec. 13, 1862. Died of wounds at Washington, D.C., Jan. 2, 1863. Interred at Soldier's Home National Cemetery, Washington, D.C. Section H, Grave 3331.

Greene, Thomas W. Pvt. Co. E. Residence, West Greenwich. Mortally wounded in action, shot in hip, at Bethesda Church, VA, June 3, 1864. Sent to hospital and borne as absent sick until Jan. 28, 1865, when he was discharged for disability from Portsmouth Grove, RI. Died of wounds at West Greenwich, RI, April 6, 1865. Interred at Wanton Greene Lot, Coventry Cemetery 128, Coventry, RI.

Greene, William H. Mus. Co. A. Residence, Providence. Died of typhoid at Baltimore, MD, April 21, 1863. Interred at Oakland Cemetery, Cranston, RI.

Hall, William A. Pvt. Co. H. Residence, Richmond. Died of typhoid in hospital at Washington, D.C., Feb. 10, 1863. Interred at Soldier's Home National Cemetery, Washington, D.C. Grave 4374.

Harrington, William. Sgt. Co. D. Residence, Scituate. Died of dysentery at hospital, Nicholasville, KY, Aug. 31, 1863. Interred at Camp Nelson National Cemetery, Nicholasville, KY. Section L, Grave 1261.

Hatfield, Richard. Pvt. Co. C. Residence, Glocester. Died of typhoid at Alexandria, VA, Nov. 19, 1862. Interred at Alexandria National Cemetery. Grave 450. Cenotaph at North Burial Ground, Providence, RI.

Hathaway, Alvin P. Pvt. Co. I. Residence, Newport. Mortally wounded in action at Petersburg, VA, June 24, 1864. Died of wounds at Mount Pleasant Hospital, Washington, D.C., June 28, 1864. Interred at Arlington National Cemetery. Grave 5555.

Healey, Horace D. Pvt. Co. G. Residence, South Kingstown. Died of dysentery at Milldale, MS, Aug. 2, 1863.

Hodson, James. Pvt. Co. H. Residence, Warwick. Killed in action at Cold Harbor, VA, June 6, 1864.

Holbrook, Joseph H. Pvt. Co. E. Residence, Glocester. Died of heat stroke near Jackson, MS, July 21, 1863. Cenotaph at Acotes Hill Cemetery, Glocester, RI.

Holloway, Thomas T. Pvt. Co. K. Residence, Foster. Died of Yazoo Fever at Union Hospital, Memphis, TN, Aug. 23, 1863. Interred at Keech-Winsor Lot, Foster Cemetery 17, Foster, RI.

Hopkins, Ashael A. Pvt. Co. K. Residence, Foster. Died of dysentery at Loudon, TN, April 11, 1864. Interred at Hopkins-Ide Lot. Foster Cemetery, 26, Foster, RI.

Hopkins, Darius A. Pvt. Co. K. Residence, Scituate. Died of Yazoo Fever at Cincinnati, OH, Sept. 29, 1863. Interred at Clayville Cemetery, Foster, RI.

Like so many Seventh Rhode Island soldiers, Private Horace D. Healey of South Kingstown died of disease serving in Mississippi.

Hopkins, John. Pvt. Co. K. Residence, Foster. Died of typhoid at regimental hospital at Newport News, VA, Mar. 1, 1863. Interred at Hopkins Lot, Foster Cemetery 74, Foster, RI.

Hopkins, John E. Pvt. Co. K. Residence, Foster. Died of dysentery at Memphis, TN, Aug. 17, 1863. Interred at Hopkins Mills Cemetery, Foster, RI.

Hopkins, William D. Sgt. Co. K. Residence, Providence. Died of dysentery at Providence, RI, Oct. 4, 1863. Interred at Swan Point Cemetery, Providence, RI.

Howarth, Abraham H. Corp. Co. C. Residence, Richmond. Mortally wounded in action at Fredericksburg, VA, Dec. 13, 1862. Died of wounds Dec.

19, 1862, at Falmouth, VA. Interred at Fredericksburg National Cemetery, Fredericksburg, VA. Grave 2344.

Hughes, James. Pvt. Co. A. Residence, Providence. Drowned in Potomac River, at Aquia Creek, Feb. 9, 1863. Interred at North Burial Ground, Providence, RI.

Hull, John K. 1st Sgt. Co. G. Residence, South Kingstown. Killed in action at Jackson, MS, July 13, 1863. Interred near Jackson, MS. Cenotaph at Riverside Cemetery, South Kingstown, RI.

Hunt, Benjamin S. Pvt. Co. F. Residence, North Kingstown. Killed in action at Fredericksburg, VA, Dec. 13, 1862. Cenotaph at Hunt-Hall Cemetery, North Kingstown Cemetery 11, North Kingstown, RI.

Johnson, William H. Pvt. Co. G. Residence, South Kingstown. Killed in action at Petersburg, VA, June 22, 1864. Interred at Poplar Grove National Cemetery. Section C, Grave 2525. Cenotaph at Elijah Johnson Lot, South Kingstown Cemetery 59, South Kingstown, RI.

Kay, James. Pvt. Co. B. Residence, Providence. Died of dysentery in Harewood Hospital, Washington, D.C., Sept. 28, 1864.

Kellen, Charles H. 2nd Lt. Co. F. Residence, Cumberland. Mortally wounded in action, shot in leg and amputated, at

Top: A graduate of Rhode Island College, and a school teacher in South Kingstown, First Sergeant John K. Hull served in Company G of the Seventh Rhode Island Volunteers. He was killed in action at Jackson, Mississippi, on July 13, 1863.

Right: Charles H. Kellen of Providence was mortally wounded at Fredericksburg serving as the first sergeant of Company F. He was given a posthumous commission as a second lieutenant for heroism on the field.

Fredericksburg, VA, Dec. 13, 1862. Died of wounds at Carver General Hospital, Dec. 29, 1862. Interred at Swan Point Cemetery, Providence, RI.

Kelly, Patrick. Pvt. Co. E. Residence, Cumberland. Killed in action at Fredericksburg, VA, Dec. 13, 1862.

Kenyon, Albert D. Pvt. Co. F. Residence, South Kingstown. Mortally wounded in action at Fredericksburg, VA, Dec. 13, 1862. Died of wounds at Falmouth, VA, Feb. 27, 1863.

Kenyon, James G. Pvt. Co. A. Residence, Charlestown. Killed in action at Petersburg, VA, June 19, 1864. Interred at Poplar Grove National Cemetery. Grave 3153.

Kenyon, John C. Pvt. Co. G. Residence, South Kingstown. Killed in action at Fredericksburg, VA, Dec. 13, 1862.

Kenyon, Joseph J. Pvt. Co. A. Residence, Hopkinton. Died of typhoid at Falmouth, VA, Nov. 24, 1862. Interred at Pine Grove Cemetery, Hopkinton, RI.

Kenyon, Thomas G. Pvt. Co. G. Residence, South Kingstown. Died of typhoid at Emory Hospital, Washington, D.C., Mar. 1, 1863. Interred at North Burial Ground, Providence, RI.

Kenyon, Thomas R. Pvt. Co. A. Residence, Hopkinton. Died of Yazoo Fever on board Steamer *David Tatum* on Mississippi River, Aug. 9, 1863.

Kenyon, Welcome H. Pvt. Co. G. Residence, South Kingstown. Died of tuberculosis contracted in the service Sept. 24, 1864, at Richmond, RI. Interred at Cross Mills Cemetery, Charlestown, RI.

Kettle, Charles A. Pvt. Co. D. Residence, Coventry. Died of dysentery in hospital at Camp

Private Joseph J. Kenyon of Hopkinton served in Company A of the Seventh. Like several members of this company, he contracted typhoid and died shortly after leaving Rhode Island.

Parole, Annapolis, MD, Mar. 19, 1865. Interred at Annapolis National Cemetery. Section C, Grave 1068.

Kilroy, John. Pvt. Co. I. Residence, Newport. Killed in action at Petersburg, VA, June 30, 1864.

Knight, Alfred Sheldon. Pvt. Co. C. Residence, Scituate. Died of pneumonia in regimental hospital at Falmouth, VA, Jan. 31, 1863. Interred at W.W. Knight Lot, Scituate Cemetery 76, Scituate, RI.

Knight, Thomas. Pvt. Co. F. Residence, Pawtucket. Mortally wounded in action at Fredericksburg, VA, Dec. 13, 1862. Died of wounds at Falmouth, VA, Dec. 15, 1862. Interred at Mineral Spring Cemetery, Pawtucket, RI.

Knowles, Charles A. Sgt. Co. G. Residence, South Kingstown. Killed in action at Fredericksburg, VA, Dec. 13, 1862. Cenotaph in James Knowles Lot, South Kingstown Cemetery 32, South Kingstown, RI.

Langworthy, Lucius C. Pvt. Co. A. Residence, Hopkinton. Died of typhoid at Hopkinton, RI, Jan. 24, 1863. Interred at Pine Grove Cemetery, Hopkinton, RI.

Leary, Jerry. Pvt. Co. H. Residence, Westerly. Killed in action at Fredericksburg, VA, Dec. 13, 1862.

Private Alfred Sheldon Knight of Scituate served in Company C, Seventh Rhode Island Volunteers. Six weeks after surviving the Battle of Fredericksburg, he died of pneumonia in a field hospital at Falmouth, Virginia. His father, William Warren Knight, paid to have his son's body brought back and laid in the family plot in Scituate.

Ledden, Daniel. Pvt. Co. H. Residence, North Providence. Killed in action at Fredericksburg, VA, Dec. 13, 1862.

Lewis, John D. Pvt. Co. A. Residence, Hopkinton. Died of typhoid at Falmouth, VA, Dec. 25, 1862. Interred at Wood River Cemetery, Richmond, RI.

Lillibridge, Amos A. Sgt. Co. A. Residence, Richmond. Killed in action at Spotsylvania Court House, VA, May 18, 1864. Cenotaph at Wood River Cemetery, Richmond, RI.

Lynch, John. Pvt. Co. B. Residence, Providence. Mortally wounded in action at Fredericksburg, VA, Dec. 13, 1862. Died of wounds at Trinity General Hospital, Dec. 25, 1862. Interred at Soldier's Home National Cemetery, Washington, D.C. Grave 3813.

Malone, John. Pvt. Co. E. Residence, Cumberland. Died of typhoid at Falmouth, VA, Dec. 16, 1862.

Maloy, Thomas. Pvt. Co. E. Residence, Tiverton. Killed in action at Fredericksburg, VA, Dec. 13, 1862.

Manchester, Alexander H. Pvt. Co. I. Residence, Bristol. Mortally wounded in action at Bethesda Church, VA, June 3, 1864. Died of wounds at Washington, D.C., June 15, 1864. Interred at North Burial Ground, Bristol, RI.

Manchester, Isaac B. Pvt. Co. I. Residence, Bristol. Died of typhoid at Armory Square Hospital, Washington, D.C., Dec. 1, 1862. Interred at North Burial Ground, Bristol, RI.

Marcoux, Joseph. Corp. Co. A. Residence, Providence. Mortally wounded in action, shot in throat, at Fredericksburg, VA, Dec. 13, 1862. Died of wounds at Washington, D.C., Jan. 7, 1863. Served in Color Guard. Interred at Soldier's Home National Cemetery, Washington, D.C. Grave 4600.

Matthewson, Nicholas W. Pvt. Co. F. Residence, West Greenwich. Killed in action at Fredericksburg, VA, Dec. 13, 1862. Cenotaph at Elm Grove Cemetery, North Kingstown, RI.

Maxon, Joel C. Pvt. Co. K. Residence, Hopkinton. Died of dysentery Sept. 24, 1863, at Hopkinton, RI. Interred at Oak Grove Cemetery, Hopkinton, RI.

May, Elisha G. Pvt. Co. G. Residence, South Kingstown. Died of dysentery at Nicholasville, KY, Aug. 29, 1863. Interred at Riverside Cemetery, South Kingstown, RI.

McCasline, Thomas. Pvt. Co. E. Residence, Pawtucket. Died of typhoid at Windmill Point, VA, Feb. 1, 1863. Interred at North Burial Ground, Providence, RI.

McDavitt, John. Pvt. Co. F. Residence, Tiverton. Mortally wounded in action at Bethesda Church, VA, June 3, 1864. Died of wounds at Harewood General Hospital, Washington, D.C., July 8, 1864. Interred at Arlington National Cemetery. Section 13, Grave 6464.

McDonald, John J. Pvt. Co. C. Residence, Glocester. Died of disease contracted in the service at Providence, RI, Aug. 29, 1866. Interred at North Burial Ground, Providence, RI.

McIlroy, Samuel. 1st Lt. Co. I. Residence, Pawtucket. Mortally wounded in action Sept. 30, 1864, at Poplar Spring Church, VA. Died of wounds Oct. 25, 1864, at City Point, VA. Interred at Mineral Spring Cemetery, Pawtucket, RI.

McKenna, Owen. Pvt. Co. D. Residence, Pawtucket. Killed in action at Spotsylvania Court House, VA, May 18, 1864. Cenotaph at St. Mary's Cemetery, Pawtucket, RI.

McQueeny, Barnard. Pvt. Co. D. Residence, Boston, MA. Deserted Sept. 10, 1862. Joined regiment from desertion July 10, 1864, and sentenced to three years hard labor at Tortugas, FL, by general court-martial. Died of yellow fever at Fort Jefferson, FL, Aug. 6, 1865.

Miller, Benjamin F. Sgt. Co. I. Residence, North Providence. Mortally wounded in action, shot in hip, June 3, 1864, at Bethesda Church, VA. Sent to Harewood Hospital, Washington, D.C. Died of wounds at Providence, RI, Nov. 11, 1866. Interred at North Burial Ground, Providence, RI

Morse, Henry L. Sgt. Co. C. Residence, Coventry. Died of dysentery at Annapolis, MD, April 12, 1864. Interred at North Burial Ground, Providence, RI.

Mulvey, Thomas. Pvt. Co. B. Residence, Providence. Killed in action at Poplar Spring Church, VA, Sept. 30, 1864.

Niles, Nelson. Pvt. Co. I. Residence, Smithfield. Died of dysentery at Smithfield, RI, Aug. 19, 1864. Interred at Intervale Cemetery, North Providence, RI.

Nye, Isaac. Corp. Co. K. Residence, Coventry. Mortally wounded in action at Spotsylvania Court House, VA, May 18, 1864. Died of wounds in hospital at Alexandria, VA, May 30, 1864. Served in Color Guard. Interred at Alexandria National Cemetery, Alexandria, VA. Grave 1985. Cenotaph in Manchester Cemetery, Coventry, RI.

Olney, Zalmon A. Pvt. Co. H. Residence, Exeter. Killed in action at Fredericksburg, VA, Dec. 13, 1862.

O'Neil, James. Pvt. Co. G. Residence, South Kingstown. Mortally wounded in action at Fredericksburg, VA, Dec. 13, 1862. Died of wounds at Falmouth, VA, Dec. 16, 1862. Interred at Fredericksburg National Cemetery, Fredericksburg, VA. Grave 3506. Cenotaph at Oak Dell Cemetery, South Kingstown, RI.

Open, Manuel. Corp. Co. G. Residence, South Kingstown. Killed in action at Spotsylvania Court House, VA, May 18, 1864. Served in Color Guard. Interred at Fredericksburg National Cemetery, Fredericksburg, VA. Grave 1143.

Pate, William. Pvt. Co. F. Residence, Mansfield, MA. Killed in action at Bethesda Church, VA, June 3, 1864. Interred at Cold Harbor National Cemetery, Mechanicsville, VA. Grave 828.

Peckham, Benjamin. Pvt. Co. I. Residence, Bristol. Died of Yazoo Fever onboard the *David Tatum*, Aug. 11, 1863. Interred at Napoleonville, AR.

Peckham, Peleg E. Capt. Co. A. Residence, Charlestown. Killed in action at Petersburg, VA, April 2, 1865. Interred at River Bend Cemetery, Westerly, RI.

Pelan, Robert T. Pvt. Co. E. Residence, Providence. Mortally wounded in action at Fredericksburg, VA, Dec. 13, 1862. Died of wounds at Falmouth, VA, Dec. 15, 1862.

Perkins, Palmer G. Pvt. Co. F. Residence, Exeter. Killed in action at Bethesda Church, VA, June 3, 1864. Interred at Cold Harbor National Cemetery, Mechanicsville, VA. Grave 823. Cenotaph at Perkins Lot, Exeter Cemetery 80, Exeter, RI.

Perry, Alpheus S. Sgt. Co. E. Residence, Cumberland. Died of typhoid at Pawtucket, RI, Feb. 16, 1863. Interred at Mineral Spring Cemetery, Pawtucket, RI.

Phillips, Ezekiel B. Pvt. Co. F. Residence, North Kingstown. Died of typhoid at Falmouth, VA, Dec. 9, 1862. Interred at Pearce Phillips Lot, North Kingstown Cemetery 15, North Kingstown, RI.

Phillips, Oliver J. Corp. Co. A. Residence, Coventry. Mortally wounded in action, shot in stomach, at Bethesda Church, VA, June 3, 1864. Died of wounds at General Hospital, Washington, D.C., July 20, 1864. Interred at Arlington National Cemetery. Section 13. Grave 6489. Cenotaph in Knotty Oak Cemetery, Coventry, RI.

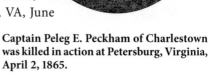

Captain Peleg E. Peckham of Charlestown was killed in action at Petersburg, Virginia, April 2, 1865.

Pierce, Allen. Pvt. Co. I. Residence, Bristol. Mortally wounded in action at Cold Harbor, VA, June 6, 1864. Died of wounds at White House, VA, June 6, 1864. Interred at Yorktown National Cemetery, Grave 424. Cenotaph at North Burial Ground, Bristol, RI.

Pierce, Christopher R. Pvt. Co. D. Residence, Coventry. Died of dysentery in camp at Milldale, MS, July 9, 1863. Cenotaph at Knotty Oak Cemetery, Coventry, RI.

Pierce, Horatio N. Pvt. Co. F. Residence, North Providence. Died of typhoid at Falmouth, VA, Dec. 19, 1862.

Place, Arnold J. Pvt. Co. H. Residence, East Greenwich. Died of typhoid at Camp Nelson, KY, Feb. 26, 1864. Interred at Camp Nelson National Cemetery, Nicholasville, KY. Section D, Grave 1259.

Pollock, William J. Pvt. Co. G. Residence, South Kingstown. Killed in action at Fredericksburg, VA, Dec. 13, 1862.

Potter, Francis W. Corp. Co. C. Residence, Cranston. Mortally wounded in action at Spotsylvania Court House, VA, May 13, 1864. Died of wounds at Fredericksburg, VA, May 20, 1864. Interred at Fredericksburg National Cemetery, Fredericksburg, VA. Grave 285.

Potter, James N. Capt. Co. C. Residence, Providence. Died of disease contracted in the service Nov. 1, 1869, at Providence, RI. Interred at Island Cemetery, Newport, RI.

Potter, Roswell H. Corp. Co. K. Residence, Providence. Died of Yazoo Fever at Milldale, MS, July 22, 1863. Interred at Vicksburg National Cemetery. Section G, Grave 5636.

Ratcliffe, Richard. Pvt. Co. C. Residence, Providence. Killed in action at Fredericksburg, VA, Dec. 13, 1862.

Rathbun, Nathan. Pvt. Co. H. Residence, East Greenwich. Mortally wounded in action at Jackson, MS, July 13, 1863. Died of wounds at U.S. Hospital, Covington, KY, Aug. 22, 1863. Interred at Camp Nelson National Cemetery, Nicholasville, KY. Section G, Grave 2012. Cenotaph at Small Maple Root Cemetery, Coventry, RI.

Reed, Frank E. Pvt. Co. F. Residence, Warwick. Died of dysentery at Milldale, MS, July 30, 1863. Interred near Milldale, MS.

Reynolds, Edward S. Corp. Co. K. Residence, Scituate. Killed in action near Cold Harbor, VA, June 2, 1864. Interred at Cold Harbor National Cemetery, Mechanicsville, VA. Unknown Grave.

Rhowerts, Charles. Corp. Co. F. Residence, Providence. Killed in action at Spotsylvania Court House, VA, May 18, 1864.

Rice, John E. Pvt. Co. H. Residence, Warwick. Killed in action at Spotsylvania Court House, VA, May 18, 1864. Interred at Fredericksburg National Cemetery, Fredericksburg, VA. Grave 1159

Rice, Samuel E. Sgt. Co. H. Residence, East Greenwich. Killed in action at Spotsylvania Court House, VA, May 18, 1864. Interred at Fredericksburg National Cemetery, Fredericksburg, VA. Grave 1161. Cenotaph in First Cemetery, East Greenwich, RI.

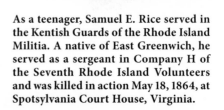

As a teenager, Samuel E. Rice served in the Kentish Guards of the Rhode Island Militia. A native of East Greenwich, he served as a sergeant in Company H of the Seventh Rhode Island Volunteers and was killed in action May 18, 1864, at Spotsylvania Court House, Virginia.

Robbins, Nathan N. Pvt. Co. C. Residence, Johnston. Died of Yazoo Fever at Big Black River, MS, July 22, 1863. Interred at Vicksburg National Cemetery. Section Q, Grave 28.

Robley, George W. Pvt. Co. B. Residence, Providence. Died of typhoid contracted in the service at Providence, RI, June 19, 1863.

Rose, George P. Pvt. Co. F. Residence, North Kingstown. Died of dysentery at North Kingstown, RI, Sept. 16, 1864, while on furlough from United States Post Hospital, Fort Wool, NY Harbor. Interred at Elm Grove Cemetery, North Kingstown, RI.

Rose, Robert N. Pvt. Co. G. Residence, South Kingstown. Mortally wounded in action at Fredericksburg, VA, Dec. 13, 1862. Died of wounds at regimental hospital, Falmouth, VA, Feb. 3, 1863. Interred at Robert Northrup Lot, North Kingstown Cemetery 88, North Kingstown, RI.

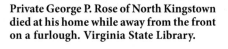

Private George P. Rose of North Kingstown died at his home while away from the front on a furlough. Virginia State Library.

Rourke, Patrick. Pvt. Co. C. Residence, Burrillville. Mortally wounded in action, shot in scalp, Dec. 13, 1862, at Fredericksburg, VA. Sent to Baltimore, MD. Deserted from hospital at Baltimore, MD, April 30, 1863, and returned to Burrillville, RI. Died of wounds at Burrillville, RI July 8, 1863. Interred at Pascoag Cemetery, Burrillville, RI.

Rowan, Thomas. Pvt. Co. B. Residence, Providence. Died of dysentery in General Hospital, Covington, KY, Aug. 13, 1863.

Salisbury, Alpheus. Pvt. Co. K. Residence, Scituate. Mortally wounded in action, shot in neck, at Fredericksburg, VA, Dec. 13, 1862. Discharged for disability Feb. 3, 1863. Died of wounds July 4, 1863, at Scituate, RI. Interred at Clayville Cemetery, Foster, RI.

Sayles, Welcome Ballou. Lt. Col. Residence, Providence. Killed in action at Fredericksburg, VA, Dec. 13, 1862. Interred at Swan Point Cemetery, Providence, RI.

Saunders, Isaac N. Pvt. Co. A. Residence, Hopkinton. Killed in action at Spotsylvania Court House, VA, May 12, 1864. Interred at Fredericksburg

National Cemetery, Fredericksburg, VA. Grave 4167. Cenotaph in Rockville Cemetery, Hopkinton, RI.

Scott, Walter R. Pvt. Co. H. Residence, Sterling, CT. Died of dysentery at U.S. General Hospital, Covington, KY, Aug. 19, 1863. Interred at Riverside Cemetery, Sterling, CT

Sherman, Daniel B. Corp. Co. D. Residence, East Greenwich. Killed in action at Spotsylvania Court House, VA, May 18, 1864. Served in Color Guard. Cenotaph at First Cemetery, East Greenwich, RI.

Simmons, George. Pvt. Co. K. Residence, Foster. Killed in action at Spotsylvania Court House, VA, May 12, 1864. Cenotaph at Walker-Randall Lot, Foster, Foster Cemetery 54, Foster, RI.

Simpson, Samuel F. Sgt. Co. I. Residence, Newport. Served as regimental color bearer. Killed in action at the North Anna River, VA, May 25, 1864.

Sisson, Benjamin F. Pvt. Co. E. Residence, West Greenwich. Killed in action at Spotsylvania Court House, VA, May 12, 1864. Cenotaph at Knotty Oak Cemetery, Coventry, RI.

Sisson, Randall, Jr. Pvt. Co. G. Residence, Richmond. Died of Yazoo Fever at Cincinnati, OH, Aug. 28, 1863. Interred at Spring Grove National Cemetery. Grave 534, Cincinnati, OH.

Smith, Albert L. 1st Lt. Co. D. Residence, Pawtucket. Died of Yazoo Fever at Nicholasville, KY, Aug. 31, 1863. Interred at Camp Nelson National Cemetery, Nicholasville, KY. Section D, Grave 1260.

Smith, Daniel. Pvt. Co. G. Residence, Warwick. Killed in action at Fredericksburg, VA, Dec. 13, 1862.

Smith, George H. Corp. Co. K. Residence, Scituate. Died of typhoid at Falmouth, VA, Jan. 3, 1863. Interred at Clayville Cemetery, Foster, RI.

Smith, Roderick D. Pvt. Co. G. Residence, South Kingstown. Killed in action at Spotsylvania Court House, VA, May 18, 1864. Interred at Fredericksburg National Cemetery, Fredericksburg, VA. Grave 1142.

Snow, Samuel J. Corp. Co. G. Residence, Exeter. Died of dysentery in hospital at Nicholasville, KY, May

Corporal Samuel J. Snow of Exeter died of dysentery in Kentucky.

1, 1863. Interred at Camp Nelson National Cemetery, Nicholasville, KY. Section G, Grave 1213. Cenotaph at Snow Lot, Exeter Cemetery 76, Exeter, RI.

Spencer, James B. Sgt. Co. H. Residence, Warwick. Died of tuberculosis at Newport News Mar. 6, 1863. Interred at Wickes Lot, East Greenwich Cemetery 72, East Greenwich, RI.

Spencer, John. Pvt. Co. F. Residence, Exeter. Died of dysentery at Camp Dennison Hospital, OH, Sept. 14, 1863. Interred at Waldschmidt Cemetery, Camp Dennison, OH. Cenotaph at Elm Grove Cemetery, North Kingstown, RI.

Spencer, William H. Pvt. Co. B. Residence, Providence. Died of Yazoo Fever onboard *David Tatum*, Aug. 11, 1863. Interred at Napoleonville, AR. Cenotaph in Moses Spencer Lot, East Greenwich Cemetery 28, East Greenwich, RI.

Steere, Benoni. Pvt. Co. D. Residence, Burrillville. Died of dysentery at Falmouth, VA, Dec. 23, 1862.

Steere, John F. Pvt. Co. B. Residence, Smithfield. Died of Yazoo Fever in Regimental Hospital at Lexington, KY, Oct. 1, 1863. Interred at Lexington National Cemetery, Lexington, KY. Grave 465.

Straight, Potter P. Pvt. Co. F. Residence, Exeter. Mortally wounded in action at Bethesda Church, VA, June 3, 1864. Died of wounds at Armory Square Hospital, Washington, D.C., June 16, 1864. Interred at Ezekiel Austin Lot, Exeter Cemetery 58, Exeter, RI.

Sweatt, Joseph S. 1st Sgt. Co. G. Residence, Boscawen, NH. Mortally wounded in action at Fredericksburg, VA, Dec. 13, 1862. Sent to Boscawen, NH, to recover. Died of wounds and typhoid at Boscawen, NH, Mar. 6, 1863. Interred at Penacook Cemetery, Boscawen, NH.

Sweetland, Job R. Pvt. Co. C. Residence, Pawtucket. Mortally wounded in action at Fredericksburg, VA, Dec. 13, 1862. Died of wounds at Washington, D.C., Feb. 27, 1863. Interred at Mineral Spring Cemetery, Pawtucket, RI.

Taylor, James J. Pvt. Co. K. Residence, Smithfield. Mortally wounded in action at Bethesda Church, VA, June 3, 1864. Died of wounds at Finley Hospital, Washington, D.C., July 6, 1864. Interred at Arlington National Cemetery. Section 13, Grave 5426.

Taylor, Richard Edwin. Pvt. Co. I. Residence, Scituate. Mortally wounded in action, shot in face, at Petersburg, VA, April 2, 1865. Died of wounds at Washington, D.C., April 16, 1865. Interred at Glenford Cemetery, Scituate, RI.

Taylor, Stephen P. Pvt. Co. H. Residence, Warwick. Died of typhoid at Annapolis, MD, April 13, 1864. Interred at First Cemetery, East Greenwich, RI.

Thomas, George Arnold. Pvt. Co. A. Residence, Hopkinton. Died of typhoid at Baltimore, MD, April 14, 1863. Interred at River Bend Cemetery, Westerly, RI.

Tourgee, William. Pvt. Co. G. Residence, South Kingstown. Died of dysentery at Nicholasville, KY, Sept. 5, 1863. Interred at Gould Tourgee Lot, South Kingstown Cemetery 35, South Kingstown, RI.

Trainor, Michael. Pvt. Co. D. Residence, Providence. Died of dysentery at Second Division, Ninth Army Corps Hospital, Washington, D.C., July 7, 1865. Interred at Alexandria National Cemetery, Alexandria, VA. Grave 3229.

Turner, Charles. Pvt. Co. E. Residence, Cumberland. Captured at Cold Harbor, VA, June 6, 1864. Died of dysentery at Andersonville Prison, GA, July 9, 1864. Interred at Andersonville National Cemetery. Grave 3075.

Underwood, Perry G. Pvt. Co. G. Residence, South Kingstown. Died of dysentery at Cincinnati, OH, Aug. 23, 1863. Interred at Spring Grove National Cemetery. Grave 191. Cenotaph at Riverside Cemetery, South Kingstown, RI.

Weeden, Richard. Pvt. Co. A. Residence, Providence. Mortally wounded in action at Fredericksburg, VA, Dec. 13, 1862. Discharged for disability Mar. 16, 1864. "Attending physician swears soldier died Oct. 4, 1868, from gun shot wounds and that he had well marked symptoms of phthisis." Interred at Warburton-Agins Lot, Johnston Cemetery 90, Johnston, RI.

Westcott, David B. 1st Sgt. Co. B. Residence, Johnston. Died of dysentery at Lexington, KY Oct. 26, 1863. Interred at Lexington National Cemetery. Grave 470.

Whipple, Olney. Pvt. Co. D. Residence, Burrillville. Died of Yazoo Fever in hospital at Nicholasville, KY, Sept. 10, 1863.

Whitcomb, Lyman. Corp. Co. B. Residence, Worcester, MA. Killed in action at Spotsylvania Court House, VA, May 17, 1864. Interred at Fredericksburg National Cemetery, Fredericksburg, VA. Grave 282.

Whitman, Olney A Corp. Co. A. Residence, Newport. Died of typhoid at Baltimore, MD, Mar. 30, 1863. Interred at Peckham West Cemetery, New Bedford, MA.

Whitman, Reuben A. Pvt. Co. D. Residence, Warwick. Died of dysentery in Second Division, Ninth Army Corps Hospital, City Point, VA, Mar. 20, 1865. Interred at City Point National Cemetery, Hopeville, VA. Section C, Grave 2190. Cenotaph in Greenwood Cemetery, Coventry, RI.

Williams, Cyrus D. Pvt. Co. B. Residence, Smithfield. Died of disease contracted in the service at Smithfield, RI, Aug. 21, 1865. Interred in Williams Lot, Smithfield Cemetery 17, Smithfield, RI.

Williams, John W. Pvt. Co. G. Residence, Newport. Died of dysentery contracted in the service at North Kingstown, RI, Oct. 14, 1865. Interred at Elm Grove Cemetery, North Kingstown, RI.

Williams, Olney D. Pvt. Co. K. Residence, Foster. Killed in action at Fredericksburg, VA, Dec. 13, 1862.

Willis, Abel, Jr. Pvt. Co. I. Residence, Bristol. Mortally wounded in action at Fredericksburg, VA, Dec. 13, 1862. Died of wounds at Washington, D.C., Dec. 28, 1862. Interred at Soldier's Home National Cemetery, Washington, D.C. Grave 2209.

Wilson, William R. Pvt. Co. H. Residence, Warwick. Died of disease contracted in the service Nov. 30, 1868 at Warwick, RI. Interred at First Cemetery, East Greenwich, RI.

Winsor, Albert A. Pvt. Co. K. Residence, Foster. Killed in action Fredericksburg, VA, Dec. 13, 1862. Cenotaph in Keech-Winsor Lot, Foster Cemetery 17, Foster, RI.

Wood, Oliver. Pvt. Co. K. Residence, Foster. Killed in action at Bethesda Church, VA, June 3, 1864. Interred at Cold Harbor National Cemetery, Mechanicsville, VA. Grave 796. Cenotaph in Line Cemetery, Foster, RI.

Wood, William T. Sgt. Co. H. Residence, Warwick. Died of dysentery at Camp Nelson, KY, Sept. 10, 1863. Interred at Brayton Cemetery, Warwick, RI.

Worden, Charles H. Pvt. Co. A. Residence, Hopkinton. Detached to Battery D, 1st Rhode Island Light Artillery, Jan. 15, 1863. Died of typhoid at Hampton General Hospital, VA, Feb. 18, 1863. Interred at Hampton National Cemetery, Hampton, VA, Section D, Grave 3292.

Wright, Harris C. Pvt. Co. B. Residence, Burrillville. Killed in action at Fredericksburg, VA, Dec. 13, 1862. Cenotaph at Locust Grove Cemetery, Providence, RI.

Young, Emor. Pvt. Co. C. Residence, Glocester. Died of disease contracted in the service at Glocester, RI, Nov. 20, 1868. Interred at Acotes Hill Cemetery, Glocester, RI.

10

Ninth Rhode Island Volunteers

Arnold, Sylvester B. Pvt. Co. K. Residence, North Kingstown. Died of typhoid at Washington, D.C., Aug. 2, 1862. Interred at Elm Grove Cemetery, North Kingstown, RI.

Colvin, Alonzo. Pvt. Co. D. Residence, Smithfield. Died of "disease contracted in the U.S. Service," at Coventry, RI, April 14, 1867. Interred at Greenwood Cemetery, Coventry, RI.

McArthur, John. Pvt. Co. C. Residence, Warwick. Died of typhoid contracted in the service at Warwick, RI, Jan. 19, 1865. Interred at St. Phillip's Episcopal Cemetery, West Warwick, RI.

Simmonds, Joseph N. Pvt. Co. I. Residence, Warren. Died of typhoid at Warren, RI, September 13, 1862. Interred at South Burial Ground, Warren, RI.

Smith, Marcus L. Pvt. Co. G. Residence, Smithfield. Died of typhoid at Smithfield, RI, Sept. 6, 1862. Interred at North Smithfield Cemetery 9, North Smithfield, RI.

Tabor, Hollis, Jr. Corp. Co. C. Residence, Warwick. Died of "brain fever" at Washington, D.C., Aug. 2, 1862. Interred at Lakewood Cemetery, Warwick, RI.

11

Tenth Rhode Island Volunteers

Atwood, William F. Pvt. Co. A. Residence, Providence. Died of peritonitis at Washington, D.C., June 29, 1862. Interred at Soldier's Home National Cemetery, Washington, D.C. Grave 2961.

Bolles, Nicholas Brown. 1st Lt. Co. H. Residence, Providence. Died of tuberculosis contracted in the service at Providence, RI, Sept. 22, 1863. Interred at Swan Point Cemetery, Providence, RI.

Meggett, Matthew McA. Pvt. Co. B. Residence, Smithfield. Died of typhoid at Washington, D.C., August 18, 1862. Interred at Slatersville Cemetery, North Smithfield, RI.

Walker, Levi C. Pvt. Co. K. Residence, Providence. Died of tuberculosis contracted in the service at New London, CT, February 23, 1864. Interred at Cedar Grove Cemetery, New London, CT.

12

Eleventh Rhode Island Volunteers

Atwood, William C. Pvt. Co. C. Residence, Providence. Died of small pox at Washington, D.C., April 19, 1863. Interred at Arlington National Cemetery, Arlington, VA. Section 13, Grave 11046. Cenotaph at North Burial Ground, Providence, RI.

Bliss, Frank. Mus. Co. B. Residence, Pawtucket. Died of typhoid onboard *John Rice*, July 3, 1863. Interred at Mineral Spring Cemetery, Pawtucket, RI.

Carpenter, J. Marshall. Pvt. Co. I. Residence, Providence. Died of typhoid at Providence, RI. July 17, 1863. Interred at North Burial Ground, Providence, RI.

Chrystal, Charles P. Pvt. Co. A. Residence, Providence. Died of disease contracted in the service at Providence, RI, unknown date, c. 1863. Interred at North Burial Ground, Providence, RI.

Clarke, William B. Pvt. Co. B. Residence, Pawtucket. Died of typhoid at Suffolk, VA, June 21, 1863.

Coyle, John. Pvt. Co. F. Residence, North Providence. Died of tuberculosis contracted in the service at Smithfield, RI, Mar. 5, 1863. Interred at Oak Hill Cemetery, Woonsocket, RI.

Dodge, Mark. Pvt. Co. A. Residence, Providence. Died of disease contracted in the service at Providence, RI, Nov. 11, 1864. Interred at North Burial Ground, Providence, RI.

Gould, Everett. Pvt. Co. K. Residence, Providence. Died of typhoid contracted in the service at Providence, RI, July 18, 1863. Interred at Williamsville Cemetery, Newfane, VT.

Grant, George W. Pvt. Co. A. Residence, Providence. Died of disease contracted in the service at Providence, RI, Jan. 2, 1864.

Hodge, Mark. Pvt. Co. A. Residence, Providence. Died of disease contracted in the service at Providence, RI, Nov. 11, 1864. Interred at North Burial Ground, Providence, RI.

Horton, Rensalaer. Pvt. Co. F. Residence, North Providence. Died of typhoid at Suffolk, VA, April 23, 1863. Interred at Mineral Spring Cemetery, Pawtucket, RI.

McGrath, Michael. Pvt. Co. F. Residence, North Providence. Died of tuberculosis contracted in the service at Johnston, RI, Dec. 25, 1862.

Northrup, Gardner. Pvt. Co. H. Residence, Providence. Died of typhoid at Washington, D.C., April 1, 1863.

Pervear, Jacob S. Hospital Steward. Residence, Pawtucket. Died of typhoid at Washington, D.C., Dec. 20, 1862. Interred at Swan Point Cemetery, Providence, RI.

Phinney, John D. Pvt. Co. D. Residence, Providence. Died of typhoid at Providence, RI, May 29, 1863. Interred at North Burial Ground, Providence, RI.

Pinckney, Isaac H. Pvt. Co. G. Residence, Providence. Died of typhoid contracted in the service at Providence, RI, Aug. 22, 1863. Interred at Swan Point Cemetery, Providence, RI.

Seamens, Frank. Corp. Co. D. Residence, Providence. Died of disease contracted in the service at Providence, RI, Oct. 11, 1863. Interred at North Burial Ground, Providence, RI.

Wyman, William J. Pvt. Co. D. Residence, Providence. Died of typhoid at Washington, D.C., Dec. 15, 1862.

13

Twelfth Rhode Island Volunteers

Arnold, George W. Sgt. Co. I. Residence, Johnston. Died of typhoid at Fairfax, VA, Dec. 8, 1862. Interred at Greenwood Cemetery, Coventry, RI.

Austin, George W. Pvt. Co. K. Residence East Greenwich. Killed in action at Fredericksburg, Dec. 13, 1862. Cenotaph at First Cemetery, East Greenwich, RI.

Austin, Stephen O. Pvt. Co. K. Residence, Providence. Died of typhoid contracted in the service at Cranston, RI, Oct. 23, 1864. Interred at Rockland Cemetery, Scituate, RI.

Babcock, Samuel. 1st Sgt. Co. D. Residence, Newport. Died of typhoid at Newport News, VA, Feb. 27, 1863. Interred at Common Burying Ground, Newport, RI.

An 1860 graduate of Yale, Sergeant George W. Arnold of Johnston died of typhoid.

Bailey, Thomas W. Pvt. Co. C. Residence, Providence. Died of typhoid at Falmouth, VA, Feb. 5, 1863. Interred at North Burial Ground, Providence, RI.

Ball, Noah D. Pvt. Co. D. Residence, New Shoreham. Died of typhoid contracted in the service at New Shoreham, RI, Aug. 10, 1863. Interred at Island Cemetery, New Shoreham, RI.

Bennett, Adams J. Pvt. Co. E. Residence, Bristol. Died of tuberculosis at Baltimore, MD, Mar. 30, 1863. Interred at North Burial Ground, Bristol, RI.

Bennett, Allen H. Corp. Co. I. Residence, Scituate. Died of tuberculosis contracted in the service at Warwick, RI, Nov. 4, 1863. Interred at Brayton Cemetery, Warwick, RI.

Bishop, Martin Van Buren. Pvt. Co. K. Residence, Glocester. Died of typhoid at Newport News, VA, Mar. 7, 1863.

Brennan, Hugh. Pvt. Co. C. Residence, Providence. Died of disease contracted in the service at Providence, RI, c. 1863. Interred at St. Francis Cemetery, Pawtucket, RI.

Briggs, Richard A. 1st Lt. Co. A. Residence, Johnston. Killed in action at Fredericksburg, Dec. 13, 1862. Interred at North Providence Cemetery 3, North Providence, RI.

Bucklin, George. Pvt. Co. K. Residence, East Providence. Mortally wounded in action, right foot amputated at Fredericksburg, VA, Dec. 13, 1862. Died of wounds at Washington,

First Lieutenant Richard A. Briggs of Johnston was killed at Fredericksburg leading Company A of the Twelfth Rhode Island.

D.C., Jan. 9, 1863. Interred at Lakeside-Carpenter Cemetery, East Providence, RI.

Burns, Michael. Pvt. Co. F. Residence, Cumberland. Killed in action at Fredericksburg, Dec. 13, 1862.

Buxton, Amasa. Pvt. Co. K. Residence, Burrillville. Died of typhoid at Washington, D.C., Feb. 10, 1863. Interred at Soldier's Home National Cemetery, Washington, D.C. Section G, Grave 4291.

Cahoone, Charles H. Pvt. Co. G. Residence Coventry. Died of typhoid at Washington, D.C., Dec. 25, 1862. Interred at Pine Grove Cemetery, Coventry, RI.

Caswell, John. Pvt. Co. D. Residence, Newport. Died of typhoid at Falmouth, VA, Jan. 5, 1863. Interred at Common Burying Ground, Newport, RI.

Clissold, Stephen. Pvt. Co. F. Mortally wounded in action, shot in head at Fredericksburg, VA, Dec. 13, 1862. Died of wounds at Falmouth, VA, Jan. 12, 1863.

Conly, Daniel. Sgt. Co. D. Residence, New Shoreham. Died of typhoid at Washington, D.C., Dec. 25, 1862.

Connelly, Terry. Pvt. Co. I. Residence, Warwick. Died of typhoid at Falmouth, VA, Feb. 5, 1863.

Crandall, Daniel A. Pvt. Co. F. Residence, South Kingstown. Mortally wounded in action at Fredericksburg, VA. Died of wounds at Philadelphia, PA, April 1, 1863. Interred at John Tucker Lot, South Kingstown Cemetery 145, South Kingstown, RI.

Davis, Jeffrey G. Sgt. Co. K. Residence, Providence. Died of disease contracted in the service at Providence, RI, Aug. 1863. Interred at North Burial Ground, Providence, RI.

Dorsay, John. Pvt. Co. C. Residence, Providence. Detached to Battery D, 1st R.I. Light Artillery. Murdered by a civilian at Camp Robinson, KY, June 6, 1863.

Duffy, John C. Pvt. Co. I. Residence, Warwick. Mortally wounded in action at Fredericksburg, VA, Dec. 13, 1862. Died of wounds at Falmouth, VA, Dec. 23, 1862. Interred at St. Mary's Cemetery, West Warwick, RI.

Gifford, Russell. Pvt. Co. C. Residence, Newport. Died of typhoid at Alexandria, VA, Feb. 20, 1863. Interred at Alexandria National Cemetery, Alexandria, VA. Grave 742.

Gilroy, Patrick. Pvt. Co. I. Residence, Newport. Mortally wounded in action at Fredericksburg, VA, Dec. 13, 1862. Died of wounds at Newport, RI, Oct. 1, 1863. Interred at Island Cemetery, Newport, RI.

Gorham, Isaac. Sgt. Co. C. Residence, Warren. Died of pneumonia contracted in the service at Bristol, RI, Aug. 1, 1863. Interred at North Burial Ground, Bristol, RI.

Gorton, Jacob. Pvt. Co. G. Residence, Coventry. Died of pneumonia at Washington, D.C., Feb. 19, 1863. Interred at Plain Meeting Cemetery, West Greenwich, RI.

Gould, Robert. Pvt. Co. D. Residence, Middletown. Died of typhoid at Washington, D.C., Feb. 14, 1863. Interred at Island Cemetery, Newport, RI.

Greene, Clark. Pvt. Co. G. Residence, Coventry. Died of typhoid at Washington, D.C., Feb. 15, 1863. Interred at Benjamin Cahoone Lot, Coventry Cemetery 101, Coventry, RI.

Grinnell, Abner. Pvt. Co. C. Residence, Newport. Mortally wounded in action at Fredericksburg, VA, Dec. 13, 1862. Died of wounds at Falmouth, VA, Dec. 15, 1862.

Hopkins, Stephen M. 1st Lt. Co. I. Residence, Burrillville. Mortally wounded in action at Fredericksburg, VA, Dec. 13, 1862. Died of wounds at Washington, D.C., Dec. 19, 1862. Interred at Marshall-Hopkins-Potter Lot, Burrillville Cemetery 12, Burrillville, RI.

Humphrey, Horatio N. Pvt. Co. K. Residence, Tiverton. Died of typhoid at Falmouth, VA, Jan. 29, 1863. Interred at Humphrey Cemetery, Tiverton Cemetery 2, Tiverton, RI.

Hutchinson, Lester. Corp. Co. C. Residence, Providence. Died of disease at Boston, MA, Oct. 26, 1862.

Jenks, Jabez E. Pvt. Co. F. Residence, North Providence. Died of typhoid at Newport News, VA, Feb. 21, 1863.

Johnson, Edward. Pvt. Co. F. Residence, Cumberland. Killed in action at Fredericksburg, VA, Dec. 13, 1862.

Keller, Richard N. Pvt. Co. F. Residence, Glocester. Mortally wounded in action, shot in arm, at Fredericksburg, VA, Dec. 13, 1862. Died of wounds at Washington, D.C., April 29, 1863.

Kellogg, William H. Pvt. Co. A. Residence, East Greenwich. Killed in action at Fredericksburg, VA, Dec. 13, 1862.

Kinnicutt, George R. Wag. Co. E. Residence, Barrington. Died of disease

Private Horatio N. Humphrey enlisted from Tiverton. He served in Company K and died of typhoid.

contracted in the service at Barrington, RI, Aug. 21, 1863. Interred at Prince's Hill Burial Ground, Barrington, RI.

Lawson, John. Pvt. Co. A. Residence, Providence. Killed in action at Fredericksburg, VA, Dec. 13, 1862.

Lewis, James G. Pvt. Co. C. Residence, Richmond. Died of typhoid at Falmouth, VA, Feb. 28, 1863. Interred at Voluntown Cemetery, Voluntown, CT.

Mason, William. Pvt. Co. B. Residence, Providence. Killed in action at Fredericksburg, VA, Dec. 13, 1862.

Mathewson, Philip. Pvt. Co. K. Residence, Glocester. Died of disease at Alexandria, VA, Dec. 14, 1862.

Mathewson, Thomas C. Pvt. Co. K. Residence, Glocester. Died of small pox contracted in the service at Warwick, RI, April 24, 1863.

McArthur, John. Pvt. Co. I. Residence, Warwick. Died of typhoid at Washington, D.C., Feb. 4, 1863.

Miller, Nathaniel L. Pvt. Co. K. Residence, Burrillville. Killed in action at Fredericksburg, VA, Dec. 13, 1862.

Mitchell, David. Pvt. Co. D. Residence, New Shoreham. Died of typhoid at Newport News, VA, Feb. 28, 1863.

Mitchell, Jesse D. Pvt. Co. D. Residence, New Shoreham. Died of typhoid at Washington, D.C., Mar. 5, 1863. Interred at Soldier's Home National Cemetery, Washington, D.C. Section G. Grave 4948.

Mitchell, John R. Pvt. Co. F. Residence, New Shoreham. Killed in action at Fredericksburg, VA, Dec. 13, 1862.

Myers, Samuel A. Pvt. Co. A. Residence, East Greenwich. Killed in action at Fredericksburg, VA, Dec. 13, 1862. Cenotaph at First Cemetery, East Greenwich, RI.

Paine, Ebenezer A.J. Pvt. Residence, Johnston. Died of disease at Washington, D.C., July 2, 1863. Interred at Arlington National Cemetery, Arlington, VA. Section 13, Grave 10401.

Pearce, Henry W. Pvt. Co. C. Residence, Providence. Died of typhoid at Falmouth, VA, Jan. 8, 1863. Interred at First Cemetery, East Greenwich, RI.

Pendleton, James M. 1st Lt. Co. B. Residence, Westerly. Died of typhoid at Westerly, RI, Mar. 11, 1863. Interred at River Bend Cemetery, Westerly, RI.

Richardson, George E. Pvt. Co. B. Residence, Cranston. Died of typhoid at Fairfax, VA, Nov. 25, 1862.

Richmond, George W. Pvt. Co. E. Residence, Barrington. Mortally wounded in action at Fredericksburg, VA, Dec. 13, 1862. Died of wounds at Washington, D.C., Feb. 15, 1863. Interred at Prince's Hill Burial Ground, Barrington, RI.

Salisbury, Alonzo F. Pvt. Co. H. Residence, Pawtucket. Died of typhoid at Falmouth, VA, Jan. 11, 1863.

Sheldon, John F. Pvt. Co. G. Residence, Coventry. Died of rheumatism at Philadelphia, PA, Feb. 25, 1863. Interred at Large Maple Root Cemetery, Coventry, RI.

Simmons, James. Pvt. Co. D. Residence, Newport. Murdered in camp at Providence, RI, Oct. 16, 1862.

Smith, Benjamin P. Pvt. Co. D. Residence, New Shoreham. Died of typhoid at Washington, D.C., Mar. 10, 1863. Interred at Soldier's Home National Cemetery, Washington, D.C. Section G, Grave 4036.

Spink, George T. Pvt. Co. A. Residence, East Greenwich. Died of dysentery at Newport News, VA, Mar. 12, 1863. Interred at Quidnessett Cemetery, North Kingstown, RI.

Sprague, Sullivan. Pvt. Co. D. Residence, New Shoreham. Killed in action at Fredericksburg, VA, Dec. 13, 1862.

Stow, Lorenzo. Corp. Co. C. Residence, Providence. Died of typhoid at Falmouth, VA, Jan. 16, 1863.

Straight, Oliver. Pvt. Co. K. Residence, South Kingstown. Died of typhoid at Falmouth, VA, Dec. 22, 1862. Interred at Dawley-Straight Lot, Exeter Cemetery 83, Exeter, RI.

Tew, James. Pvt. Co. I. Residence, Charlestown. Died of disease at Washington, D.C., Jan. 5, 1863. Interred at John Tew Lot, West Warwick Cemetery 6, West Warwick, RI.

Tinkham, Thomas. Pvt. Co. A. Residence, Scituate. Died of typhoid at Falmouth, VA, Jan. 13, 1863. Interred at Tinkham Lot, Scituate Cemetery 23, Scituate, RI.

Tourgee, George R. Pvt. Co. G. Residence, Coventry. Died of disease Aug. 1863 at Coventry, RI. Interred at Knotty Oak Cemetery, Coventry, RI.

Webb, Charles H. Pvt. Co. I. Residence, Johnston. Died of dysentery at Washington, D.C., Feb. 12, 1863. Interred at Soldier's Home National Cemetery, Washington, D.C. Grave 2637.

Whiting, Samuel S. Mortally wounded in action at Fredericksburg, VA, Dec. 13, 1862. Died of wounds at Portsmouth Grove Hospital, Jan. 15, 1863. Interred at First Cemetery, East Greenwich, RI.

Typhoid was the leading killer of men in the Twelfth. Among the victims was Private Frank J. Wilder of Scituate who served in Company A; he was only 17.

Whitman, Hiram. Pvt. Co. A. Residence, East Greenwich. Killed in action at Fredericksburg, VA, Dec. 13, 1862. Cenotaph at First Cemetery, East Greenwich, RI.

Wilbur, Edward J. Pvt. Co. C. Residence, Providence. Killed in a railroad accident, Oct. 23, 1862. Interred at Brayton Cemetery, Warwick, RI.

Wilder, Frank J. Pvt. Co. A. Residence, Scituate. Died of typhoid at Aquia Creek, VA, Jan. 26, 1863. Interred at Westcott Lot, Scituate Cemetery 1, Scituate, RI.

Williams, Gilbert O. Pvt. Co. K. Residence, Burrillville. Died of typhoid at Newport News, VA, Mar. 11, 1863. Interred at Rufus Williams Lot, Burrillville Cemetery 22, Burrillville, RI.

Wood, George W. Pvt. Co. A. Residence, Warwick. Died of typhoid at Falmouth, VA, Jan. 15, 1863. Interred at Brayton Cemetery, Warwick, RI.

14

Fourteenth Rhode Island Heavy Artillery

Abbott, William L. Pvt. Co. D. Residence, Providence. Died of typhoid at Plaquemine, LA, Aug. 2, 1864. Interred at Fort Jackson Post Cemetery, Plaquemines Parish, LA.

Allen, Henry. Pvt. Co. M. Residence, Hopkinton. Died of dysentery at Camp Parapet, LA, Aug. 19, 1864. Interred at Shrewsbury Cemetery, Shrewsbury, LA.

Allen, Robert B. Pvt. Co. A. Residence, Portland, ME. Died of typhoid at Fort Jackson, LA, Sept. 26, 1864. Interred at Fort Jackson Post Cemetery, Plaquemines Parish, LA.

Allen, William. Pvt. Co. F. Residence, Providence. Died of small pox at New Orleans, LA, Dec. 18, 1864. Interred at Chalmette National Cemetery, New Orleans, LA.

Anderson, Cornelius. Corp. Co. B. Residence, Flushing, NY. Died of typhoid at Fort Jackson, LA, Sept. 3, 1864. Interred at Fort Jackson Post Cemetery, Plaquemines Parish, LA.

Anderson, William P. Pvt. Co. F. Residence, Providence. Died of tuberculosis at Plaquemine, LA, Jan. 28, 1865. Interred at Plaquemine Post Burying Ground, Plaquemine, LA.

Anthony, Henry G. Pvt. Co. D. Residence, Uxbridge, MA. Died of phthisis at Fort Jackson, LA, Nov. 19, 1864. Interred at Fort Jackson Post Cemetery, Plaquemines Parish, LA.

Anthony, Jerome. Pvt. Co. D. Residence, Uxbridge, MA. Died of dysentery at Fort Jackson, LA, Sept. 16, 1864. Interred at Fort Jackson Post Cemetery, Plaquemines Parish, LA.

Anthony, Leander E. Pvt. Co. L. Residence, Uxbridge, MA. Died of cholera at Camp Parapet, LA, June 26, 1864. Interred at Shrewsbury Cemetery, Shrewsbury, LA.

Atwood, Alexander. Sgt. Co. E. Residence, Providence. Died of dysentery at Donaldsonville, LA, Aug. 28, 1865. Interred at Donaldsonville Post Burying Ground, Donaldsonville, LA.

Babcock, Isaac. Pvt. Co. A. Residence, South Kingstown. Died of rheumatism at New Orleans, LA, Oct. 10, 1864.

Baker, Lewis. Pvt. Co. D. Residence, New York, NY. Died of typhoid at Fort Jackson, LA, Aug. 22, 1864. Interred at Fort Jackson Post Cemetery, Plaquemines Parish, LA.

Banks, Henry. Pvt. Co. A. Residence, Providence. Died of tuberculosis at Camp Parapet, LA, June 13, 1864. Interred at Shrewsbury Cemetery, Shrewsbury, LA.

Barret, Albert. Pvt. Co. I. Residence, Buffalo, NY. Died of disease at Camp Parapet, LA, Aug. 6, 1864. Interred at Shrewsbury Cemetery, Shrewsbury, LA.

Barrett, Henry. Pvt. Co. M. Residence, Schoharie, NY. Died of dysentery at Camp Parapet, LA, Dec. 28, 1864. Interred at Shrewsbury Cemetery, Shrewsbury, LA.

Bayard, Jacob. Pvt. Co. B. Residence, Flushing, NY. Died of dysentery at Camp Parapet, LA, June 25, 1864. Interred at Shrewsbury Cemetery, Shrewsbury, LA.

Bell, John. Pvt. Co. D. Residence, New York, NY. Died of pneumonia at Fort Jackson, LA, Aug. 20, 1864. Interred at Fort Jackson Post Cemetery, Plaquemines Parish, LA.

Benson, Lafayette G.M. Pvt. Co. K. Residence, Randolph, IN. Died of dysentery at Camp Parapet, LA, Nov. 11, 1864. Interred at Shrewsbury Cemetery, Shrewsbury, LA.

Betson, William. Pvt. Co. L. Residence, Prince George, MD. Died of tuberculosis at Dutch Island, Rhode Island, Mar. 11, 1864. Interred at Long Island National Cemetery, East Farmingdale, NY.

Boardley, James. Pvt. Co. I. Residence, Tuscaloosa, AL. Died of typhoid at Camp Parapet, LA, June 8, 1864. Interred at Shrewsbury Cemetery, Shrewsbury, LA.

Bogart, George W. Pvt. Co. L. Residence, Providence. Died of disease at Camp Parapet, LA, Aug. 7, 1864. Interred at Shrewsbury Cemetery, Shrewsbury, LA.

Brewster, Alfred. Pvt. Co. I. Residence, Providence. Died of typhoid at Camp Parapet, LA, Nov. 14, 1864. Interred at Shrewsbury Cemetery, Shrewsbury, LA.

Brister, Abner W. Pvt. Co. B. Residence, Boston, MA. Died of malaria at Fort Jackson, LA, Aug. 23, 1864. Interred at Fort Jackson Post Cemetery, Plaquemines Parish, LA.

Brown, George W. Pvt. Co. M. Residence, Alexandria, VA. Died of dysentery at Camp Parapet, LA, Jan. 16, 1865. Interred at Shrewsbury Cemetery, Shrewsbury, LA.

Brown, James Peck. 2nd Lt. Co. H. Residence, Rehoboth, MA. Died of malaria at Donaldsonville, LA, Aug. 23, 1865. Interred at Village Cemetery, Rehoboth, MA.

Brown, John E. Corp. Co. F. Residence, Providence. Died of malaria at Plaquemine, LA, Aug. 31, 1864. Interred at Plaquemine Post Burying Ground, Plaquemine, LA.

Brown, John W. Pvt. Co. H. Residence, Newark, NJ. Died of malaria at Camp Parapet, LA, Feb. 21, 1864. Interred at Shrewsbury Cemetery, Shrewsbury, LA.

Brown, Joshua M. Corp. Co. H. Residence, Providence. Died of kidney disease at Plaquemine, LA, Mar. 3, 1865. Interred at Plaquemine Post Burying Ground, Plaquemine, LA.

Bush, Henry. Pvt. Co. B. Residence, Bridgeport, CT. Died of typhoid at Fort Jackson, LA, Aug. 31, 1864. Interred at Fort Jackson Post Cemetery, Plaquemines Parish, LA.

Bush, William. Pvt. Co. B. Residence, Bridgeport, CT. Died of disease at Dutch Island, RI, Oct. 4, 1863. Interred at Long Island National Cemetery, East Farmingdale, NY.

Butler, John. Pvt. Co. B. Residence, Washington, NY. Died of small pox at New Orleans, LA, June 4, 1864. Interred at Chalmette National Cemetery, New Orleans, LA. Grave 11243.

Caesar, Ralph. Pvt. Co. I. Residence, Providence. Died of typhoid at Camp Parapet, LA, June 29, 1865. Interred at Shrewsbury Cemetery, Shrewsbury, LA.

Cambridge, William H. Pvt. Co. E. Residence, New York, NY. Died of phthisis at English Turn, LA, Mar. 15, 1864. Interred at English Turn Post Burying Grounds, English Turns, LA.

Carr, Leveran. Pvt. Co. D. Residence, Providence. Died of pneumonia at Fort Esperanza, TX, Mar. 30, 1864. Interred at Fort Esperanza Burying Ground, Matagorda Island, TX.

Carroll, Dennis. Pvt. Co. L. Residence, Providence. Died of disease at Dutch Island, Rhode Island, Jan. 6, 1864. Interred at Long Island National Cemetery, East Farmingdale, NY.

Carter, William H. Pvt. Co. F. Residence, Providence. Died of tuberculosis at English Turn, LA, Mar. 13, 1864. Interred at English Turn Post Burying Grounds, English Turns, LA.

Cartwright, John W. Corp. Co. M. Residence, New York, NY. Died of malaria at New Orleans, LA, Sept. 2, 1865. Interred at Chalmette National Cemetery, New Orleans, LA.

Charles, John. Pvt. Co. A. Residence, South Kingstown. Died of typhoid at New Orleans, LA, July 29, 1864. Interred at Chalmette National Cemetery, New Orleans, LA. Grave 11755.

Chase, William. Corp. Co. A. Residence, Providence. Died of typhoid at Fort Jackson, LA, Aug. 13, 1864. Interred at Fort Jackson Post Cemetery, Plaquemines Parish, LA.

Cheese, Thomas S. Sgt. Co. A. Residence, Providence. Died of disease at New Orleans, LA, July 8, 1864. Interred at Chalmette National Cemetery, New Orleans, LA.

Cisco, Charles. Pvt. Co. A. Residence, Providence. Murdered at Fort Jackson, LA, July 26, 1864. Interred at Fort Jackson Post Cemetery, Plaquemines Parish, LA.

Clare, Austin. Pvt. Co. H. Residence, Providence. Died of dropsy at Plaquemine, LA, May 6, 1865. Interred at Plaquemine Post Burying Ground, Plaquemine, LA.

Claxton, Robert. Pvt. Co. F. Residence, Providence. Died of dropsy at Plaquemine, LA, Sept. 9, 1864. Interred at Plaquemine Post Burying Ground, Plaquemine, LA.

Clay, William. Pvt. Co. M. Residence, Philadelphia, PA. Died of dysentery at New Orleans, LA, Sept. 3, 1864. Interred at Chalmette National Cemetery, New Orleans, LA. Grave 11177.

Clayton, Charles L. Pvt. Co. E. Died of phthisis at English Turn, LA, Mar. 6, 1864. Interred at English Turn Post Burying Grounds, English Turns, LA.

Cleggett, William T. Pvt. Co. M. Residence, Rochester, NY. Died of apoplexy at Camp Parapet, LA, Nov. 10, 1864. Interred at Shrewsbury Cemetery, Shrewsbury, LA.

Cole, Philip. Pvt. Co. L. Residence, Providence. Died of small pox at Dutch Island, RI, Mar. 10, 1864. Interred at Long Island National Cemetery, East Farmingdale, NY.

Coleman, James L. Residence, Providence. Died of malaria at Fort Jackson, LA, Oct. 21, 1864. Interred at Fort Jackson Post Cemetery, Plaquemines Parish, LA.

Congdon, James. Pvt. Co. M. Residence, Windham, CT. Died of diphtheria at Camp Parapet, LA, Nov. 22, 1864. Interred at Shrewsbury Cemetery, Shrewsbury, LA.

Copeland, Allen. Pvt. Co. K. Residence, Providence. Died of tuberculosis at Camp Parapet, LA, Oct. 3, 1864. Interred at Shrewsbury Cemetery, Shrewsbury, LA.

Corson, John. Pvt. Co. A. Residence, New York, NY. Died of typhoid at Fort Jackson, LA, Aug. 23, 1864. Interred at Fort Jackson Post Cemetery, Plaquemines Parish, LA.

Cox, Edward A. Pvt. Co. F. Residence, Providence. Died of tuberculosis at English Turn, LA, Mar. 8, 1864. Interred at English Turn Post Burying Grounds, English Turns, LA.

Cummings, Francis. Pvt. Co. H. Residence, Bridgeport, CT. Died of dropsy at Plaquemine, LA, Aug. 21, 1864. Interred at Plaquemine Post Burying Ground, Plaquemine, LA.

Dailey, Gustavus. Pvt. Co. D. Residence, Woodstock, CT. Died of typhoid at Fort Jackson, LA, Nov. 9, 1864. Interred at Fort Jackson Post Cemetery, Plaquemines Parish, LA.

Davis, Abraham. Pvt. Co. B. Residence, Bedford, MA. Died of phthisis at Fort Jackson, LA, Aug. 17, 1864. Interred at Fort Jackson Post Cemetery, Plaquemines Parish, LA.

Davis, Hamilton F. Sgt. Co. G. Residence, Providence. Died of typhoid at Plaquemine, LA, June 24, 1865. Interred at Plaquemine Post Burying Ground, Plaquemine, LA.

Davis, Hannibal F. Pvt. Co. G. Residence, Providence. Died of dysentery at Plaquemine, LA, Sept. 5, 1864. Interred at Plaquemine Post Burying Ground, Plaquemine, LA.

Debois, Thomas B. Pvt. Co. L. Residence, Providence. Died of dysentery at Camp Parapet, LA, July 16, 1865. Interred at Shrewsbury Cemetery, Shrewsbury, LA.

Degroot, David. Pvt. Co. B. Residence, Orange, NY. Died of dysentery at Fort Jackson, LA, Oct. 11, 1864. Interred at Fort Jackson Post Cemetery, Plaquemines Parish, LA.

DeMars, Geraldo. Pvt. Co. E. Residence, Hartford, CT. Died of tuberculosis at Plaquemine, LA, Nov. 24, 1864. Interred at Plaquemine Post Burying Ground, Plaquemine, LA.

Demming, William. Pvt. Co. C. Residence, Lebanon, CT. Died of dysentery at Fort Jackson, LA, Nov. 19, 1864. Interred at Fort Jackson Post Cemetery, Plaquemines Parish, LA.

Demon, John. Pvt. Co. E. Residence, Fishkill, NY. Died of tuberculosis at Plaquemine, LA, Feb. 8, 1865. Interred at Plaquemine Post Burying Ground, Plaquemine, LA.

Denny, Woodhall. Pvt. Co. I. Residence, Providence. Died of dysentery at Camp Parapet, LA, Jan. 16, 1865. Interred at Shrewsbury Cemetery, Shrewsbury, LA.

Depew, Hugh. Pvt. Co. K. Residence, Pennellville, NY. Died of disease at New York, NY, Oct. 3, 1865. Interred at Cypress Hills National Cemetery, Brooklyn, NY. Grave 3196.

Derrick, William P. Pvt. Co. I. Residence, Providence. Died of diphtheria at Camp Parapet, LA, Sept. 15, 1864. Interred at Shrewsbury Cemetery, Shrewsbury, LA.

Dewitt, William. Pvt. Co. L. Residence, Providence. Died of dysentery at Camp Parapet, LA, June 24, 1865. Interred at Shrewsbury Cemetery, Shrewsbury, LA.

Dixon, Hezekiah, Jr. Pvt. Co. M. Residence for Rochester, NY. Executed for assaulting an officer at Camp Parapet, LA, April 30, 1864. Interred at Shrewsbury Cemetery, Shrewsbury, LA.

Dolphin, James. Pvt. Co. G. Residence, Providence. Died of typhoid at Plaquemine, LA, Aug. 4, 1864. Interred at Plaquemine Post Burying Ground, Plaquemine, LA.

Dorsey, John H. Pvt. Co. M. Residence, Baltimore, MD. Died of disease at New Orleans, LA, July 7, 1864. Interred at Chalmette National Cemetery, New Orleans, LA. Grave 11278.

Dubois, Hiram. Pvt. Co. B. Residence, Ulster, NY. Died of small pox at New Orleans, LA, July 15, 1864. Interred at Shrewsbury Cemetery, Shrewsbury, LA.

Dusenbuy, Lewis. Pvt. Co. I. Residence, Providence. Died of dysentery at Camp Parapet, LA, Dec. 21, 1864. Interred at Shrewsbury Cemetery, Shrewsbury, LA.

Edwards, David. Pvt. Co. D. Residence, Providence. Died of tuberculosis at Fort Jackson, LA, July 31, 1864. Interred at Fort Jackson Post Cemetery, Plaquemines Parish, LA.

Edwards, Nathaniel. Mus. Co. C. Residence, New York, NY. Died of typhoid at Fort Jackson, LA, Sept. 1, 1864. Interred at Fort Jackson Post Cemetery, Plaquemines Parish, LA.

Elkey, Austin E. Pvt. Co. E. Residence, Danbury, CT. Died of typhoid at Plaquemine, LA, July 10, 1864. Interred at Plaquemine Post Burying Ground, Plaquemine, LA.

Elkey, George. Pvt. Co. F. Residence, Granby, CT. Died of disease at Camp Parapet, LA, Oct. 4, 1865. Interred at Shrewsbury Cemetery, Shrewsbury, LA.

Ellis, Charles H. Pvt. Co. F. Residence, Providence. Died of tuberculosis at Plaquemine, LA, Aug. 3, 1864. Interred at Plaquemine Post Burying Ground, Plaquemine, LA.

Erls, Thomas C. Pvt. Co. K. Residence, Providence. Died of typhoid at Camp Parapet, LA, Aug. 26, 1865. Interred at Shrewsbury Cemetery, Shrewsbury, LA.

Everson, Peter. Pvt. Co. M. Residence, New York, NY. Died of "convulsions" at Fort Jackson, LA, Nov. 5, 1864. Interred at Fort Jackson Post Cemetery, Plaquemines Parish, LA.

Fairfax, Thomas C. Pvt. Co. M. Residence, Alexandria, VA. Died of typhoid at Camp Parapet, LA, Oct. 14, 1864. Interred at Shrewsbury Cemetery, Shrewsbury, LA.

Farnum, Samuel. Capt. Co. C. Residence, Uxbridge, MA. Drowned in the sinking of the *Atlanta* while returning to Providence for muster out, Oct. 15, 1865. Cenotaph at Friends Burying Ground, Uxbridge, MA.

Fields, David. Pvt. Co. D. Residence, New York, NY. Died of typhoid at Fort Esperanza, TX, May 19, 1864. Interred at Fort Esperanza Burying Ground, Matagorda Island, TX.

Fisher, Franklin. Corp. Co. K. Residence, Providence. Died of "congestion of the brains" at Camp Parapet, LA, June 21, 1864. Interred at Shrewsbury Cemetery, Shrewsbury, LA.

Fisher, Lewis. Corp. Co. K. Residence, Providence. Died of disease on board the *Cahawba* Dec. 20, 1863.

Fleming, William J. Pvt. Co. L. Residence, Providence. Died of disease at New York, NY. Oct. 20, 1865. Interred at Cypress Hills National Cemetery, Brooklyn, NY. Grave 3214.

Fletcher, David R. Pvt. Co. L. Residence, Providence. Died of tuberculosis at Camp Parapet, LA, June 5, 1864. Interred at Shrewsbury Cemetery, Shrewsbury, LA.

Fletcher, Roderick L. Pvt. Co. L. Residence, Providence. Died of tuberculosis at Camp Parapet, LA, July 1, 1864. Interred at Shrewsbury Cemetery, Shrewsbury, LA.

Fletcher, Samuel. Pvt. Co. K. Residence, Providence. Died of typhoid at Camp Parapet, LA, July 5, 1864. Interred at Shrewsbury Cemetery, Shrewsbury, LA.

Fletcher, Western. Pvt. Co. M. Residence, Cleveland, OH. Died of typhoid at Camp Parapet, LA, June 18, 1865. Interred at Shrewsbury Cemetery, Shrewsbury, LA.

Frazier, John H. Pvt. Co. E. Residence, Pine Plains, NY. Accidentally shot and killed at Camp Parapet, LA, June 27, 1864. Interred at Shrewsbury Cemetery, Shrewsbury, LA.

Freeman, Albert J. Pvt. Co. D. Residence, Middletown, NY. Died of disease at Fort Jackson, LA, Sept. 20, 1864. Interred at Fort Jackson Post Cemetery, Plaquemines Parish, LA.

Freeman, Amos G. Corp. Co. M. Residence, Providence. Died of typhoid at Camp Parapet, LA, Aug. 4, 1864. Interred at Shrewsbury Cemetery, Shrewsbury, LA.

Freeman, Charles. Pvt. Co. A. Residence, Bristol. Died of pneumonia at Donaldsonville, LA, July 19, 1864. Interred at Chalmette National Cemetery, New Orleans, LA. Grave 11744.

Freeman, Peter. Pvt. Co. A. Residence, Providence. Died of tuberculosis at Providence, RI, Feb. 11, 1864.

Fry, James. Pvt. Co. A. Residence, East Greenwich. Died of malaria at Fort Jackson, LA, Sept. 9, 1864. Interred at Fort Jackson Post Cemetery, Plaquemines Parish, LA.

Fry, Lewis J. Sgt. Co. D. Residence, Reading, PA. Died of disease at Fort Jackson, LA, Aug. 27, 1864. Interred at Fort Jackson Post Cemetery, Plaquemines Parish, LA.

Furber, Newton. Pvt. Co. H. Residence, Lexington, KY. Died of malaria at Plaquemine, LA, Sept. 1, 1864. Interred at Plaquemine Post Burying Ground, Plaquemine, LA.

Gaines, John. Pvt. Co. C. Residence, Philadelphia, PA. Died of malaria at Fort Jackson, LA, Aug. 24, 1864. Interred at Fort Jackson Post Cemetery, Plaquemines Parish, LA.

Gardner, Benjamin C. Pvt. Co. A. Residence, North Kingstown. Died of malaria at Fort Jackson, LA, Aug. 22, 1864. Interred at Fort Jackson Post Cemetery, Plaquemines Parish, LA.

Gardner, Henry F. Pvt. Co. M. Residence, Warren. Died of typhoid at Key West, FL, Feb. 23, 1865. Interred at Fort Jefferson Parade Ground, Fort Jefferson, FL.

Gardner, Henry J. Pvt. Co. A. Residence, South Kingstown. Died of typhoid at Fort Jackson, LA, Sept. 24, 1864. Interred at Fort Jackson Post Cemetery, Plaquemines Parish, LA.

Gardner, Joseph C. Pvt. Co. D. Residence, Swansea, MA. Died of tuberculosis at Brashear, LA, June 24, 1865. Interred at Fort Brashear Cemetery, Morgan City, LA.

Gardner, Willard C. Pvt. Co. A. Residence, Providence. Died of dysentery at Fort Jackson, LA, Sept. 11, 1864. Interred at Fort Jackson Post Cemetery, Plaquemines Parish, LA.

Geer, Henry. Pvt. Co. C. Residence, Canterbury, CT. Died of typhoid at Fort Jackson, LA, July 19, 1864. Interred at Fort Jackson Post Cemetery, Plaquemines Parish, LA.

Gibson, Edward H. Pvt. Co. I. Residence, Providence. Died of disease at Camp Parapet, LA, Aug. 22, 1864. Interred at Shrewsbury Cemetery, Shrewsbury, LA.

Giles, James. Pvt. Co. D. Residence, New York, NY. Died of disease at New Orleans, LA, June 15, 1864. Interred at Chalmette National Cemetery, New Orleans, LA. Grave 11709.

Good, Hezekiah. Pvt. Co. L. Residence, Providence. Died of "debility" at Portsmouth Grove Hospital, Portsmouth, RI, Oct. 1, 1864. Interred at Long Island National Cemetery, East Farmingdale, NY.

Gordon, John. Pvt. Co. K. Residence, Providence. Died of dysentery at Camp Parapet, LA, Aug. 18, 1865. Interred at Shrewsbury Cemetery, Shrewsbury, LA.

Graham, Melville. Pvt. Co. A. Residence, Providence. Died of disease at Key West, FL, Dec. 6, 1864. Interred at Fort Jefferson Parade Ground, Fort Jefferson, FL.

Grant, William A. Pvt. Co. E. Residence, Tarrytown, NY. Died of malaria at Plaquemine, LA, Sept. 9, 1864. Interred at Plaquemine Post Burying Ground, Plaquemine, LA.

Green, George. Pvt. Co. E. Residence, Pleasant Valley, NY. Died of malaria at Plaquemine, LA, June 1, 1864. Interred at Plaquemine Post Burying Ground, Plaquemine, LA.

Green, John. Pvt. Co. K. Residence, Providence. Committed suicide at Camp Parapet, LA, May 16, 1864. Interred at Shrewsbury Cemetery, Shrewsbury, LA.

Greene, Albert. Pvt. Co. A. Residence, Providence. Died of dysentery at Fort Jackson, LA, Sept. 16, 1864. Interred at Fort Jackson Post Cemetery, Plaquemines Parish, LA.

Greer, Richard. Pvt. Co. M. Residence, Newark, NJ. Died of typhoid at Camp Parapet, LA, June 17, 1864. Interred at Shrewsbury Cemetery, Shrewsbury, LA.

Griffin, Charles. Pvt. Co. M. Residence, Lexington, KY. Died of malaria at Camp Parapet, LA, Oct. 16, 1864. Interred at Shrewsbury Cemetery, Shrewsbury, LA.

Griffin, Henry A. Pvt. Co. M. Residence, Attleboro, MA. Died of dysentery at Camp Parapet, LA, Dec. 31, 1864. Interred at Shrewsbury Cemetery, Shrewsbury, LA.

Hagamore, George. Pvt. Co. F. Residence, Providence. Died of kidney disease at Plaquemine, LA, July 7, 1864. Interred at Plaquemine Post Burying Ground, Plaquemine, LA.

Haird, John. Pvt. Co. L. Residence, Providence. Died of typhoid at Camp Parapet, LA, Aug. 1, 1864. Interred at Shrewsbury Cemetery, Shrewsbury, LA.

Hall, Nathaniel. Pvt. Co. M. Residence, Alexandria, VA. Died of typhoid at Camp Parapet, LA, Sept. 4, 1864. Interred at Shrewsbury Cemetery, Shrewsbury, LA.

Hallam, Chester H. Pvt. Co. B. Residence, Hartford, CT. Died of typhoid at Fort Jackson LA, Mar. 1, 1865. Interred at Fort Jackson Post Cemetery, Plaquemines Parish, LA.

Hamblin, Julius P. Sgt. Co. A. Residence, Providence. Died of typhoid at Fort Jackson, LA, Sept. 5, 1864. Interred at Fort Jackson Post Cemetery, Plaquemines Parish, LA.

Hardy, Charles H. Corp. Co. K. Residence, Providence. Died of dysentery at Camp Parapet, LA, Dec. 21, 1864. Interred at Shrewsbury Cemetery, Shrewsbury, LA.

Harris, Charles W. Pvt. Co. F. Residence, Providence. Died of dropsy at Plaquemine, LA, Aug. 11, 1864. Interred at Plaquemine Post Burying Ground, Plaquemine, LA.

Harway, Prince A. Pvt. Co. H. Residence, Providence. Died of pneumonia at New Orleans, LA, July 8, 1864. Interred at Chalmette National Cemetery, New Orleans, LA.

Hatfield, George. Pvt. Co. A. Residence, Sherman, CT. Died of typhoid at Dutch Island, RI, Nov. 23, 1863. Interred at Long Island National Cemetery, East Farmingdale, NY.

Hawes, Alexander. Pvt. Co. H. Residence, Providence. Died of pneumonia at New Orleans, LA, Feb. 4, 1864. Interred at Shrewsbury Cemetery, Shrewsbury, LA.

Hazel, Allen. Pvt. Co. I. Residence, Providence. Died of disease at Camp Parapet, LA, May 28, 1864. Interred at Shrewsbury Cemetery, Shrewsbury, LA.

Hector, William H. Pvt. Co. A. Residence, Worcester, MA. Died of typhoid at Fort Jackson, LA, Sept. 5, 1864. Interred at Fort Jackson Post Cemetery, Plaquemines Parish, LA.

Henry, James F. Pvt. Co. M. Residence, Bath, NY. Died of dysentery at New Orleans, LA, Aug. 7, 1864. Interred at Chalmette National Cemetery, New Orleans, LA. Grave 11769.

Henson, Joseph H. Pvt. Co. H. Residence, Providence. Died of malaria at Plaquemine, LA, Sept. 10, 1864. Interred at Plaquemine Post Burying Ground, Plaquemine, LA.

Hicks, John J. Pvt. Co. D. Residence, Cumberland. Died of tuberculosis at Fort Jackson, LA, Nov. 1, 1864. Interred at Fort Jackson Post Cemetery, Plaquemines Parish, LA.

Hicks, Lanson E. Corp. Co. F. Residence, Providence. Died of typhoid at Plaquemine, LA, July 11, 1864. Interred at Plaquemine Post Burying Ground, Plaquemine, LA.

Hicks, Peter. Pvt. Co. H. Residence, Providence. Died of rheumatism at New Orleans, LA, May 17, 1864. Interred at Chalmette National Cemetery, New Orleans, LA. Grave 11202.

Hill, Henry C. Pvt. Co. M. Residence, Taunton, MA. Died of malaria at Camp Parapet, LA, Sept. 21, 1864. Interred at Shrewsbury Cemetery, Shrewsbury, LA.

Hill, James. Pvt. Co. B. Residence, Taunton, MA. Died of typhoid at Fort Jackson, LA, Aug. 21, 1864. Interred at Fort Jackson Post Cemetery, Plaquemines Parish, LA.

Hinkman, John. Pvt. Co. D. Residence, Flushing, NY. Died of typhoid at Camp Parapet, LA, June 12, 1864. Interred at Shrewsbury Cemetery, Shrewsbury, LA.

Hogan, Frederick. Pvt. Co. D. Residence, New Bedford, MA. Died of tuberculosis at New Orleans, LA, Nov. 9, 1864. Interred at Shrewsbury Cemetery, Shrewsbury, LA.

Hollis, Robert. Mus. Co. B. Residence, Enfield, CT. Died of typhoid at Fort Jackson, LA, Aug. 23, 1864. Interred at Fort Jackson Post Cemetery, Plaquemines Parish, LA.

Holmes, Nelson. Pvt. Co. B. Residence, New York, NY. Died of typhoid at New Orleans, LA, June 6, 1864. Interred at Shrewsbury Cemetery, Shrewsbury, La.

Holmes, Thomas. Pvt. Co. C. Residence, Providence. Died of syphilis at Camp Parapet, LA, Oct. 14, 1864. Interred at Shrewsbury Cemetery, Shrewsbury, LA.

Honeycutt, Greenberry. Pvt. Co. M. Residence, Cleveland, OH. Died of dysentery at New Orleans, LA, July 24, 1864. Interred at Shrewsbury Cemetery, Shrewsbury, LA.

Hopper, Benjamin H. Pvt. Co. F. Residence, Providence. Died of tuberculosis at Plaquemine, LA, April 5, 1864. Interred at Plaquemine Post Burying Ground, Plaquemine, LA.

Hornbeck, Theodore. Pvt. Co. M. Residence, New York, NY. Died of typhoid at Camp Parapet, LA, Sept. 30, 1864. Interred at Shrewsbury Cemetery, Shrewsbury, LA.

Howland, George. Pvt. Co. M. Residence, Ontario, NY. Died of "congestion of the brain" at Camp Parapet, LA, Nov. 7, 1864. Interred at Shrewsbury Cemetery, Shrewsbury, LA.

Humbert, William L. Corp. Co. A. Residence, Providence. Died of malaria at Fort Jackson, LA, Sept. 5, 1864. Interred at Fort Jackson Post Cemetery, Plaquemines Parish, LA.

Huntington, Hiram. Pvt. Co. A. Residence, Providence. Died of malaria at Fort Jackson, LA, Aug. 27, 1864. Interred at Fort Jackson Post Cemetery, Plaquemines Parish, LA.

Irons, Robert. Pvt. Co. A. Residence, Providence. Died of typhoid at Fort Jackson, LA, Oct. 17, 1864. Interred at Fort Jackson Post Cemetery, Plaquemines Parish, LA.

Irving, William. Pvt. Co. C Residence, Providence. Died of dropsy at Fort Jackson, LA, Nov. 12, 1864. Interred at Fort Jackson Post Cemetery, Plaquemines Parish, LA.

Isaac, John. Pvt. Co. G. Residence, Providence. Died of jaundice at New Orleans, LA, April 1, 1864. Interred at Shrewsbury Cemetery, Shrewsbury, LA.

Jackson, Adelbert. Pvt. Co. G. Residence, Providence. Died of typhoid at Plaquemine, LA, June 27, 1864. Interred at Plaquemine Post Burying Ground, Plaquemine, LA.

Jackson, Albert G. Corp. Co. B. Residence, Hartford, CT. Died of dysentery at Matagorda Island, TX, May 5, 1864. Interred at Fort Esperanza Burying Ground, Matagorda Island, TX.

Jackson, David. Pvt. Co. F. Residence, Providence. Died of disease at Camp Parapet, LA, May 24, 1864. Interred at Shrewsbury Cemetery, Shrewsbury, LA.

Jackson, Erastus. Pvt. Co. F. Residence, Hartford, CT. Died of typhoid at Plaquemine, LA, Oct. 13, 1864. Interred at Plaquemine Post Burying Ground, Plaquemine, LA.

Jackson, James M. Pvt. Co. D. Residence, Westbury, NY. Died of malaria at Fort Jackson, LA, Sept. 9, 1864. Interred at Fort Jackson Post Cemetery, Plaquemines Parish, LA.

Jackson, Lanson. Pvt. Co. D. Residence, Jerusalem, NY. Died of typhoid at New Orleans, LA, July 7, 1864. Interred at Shrewsbury Cemetery, Shrewsbury, LA.

Jackson, Leonard. Pvt. Co. D. Residence, Montgomery, NY. Died of disease at New Orleans, LA, Sept. 21, 1864. Interred at Chalmette National Cemetery, New Orleans, LA. Grave 10815.

Jackson, Samuel. Pvt. Co. G. Residence, Providence. Died of typhoid at Plaquemine, LA, May 27, 1864. Interred at Plaquemine Post Burying Ground, Plaquemine, LA.

Jackson, Sylvester. Pvt. Co. F. Residence, Providence. Died of rheumatism at Plaquemine, LA, April 24, 1865. Interred at Plaquemine Post Burying Ground, Plaquemine, LA.

Jackson, Theodore. Pvt. Co. B. Residence, New York, NY. Died of dysentery at New Orleans, LA, June 19, 1864. Interred at Chalmette National Cemetery, New Orleans, LA. Grave 11720.

Jackson, William C. Pvt. Co. C. Residence, Bridgeport, CT. Died of malaria at Fort Jackson, LA, Sept. 25, 1864. Interred at Fort Jackson Post Cemetery, Plaquemines Parish, LA.

Jackson, William H. Pvt. Co. A. Residence, New York, NY. Died of dysentery at Brashear City, LA, June 21, 1865. Interred at Fort Brashear Post Cemetery, Morgan City, LA.

Jarvis, Samuel. Sgt. Co. A. Residence, Providence. Died of malaria at Fort Jackson, LA, Oct. 23, 1864. Interred at Fort Jackson Post Cemetery, Plaquemines Parish, LA.

Jefferson, Samuel O. Pvt. Co. G. Residence, Providence. Captured and murdered in cold blood by Rebels at Plaquemine, LA, Aug. 6, 1864. Interred at Plaquemine Post Burying Ground, Plaquemine, LA.

Johnson, Charles H. Pvt. Co. K. Residence, Providence. Died of typhoid at Camp Parapet, LA, June 2, 1864. Interred at Shrewsbury Cemetery, Shrewsbury, LA.

Johnson, Edward. Pvt. Co. D. Residence, Monmouth, NJ. Died of tuberculosis at Fort Jackson, LA, Oct. 9, 1864. Interred at Fort Jackson Post Cemetery, Plaquemines Parish, LA.

Johnson, George H. Pvt. Co. A. Residence, Newport. Died of tuberculosis at Fort Jackson, LA, Oct. 15, 1864. Interred at Fort Jackson Post Cemetery, Plaquemines Parish, LA.

Johnson, John. Pvt. Co. L. Residence, Providence. Died of bronchitis at Dutch Island, RI, Mar. 10, 1864. Interred at Long Island National Cemetery, East Farmingdale, NY.

Johnson, Joseph W. Pvt. Co. K. Residence, Providence. Died of typhoid at Camp Parapet, LA, Nov. 24, 1864. Interred at Shrewsbury Cemetery, Shrewsbury, LA.

Johnson, Peter H. Pvt. Co. K. Residence, Providence. Died of typhoid at Camp Parapet, LA, Oct. 7, 1864. Interred at Shrewsbury Cemetery, Shrewsbury, LA.

Jones, Abraham. Pvt. Co. D. Residence, Flushing, NY. Died of typhoid at Fort Esperanza, TX, April 5, 1864. Interred at Fort Esperanza Burying Ground, Matagorda Island, TX.

Jones, George W. Pvt. Co. D. Residence, Jamaica, NY. Died of malaria at Fort Jackson, LA, Aug. 25, 1864. Interred at Fort Jackson Post Cemetery, Plaquemines Parish, LA.

Jones, James E. Pvt. Co. I. Residence, Providence. Died of dysentery at Camp Parapet, LA, Oct. 26, 1864. Interred at Shrewsbury Cemetery, Shrewsbury, LA.

Jones, James F. Pvt. Co. M. Residence, Richmond, IN. Died of tuberculosis at Camp Parapet, LA, Nov. 30, 1864. Interred at Shrewsbury Cemetery, Shrewsbury, LA.

Jones, Mervin. Pvt. Co. D. Residence, Flushing, NY. Died of scrofula at New Orleans, LA, Oct. 3, 1864. Interred at Shrewsbury Cemetery, Shrewsbury, LA.

Jones, William. Pvt. Co. G. Residence, Providence. Died of disease at Camp Parapet, LA, Sept. 28, 1865. Interred at Shrewsbury Cemetery, Shrewsbury, LA.

Jones, Willis. Sgt. Co. E. Residence, Providence. Accidentally shot and killed in camp at Plaquemine, LA, June 21, 1864. Interred at Plaquemine Post Burying Ground, Plaquemine, LA.

Keller, John. Pvt. Co. H. Residence, Providence. Died of tuberculosis at Plaquemine, LA, June 30, 1864. Interred at Plaquemine Post Burying Ground, Plaquemine, LA.

Kellman, James H. Pvt. Co. E. Residence, Schoharie, NY. Died of phthisis at English Turn, LA, Mar. 15, 1864. Interred at English Turn Post Burying Grounds, English Turns, LA.

Kenney, Henry J. Pvt. Co. L. Residence, Providence. Died of tuberculosis at Dutch Island, RI, Mar. 17, 1864. Interred at Long Island National Cemetery, East Farmingdale, NY.

Kenney, William. Pvt. Co. M. Residence, Alexandria, VA. Died of typhoid at Camp Parapet, LA, Oct. 25, 1865. Interred at Shrewsbury Cemetery, Shrewsbury, LA.

King, Anthony. Pvt. Co. G. Residence, Providence. Captured and murdered in cold blood by Rebels at Plaquemine, LA, Aug. 6, 1864. Interred at Plaquemine Post Burying Ground, Plaquemine, LA.

King, Cornelius. Mus. Co. E. Residence, Providence. Died of tuberculosis at Plaquemine, LA, June 29, 1864. Interred at Plaquemine Post Burying Ground, Plaquemine, LA.

Labiel, William H. Pvt. Co. K. Residence, Providence. Died of dysentery at New Orleans, LA, Aug. 4, 1864. Interred at Plaquemine Post Burying Ground, Plaquemine, LA.

Lambert, Andrew. Pvt. Co. H. Residence, Providence. Died of typhoid at Plaquemine, LA, Aug. 5, 1864. Interred at Plaquemine Post Burying Ground, Plaquemine, LA.

Laws, Leven. Pvt. Co. A. Residence, Portland, ME. Died of typhoid at Fort Jackson, LA, Sept. 13, 1864. Interred at Fort Jackson Post Cemetery, Plaquemines Parish, LA.

Lee, Henry. Pvt. Co. M. Residence, Shenandoah, VA. Died of typhoid at Camp Parapet, LA, Oct. 2, 1864. Interred at Shrewsbury Cemetery, Shrewsbury, LA.

Lee, Henry. Pvt. Co. M. Residence, Providence. Died of dropsy at Camp Parapet, LA, Nov. 3, 1864. Interred at Shrewsbury Cemetery, Shrewsbury, LA.

Lee, John W. Corp. Co. K. Residence, Providence. Died of phthisis at Camp Parapet. LA, Dec. 10, 1864. Interred at Shrewsbury Cemetery, Shrewsbury, LA.

Lenisen, Philip. Pvt. Co. G. Died of diphtheria at Camp Parapet, LA, Feb. 9, 1864. Interred at Shrewsbury Cemetery, Shrewsbury, LA.

Lewis, Jesse. Pvt. Co. I. Residence, Providence. Died of typhoid at Camp Parapet, LA, Dec. 7, 1864. Interred at Shrewsbury Cemetery, Shrewsbury, LA.

Lippitt, George. Pvt. Co. A. Residence, South Kingstown. Died of typhoid at Fort Jackson, LA, Aug. 8, 1864. Interred at Fort Jackson Post Cemetery, Plaquemines Parish, LA.

Livingston, Oscar. Capt. Co. M. Residence, Providence. Drowned in the sinking of the *Atlanta* while returning to Providence for muster out, Oct. 15, 1865.

Loncks, John A. Corp. Co. K. Residence, Providence. Died of typhoid at New Orleans, LA, Sept. 6, 1864. Interred at Shrewsbury Cemetery, Shrewsbury, LA.

Lowe, Ishmael R. Pvt. Co. C. Residence, Warwick. Died of syphilis at New Orleans, LA, June 21, 1864. Interred at Shrewsbury Cemetery, Shrewsbury, LA.

Lucas, James. Pvt. Co. I. Residence, Providence. Died of apoplexy at Camp Parapet, LA, Feb. 10, 1865. Interred at Shrewsbury Cemetery, Shrewsbury, LA.

Lunn, Amos A. Pvt. Co. D. Residence, Crawford, NY. Died of dysentery at Fort Jackson, LA, Oct. 21, 1864. Interred at Fort Jackson Post Cemetery, Plaquemines Parish, LA.

Mann, Stephen. Pvt. Co. H. Residence, Providence. Died of rheumatism at Plaquemine, LA, June 24, 1864. Interred at Plaquemine Post Burying Ground, Plaquemine, LA.

Mann, William H. Sgt. Co. L. Residence, Providence. Died of typhoid at Camp Parapet, LA, Aug. 1, 1864. Interred at Shrewsbury Cemetery, Shrewsbury, LA.

Martin, Thomas. Pvt. Co. B. Residence, New York, NY. Died of malaria at Fort Jackson, LA, Sept. 12, 1864. Interred at Fort Jackson Post Cemetery, Plaquemines Parish, LA.

Mason, Henry. Corp. Co. I. Residence, Providence. Died of typhoid at Camp Parapet, LA, Sept. 18, 1864. Interred at Shrewsbury Cemetery, Shrewsbury, LA.

Mason, Isaac. Pvt. Co. C. Residence, Warwick. Died of typhoid at Matagorda Island, TX, May 26, 1864. Interred at Fort Esperanza Burying Ground, Matagorda Island, TX.

Mason, Samuel. Pvt. Co. G. Residence, Providence. Captured and murdered in cold blood by Rebels at Plaquemine, LA, Aug. 6, 1864. Interred at Plaquemine Post Burying Ground, Plaquemine, LA.

Mason, Samuel. Sgt. Co. H. Residence, Providence. Died of dysentery at Plaquemine, LA, Sept. 15, 1864. Interred at Plaquemine Post Burying Ground, Plaquemine, LA.

McCarty, Henry. Pvt. Co. F. Residence, Providence. Died of dysentery at Plaquemine, LA, May 20, 1865. Interred at Plaquemine Post Burying Ground, Plaquemine, LA.

McClow, James. Pvt. Co. E. Residence, Burlington, NJ. Died of tuberculosis at English Turn, LA, Feb. 4, 1864. Interred at English Turn Post Burying Grounds, English Turns, LA.

McGill, William. Pvt. Co. L. Residence, Providence. Died of tuberculosis at Camp Parapet, LA, Feb. 9, 1865. Interred at Shrewsbury Cemetery, Shrewsbury, LA.

Merrick, John. Pvt. Co. B. Residence, Providence. Died of phthisis at Portsmouth Grove Hospital, Portsmouth, RI, Jan. 23, 1864. Interred at Long Island National Cemetery, East Farmingdale, NY.

Miller, Benjamin. Pvt. Co. L. Residence, Providence. Died of typhoid at Camp Parapet, LA, July 21, 1865. Interred at Shrewsbury Cemetery, Shrewsbury, LA.

Mills, William W. Pvt. Co. K. Residence, Providence. Died of dysentery at Camp Parapet, LA, May 12, 1864. Interred at Shrewsbury Cemetery, Shrewsbury, LA.

Miltier, Solomon. Pvt. Co. A. Residence, Providence. Died of disease at New Orleans, LA, June 4, 1864. Interred at Shrewsbury Cemetery, Shrewsbury, LA.

Mix, Collins. Pvt. Co. F. Residence, New Haven, CT. Died of tuberculosis at New Orleans, LA, May 30, 1864. Interred at Chalmette National Cemetery, New Orleans, LA.

Moody, Joseph. Pvt. Co. C. Residence, Canterbury, CT. Died of dysentery at New Orleans, LA, May 31, 1864. Interred at Chalmette National Cemetery, New Orleans, LA. Grave 11235.

Moore, Charles C. Pvt. Co. D. Residence, Buffalo, NY. Died of pneumonia at Fort Jackson, LA, Aug. 11, 1864. Interred at Fort Jackson Post Cemetery, Plaquemines Parish, LA.

Moore, Charles H. Corp. Co. M. Residence, Providence. Died of malaria at Camp Parapet, LA, Oct. 12, 1864. Interred at Shrewsbury Cemetery, Shrewsbury, LA.

Moore, George. Pvt. Co. M. Residence, Saratoga, NY. Died of "congestion of the brain" at Camp Parapet, LA, Sept. 23, 1864. Interred at Shrewsbury Cemetery, Shrewsbury, LA.

Morrison, William A. Pvt. Co. M. Residence, Pittsburgh, PA. Died of typhoid at Camp Parapet, LA, July 15, 1864. Interred at Shrewsbury Cemetery, Shrewsbury, LA.

Morton, Willis. Pvt. Co. L. Residence, Providence. Died of "congestion of the brain" at Camp Parapet, LA, Nov. 6, 1864. Interred at Shrewsbury Cemetery, Shrewsbury, LA.

Munroe, Charles W. 1st Lt. Co. K. Residence, Providence. Died of disease contracted in the service at Providence, RI, Mar. 20, 1868. Interred at North Burial Ground, Providence, RI.

Myers, Aaron C. Pvt. Co. M. Residence, Munroe, NY. Died of diphtheria at Camp Parapet, LA, Dec. 31, 1864. Interred at Shrewsbury Cemetery, Shrewsbury, LA.

Nelson, Charles C. Pvt. Co. K. Residence, Providence. Died of "fits" at Camp Parapet, LA, July 1, 1865. Interred at Shrewsbury Cemetery, Shrewsbury, LA.

Newcomb, William W. Residence, Providence. Died of disease at Camp Parapet, LA, Aug. 4, 1864. Interred at Shrewsbury Cemetery, Shrewsbury, LA.

Niles, Edward F. Pvt. Co. A. Residence, South Kingstown. Died of malaria at Fort Jackson, LA, Aug. 26, 1864. Interred at Fort Jackson Post Cemetery, Plaquemines Parish, LA.

Niles, Simon. Sgt. Co. A. Residence, South Kingstown. Died of dysentery contracted in the service at South Kingstown, RI, Nov. 21, 1865. Interred at Simon Niles Lot, South Kingstown Cemetery 81, South Kingstown, RI.

Nite, Joseph T. Pvt. Co. H. Residence, Providence. Died of tuberculosis at Plaquemine, LA, Nov. 11, 1864. Interred at Plaquemine Post Burying Ground, Plaquemine, LA.

Noka, Jeremiah. Artificer. Co. A. Residence, Charlestown. Died of malaria at Fort Jackson, LA, Oct. 9, 1864. Interred at Fort Jackson Post Cemetery, Plaquemines Parish, LA.

Norris, George. Pvt. Co. D. Residence, Adams County, PA. Died of dysentery at Fort Jackson, LA, Sept. 27, 1864. Interred at Fort Jackson Post Cemetery, Plaquemines Parish, LA.

Outland, Milton. Corp. Co. K. Residence, Providence. Died of dysentery at New York, NY. Oct. 3, 1865. Interred at Cypress Hills National Cemetery, Brooklyn, NY. Grave 3197.

Page, Poke. Pvt. Co. D. Residence, Jackson, MS. Died of tuberculosis at Brashear City, LA, June 24, 1865. Interred at Fort Brashear Post Cemetery, Morgan City, LA.

Paine, Arthur. Pvt. Co. M. Residence, New York, NY. Died of typhoid at Camp Parapet, LA, June 26, 1864. Interred at Shrewsbury Cemetery, Shrewsbury, LA.

Paine, Valentine. Corp. Co. A. Residence, Providence. Died of tuberculosis at Fort Jackson, LA, Sept. 24, 1864. Interred at Fort Jackson Post Cemetery, Plaquemines Parish, LA.

Palmer, Oliver. Pvt. Co. D. Residence, Hartford. Died of typhoid at New Orleans, LA, Aug. 20, 1864. Interred at Shrewsbury Cemetery, Shrewsbury, LA.

Pell, John. Sgt. Co. L. Residence, Providence. Died of dysentery at Camp Parapet, LA, Nov. 1, 1864. Interred at Shrewsbury Cemetery, Shrewsbury, LA.

Peters, Charles H. Pvt. Co. I. Residence, Providence. Died of dysentery at Camp Parapet, LA, Oct. 24, 1865. Interred at Shrewsbury Cemetery, Shrewsbury, LA.

Peters, John W. Pvt. Co. D. Residence, Norwich, CT. Died of tuberculosis at Fort Jackson, LA, Aug. 29, 1864. Interred at Fort Jackson Post Cemetery, Plaquemines Parish, LA.

Peterson, Walter. Pvt. Co. G. Residence, Providence. Died of tuberculosis at Plaquemine, LA, April 18, 1865. Interred at Plaquemine Post Burying Ground, Plaquemine, LA.

Pierce, George A. 1st Lt. Co. M. Residence, Smithfield. "Died in Central Falls, Nov. 19, 1870 of malarious fever contracted in Louisiana." Interred at Moshassuck Cemetery, Central Falls, RI.

Pierce, George W. Pvt. Co. A. Residence, New York, NY. Died of tuberculosis at Providence, RI, Jan. 3, 1864. Interred at North Burial Ground, Providence, RI.

Poole, Fielding. Pvt. Co. M. Residence, Shenandoah, VA. Died of "congestion of the brain" at Camp Parapet, LA, July 30, 1864. Interred at Shrewsbury Cemetery, Shrewsbury, LA.

Potter, Frederick A. Pvt. Co. A. Residence, South Kingstown. Died of pneumonia at Fort Jackson, July 8, 1864. Interred at Fort Jackson Post Cemetery, Plaquemines Parish, LA.

Powers, John. Pvt. Co. C. Residence, Hartford, CT. Died of malaria at Fort Jackson, LA, Aug. 22, 1864. Interred at Fort Jackson Post Cemetery, Plaquemines Parish, LA.

Profitt, Charles M. Pvt. Co. A. Residence, Providence. Died of dysentery at Fort Jackson, LA, Sept. 13, 1864. Interred at Fort Jackson Post Cemetery, Plaquemines Parish, LA.

Quinn, James. Pvt. Co. A. Residence, Providence. Executed for mutinous behavior at Camp Parapet, LA, Nov. 15, 1864. Interred at Shrewsbury Cemetery, Shrewsbury, LA.

Randall, Hannibal. Pvt. Co. D. Residence, Bridgeport, CT. Died of tuberculosis at Fort Jackson, LA, Aug. 25, 1864. Interred at Fort Jackson Post Cemetery, Plaquemines Parish, LA.

Randall, Joseph B. Pvt. Co. L. Residence, Providence. Died of typhoid at Fort Jackson, LA, May 17, 1865. Interred at Fort Jackson Post Cemetery, Plaquemines Parish, LA.

Randall, Richard. Pvt. Co. D. Residence, Prescott, CT. Died on enteritis at Fort Jackson, LA, Oct. 31, 1864. Interred at Fort Jackson Post Cemetery, Plaquemines Parish, LA.

Rawson, Anthony Richmond. Capt. Co. K. Residence, Providence. Died of neuralgia at Providence, RI, May 5, 1864. Interred at Swan Point Cemetery, Providence, RI.

Reading, Stephen. Pvt. Co. H. Residence, Providence. Died of a concussion at Plaquemine, LA, Mar. 20, 1865. Interred at Plaquemine Post Burying Ground, Plaquemine, LA.

Redder, Jacob W. Pvt. Co. I. Residence, Providence. Died of smallpox at New Orleans, LA, April 30, 1864. Interred at Shrewsbury Cemetery, Shrewsbury, LA.

Reed, Charles P. Pvt. Co. C. Residence, New York, NY. Died of dropsy at Fort Jackson, LA, Dec. 2, 1864. Interred at Fort Jackson Post Cemetery, Plaquemines Parish, LA.

Reynolds, Albert. Pvt. Co. D. Residence, Sterling, CT. Died of tuberculosis at New Orleans, LA, Dec. 29, 1864. Interred at Shrewsbury Cemetery, Shrewsbury, LA.

Reynolds, Edward. Pvt. Co. A. Residence, Providence. Died of dysentery at Fort Jackson, LA, Sept. 21, 1864. Interred at Fort Jackson Post Cemetery, Plaquemines Parish, LA.

The Fourteenth Rhode Island Heavy Artillery lost more men than any other Rhode Island regiment. Among the victims was Captain Anthony Richmond Rawson of Providence.

Rhodes, John. Mus. Co. B. Residence, Providence. Died of dysentery at Fort Jackson, LA, Sept. 8, 1864. Interred at Fort Jackson Post Cemetery, Plaquemines Parish, LA.

Rice, John. Pvt. Co. I. Residence, Providence. Died of dysentery at Camp Parapet, LA, Aug. 1, 1864. Interred at Shrewsbury Cemetery, Shrewsbury, LA.

Ricks, Harrison. Pvt. Co. C. Residence, Providence. Died of phthisis at New Orleans, LA, Jan. 6, 1864. Interred at Shrewsbury Cemetery, Shrewsbury, LA.

Ricks, Stephen T. Pvt. Co. C. Residence, Brooklyn, NY. Died of dysentery at Fort Jackson, LA, Nov. 10, 1864. Interred at Fort Jackson Post Cemetery, Plaquemines Parish, LA.

Robbins, William. Pvt. Co. G. Residence, Providence. Died of tuberculosis at Plaquemine, LA, Nov. 4, 1864. Interred at Plaquemine Post Burying Ground, Plaquemine, LA.

Roberts, Charles A. Pvt. Co. L. Residence, Providence. Died of tuberculosis at Dutch Island, RI, Feb. 13, 1864. Interred at Long Island National Cemetery, East Farmingdale, NY.

Rooms, James. Pvt. Co. A. Residence, North Kingstown. Died of tuberculosis at Fort Jackson, LA, Aug. 25, 1864. Interred at Fort Jackson Post Cemetery, Plaquemines Parish, LA.

Sanford, James. Pvt. Co. L. Residence, Providence. Died of pneumonia at Camp Parapet, LA, May 14, 1864. Interred at Shrewsbury Cemetery, Shrewsbury, LA.

Saunders, Aaron. Pvt. Co. E. Residence, Allentown, NH. Died of tuberculosis at Dutch Island, RI, Nov. 29, 1863. Interred at Long Island National Cemetery, East Farmingdale, NY.

Saunders, John. Pvt. Co. H. Residence, Providence. Died of dropsy at Camp Parapet, LA, Mar. 29, 1864. Interred at Shrewsbury Cemetery, Shrewsbury, LA.

Scott, J. Wesley. Pvt. Co. I. Residence, Providence. Died of "congestion of the brain" at Camp Parapet, LA, Sept. 18, 1864. Interred at Shrewsbury Cemetery, Shrewsbury, LA.

Scott, Norris. Pvt. Co. F. Residence, Providence. Died of tuberculosis at Plaquemine, LA, Sept. 12, 1864. Interred at Plaquemine Post Burying Ground, Plaquemine, LA.

Scudder, William G. Pvt. Co. K. Residence, Providence. Died of dysentery at Camp Parapet, LA, May 20, 1864. Interred at Shrewsbury Cemetery, Shrewsbury, LA.

Seaman, Elias. Pvt. Co. D. Residence, Flushing, NY. Died of disease at Fort Jackson, LA, Aug. 22, 1864. Interred at Fort Jackson Post Cemetery, Plaquemines Parish, LA.

Seaton, George. Pvt. Co. L. Residence, Providence. Died of dysentery at Camp Parapet, LA, Aug. 25, 1865. Interred at Shrewsbury Cemetery, Shrewsbury, LA.

Sharper, John N. Pvt. Co. G. Residence, Herkimer, NY. Died of disease contracted in the service April 5, 1866 at Herkimer, NY. Interred at Oak Hill Cemetery, Herkimer, NY.

Sills, Edward H. Pvt. Co. I. Residence, Providence. Died of typhoid at Camp Parapet, LA, Oct. 31, 1864. Interred at Shrewsbury Cemetery, Shrewsbury, LA.

Simms, James W. Pvt. Co. L. Residence, Providence. Died of typhoid at Camp Parapet, LA, Aug. 19, 1865. Interred at Shrewsbury Cemetery, Shrewsbury, LA.

Simons, Henry. Capt. Co. B. Residence, Providence. Died of typhoid at New Orleans, LA, Oct. 6, 1864. Interred at North Burial Ground, Providence, RI.

Simons, John. Pvt. Co. D. Residence, Norwich, CT. Died of malaria at Fort Jackson, LA, Sept. 28, 1864. Interred at Fort Jackson Post Cemetery, Plaquemines Parish, LA.

Simons, William H. Pvt. Co. D. Residence, Norwich, CT. Died of malaria at Fort Jackson, LA, Aug. 20, 1865. Interred at Fort Jackson Post Cemetery, Plaquemines Parish, LA.

Smerdus, Isaac. Sgt. Co. D. Residence, Poughkeepsie, NY. Died of hepatitis at New Orleans, LA, Aug. 17, 1864. Interred at Shrewsbury Cemetery, Shrewsbury, LA.

Smith, Alfred E. Pvt. Co. C. Residence, Stony Brook, NY. Died of smallpox at New Orleans, LA, Aug. 5, 1864. Interred at Chalmette National Cemetery, New Orleans, LA. Grave 11768.

Pvt. John N. Sharper died of disease at his home in Herkimer, NY, in 1866. His image is one of only a few identified photographs of enlisted men from the Fourteenth Rhode Island Heavy Artillery. Library of Congress.

Smith, Benjamin F. Pvt. Co. G. Residence, Providence. Died of tuberculosis at Dutch Island, RI, Jan. 31, 1864. Interred at Long Island National Cemetery, East Farmingdale, NY.

Smith, David. Pvt. Co. I. Residence, Providence. Died of typhoid at Camp Parapet, LA, Oct. 2, 1864. Interred at Shrewsbury Cemetery, Shrewsbury, LA.

Smith, David. Pvt. Co. K. Residence, Providence. Died of typhoid at Camp Parapet, LA, May 6, 1865. Interred at Shrewsbury Cemetery, Shrewsbury, LA.

Smith, Henry. Pvt. Co. B. Residence, Providence. Died of pleurisy at Providence, RI, Dec. 1, 1864. Interred at North Burial Ground, Providence, RI.

Smith, Jacob. Pvt. Co. C. Residence, New York, NY. Died of tuberculosis at Fort Jackson, LA, Dec. 10, 1864. Interred at Fort Jackson Post Cemetery, Plaquemines Parish, LA.

Smith, James L. Pvt. Co. I. Residence, Providence. Died of dysentery at New Orleans, LA, July 24, 1864. Interred at Shrewsbury Cemetery, Shrewsbury, LA.

Smith, John M. Pvt. Co. G. Residence, Providence. Died of typhoid at Plaquemine, LA, Sept. 15, 1864. Interred at Plaquemine Post Burying Ground, Plaquemine, LA.

Smith, Joseph. Sgt. Co. H. Residence, Providence. Shot while trying to escape from prison at Donaldsonville, LA, June 29, 1865.

Smith, Lemuel H. Pvt. Co. E. Residence, Windsor, CT. Died of pneumonia at Dutch Island, RI, Jan. 4, 1864. Interred at Long Island National Cemetery, East Farmingdale, NY.

Smothers, Francis. Pvt. Co. G. Residence, Providence. Died of typhoid at Plaquemine, LA, Nov. 9, 1864. Interred at Plaquemine Post Burying Ground, Plaquemine, LA.

Stanton, William J. Pvt. Co. I. Residence, Providence. Died of typhoid at Camp Parapet, LA, Oct. 13, 1864. Interred at Shrewsbury Cemetery, Shrewsbury, LA.

Stevenson, Robert M. Pvt. Co. K. Residence, Providence. Died of typhoid at New Orleans, LA, Aug. 14, 1864. Interred at Chalmette National Cemetery, New Orleans, LA. Grave 11778.

Steward, Elijah A. Pvt. Co. I. Residence, Providence. Died of dysentery at Camp Parapet, LA, Dec. 22, 1864. Interred at Shrewsbury Cemetery, Shrewsbury, LA.

Sullivan, John. Pvt. Co. G. Residence, Providence. Died of typhoid at Plaquemine, LA, May 20, 1864. Interred at Plaquemine Post Burying Ground, Plaquemine, LA.

Summerset, Lemuel. Pvt. Co. D. Residence, New York, NY. Died of tuberculosis at Fort Jackson, LA, Oct. 10, 1864. Interred at Fort Jackson Post Cemetery, Plaquemines Parish, LA.

Sutphens, Thomas. Pvt. Co. F. Residence, Providence. Died of cholera at English Turn, LA, Mar. 21, 1864. Interred at English Turn Post Burying Grounds, English Turns, LA.

Talbot, Phillip W. Corp. Co. K. Residence, Providence. Died of diphtheria at Camp Parapet, LA, Dec. 14, 1864. Interred at Shrewsbury Cemetery, Shrewsbury, LA.

Tanner, James. Pvt. Co. I. Residence, Providence. Died of typhoid at Camp Parapet, LA, Oct. 11, 1864. Interred at Shrewsbury Cemetery, Shrewsbury, LA.

Tansey, William F. 1st Lt. Co. K. Residence, Providence. Drowned in the sinking of the *Atlanta* while returning to Providence for muster out, Oct. 15, 1865.

Telegrove, John. Pvt. Co. A. Residence, Providence. Died of phthisis at Matagorda Island, TX, April 2, 1864. Interred at Fort Esperanza Burying Ground, Matagorda Island, TX.

Tembroke, Samuel. Co. A. Residence, Providence. Died of dysentery at Fort Jackson, LA, Aug. 13, 1864. Interred at Fort Jackson Post Cemetery, Plaquemines Parish, LA.

Terrell, Robert. Pvt. Co. M. Residence, Cleveland, OH. Died of malaria at Camp Parapet, LA, Oct. 17, 1864. Interred at Shrewsbury Cemetery, Shrewsbury, LA.

Thomas, John. Pvt. Co. E. Residence, Delaware. Died of dysentery at Donaldsonville, LA, Sept. 6, 1865. Interred at Donalsonville Post Burying Ground, Donaldsonville, LA.

Thomas, Judson. Mus. Co. K. Residence, Providence. Died of dysentery at Camp Parapet, LA, Oct. 6, 1864. Interred at Shrewsbury Cemetery, Shrewsbury, LA.

Thompson, Hiram J. Corp. Co. I. Residence, Providence. Struck by lightning and killed at Camp Parapet, LA, July 12, 1864. Interred at Shrewsbury Cemetery, Shrewsbury, LA.

Thorn, Floyd. Pvt. Co. D. Residence, New York, NY. Died of typhoid at Fort Jackson, LA, Aug. 5, 1864. Interred at Fort Jackson Post Cemetery, Plaquemines Parish, LA.

Tierce, Simeon A. Pvt. Co. E. Residence, Harrison, NY. Died of typhoid at Plaquemine, LA, July 8, 1864. Interred at Plaquemine Post Burying Ground, Plaquemine, LA.

Tossett, Charles. Mus. Co. D. Residence, Norwich, CT. Died of disease at Fort Jackson, LA, Sept. 20, 1864. Interred at Fort Jackson Post Cemetery, Plaquemines Parish, LA.

Townsend, Daniel. Pvt. Co. C. Residence, Providence. Died of a liver infection at Fort Jackson, LA, April 21, 1865. Interred at Fort Jackson Post Cemetery, Plaquemines Parish, LA.

Townsend, John. Pvt. Co. D. Residence, Washington, NY. Died of malaria at Fort Jackson, LA, Aug. 30, 1864. Interred at Fort Jackson Post Cemetery, Plaquemines Parish, LA.

Tuttle, Samuel. Pvt. Co. B. Residence, Orange, NY. Died of tuberculosis at Fort Jackson, LA, Nov. 21, 1864. Interred at Fort Jackson Post Cemetery, Plaquemines Parish, LA.

Valentine, John S. Pvt. Co. I. Residence, Providence. Died of typhoid at Camp Parapet, LA, Feb. 1, 1865. Interred at Shrewsbury Cemetery, Shrewsbury, LA.

Walker, James. Pvt. Co. I. Residence, Providence. Died of tuberculosis at Dutch Island, RI, Feb. 18, 1864. Interred at Long Island National Cemetery, East Farmingdale, NY.

Walker, Josiah. Sgt. Co. I. Residence, Providence. Died of a ruptured blood vessel at Dutch Island, RI, Mar. 12, 1864. Interred at Long Island National Cemetery, East Farmingdale, NY.

Wallace, George. Pvt. Co. A. Residence, New York, NY. Died of pneumonia at Fort Esperanza, TX, Jan. 14, 1864. Interred at Fort Esperanza Burying Ground, Matagorda Island, TX.

Wardlow, John E. 1st Lt. Co. E. Residence, Providence. Died of heart disease contracted in the service at New York, NY, Mar. 10, 1867. Interred at Oak Grove Cemetery, Pawtucket, RI.

Warmsley, Daniel. Pvt. Co. A. Residence, North Kingstown. Died of typhoid at Fort Esperanza, TX, April 4, 1864. Interred at Fort Esperanza Burying Ground, Matagorda Island, TX.

Warmsley, James. Pvt. Co. A. Residence, North Kingstown. Died of

Hard service with Battery B, First Rhode Island Light Artillery could not prepare Lieutenant John E. Wardlow for the rigors of campaigning in Louisiana with the Fourteenth Rhode Island Heavy Artillery. He died in 1867 of a disease he contracted in the South.

typhoid at Fort Jackson, LA, April 24, 1864. Interred at Fort Jackson Post Cemetery, Plaquemines Parish, LA.

Warren, John. Pvt. Co. I. Residence, Providence. Died of hydrothorax at Camp Parapet, LA, Sept. 9, 1864. Interred at Shrewsbury Cemetery, Shrewsbury, LA.

Washington, George. Pvt. Co. K. Residence, Providence. Died of tuberculosis at Dutch Island, RI, Feb. 19, 1864. Interred at Long Island National Cemetery, East Farmingdale, NY.

Washington, George. Pvt. Co. L. Residence, Providence. Died of typhoid at Camp Parapet, LA, Aug. 5, 1864. Interred at Shrewsbury Cemetery, Shrewsbury, LA.

Washington, William. Pvt. Co. L. Residence, Providence. Died of tuberculosis at Camp Parapet, LA, Sept. 12, 1865. Interred at Shrewsbury Cemetery, Shrewsbury, LA.

Watkins, Stephen L. Pvt. Co. M. Residence, New York, NY. Died of epilepsy "as sea" April 12, 1864.

Watts, George E. Pvt. Co. E. Residence, Buffalo, NY. Died of dysentery at Camp Parapet, LA, Sept. 17, 1865. Interred at Shrewsbury Cemetery, Shrewsbury, LA.

Weddinston, James H. Pvt. Co. D. Residence, New Haven, CT. Died of scrofula at Fort Jackson, LA, Oct. 7, 1864. Interred at Fort Jackson Post Cemetery, Plaquemines Parish, LA.

Weeden, Charles H.W. Pvt. Co. A. Residence, North Kingstown. Died of kidney disease at Dutch Island, RI, Oct. 15, 1863. Interred at Long Island National Cemetery, East Farmingdale, NY.

Welden, Stephen. Pvt. Co. D. Residence, Stanford, NY. Died of dysentery at Fort Jackson, LA, Aug. 6, 1864. Interred at Fort Jackson Post Cemetery, Plaquemines Parish, LA.

West, Job. Pvt. Co. G. Residence, Providence. Died of tuberculosis at Plaquemine, LA, April 28, 1864. Interred at Plaquemine Post Burying Ground, Plaquemine, LA.

West, William H. Pvt. Co. D. Residence, Salem, CT. Died of "fits" at Fort Jackson, LA, Sept. 22, 1864. Interred at Fort Jackson Post Cemetery, Plaquemines Parish, LA.

Westley, Andrew. Pvt. Co. K. Residence, Providence. Died of dysentery at Camp Parapet, LA, July 30, 1864. Interred at Shrewsbury Cemetery, Shrewsbury, LA.

Wheatley, Joshua. Pvt. Co. L. Residence, Providence. Died of tuberculosis at Camp Parapet, LA, June 2, 1864. Interred at Shrewsbury Cemetery, Shrewsbury, LA.

White, Anthony T. Pvt. Co. I. Residence, Providence. Died of disease at Camp Parapet, LA, Jan. 1, 1865. Interred at Shrewsbury Cemetery, Shrewsbury, LA.

White, Willis. Pvt. Co. I. Residence, Providence. Died of dysentery at Camp Parapet, LA, June 4, 1864. Interred at Shrewsbury Cemetery, Shrewsbury, LA.

Whitfield, Joseph H. Pvt. Co. M. Residence, Buffalo, NY. Died of "congestion of the brain" at Dutch Island, RI, Feb. 29, 1864. Interred at Long Island National Cemetery, East Farmingdale, NY.

Williams, Abraham. Pvt. Co. C. Residence, Bay Bridge, NY. Died of smallpox at New Orleans, LA, Aug. 3, 1864. Interred at Shrewsbury Cemetery, Shrewsbury, LA.

Williams, Edward. Pvt. Co. A. Residence, Providence. Died of typhoid at Fort Jackson, LA, Aug. 26, 1864. Interred at Fort Jackson Post Cemetery, Plaquemines Parish, LA.

Williams, Edward. Pvt. Co. L. Residence, Providence. Died of smallpox at Dutch Island, RI, Mar. 8, 1864. Interred at Long Island National Cemetery, East Farmingdale, NY.

Williams, Richard. Pvt. Co. B. Residence, New York, NY. Died of dysentery at New Orleans, LA, Sept. 17, 1864. Interred at Chalmette National Cemetery, New Orleans, LA. Grave 9642.

Williamson, Thomas. Pvt. Co. F. Residence, Providence. Died of phthisis at New Orleans, LA, April 2, 1864. Interred at Shrewsbury Cemetery, Shrewsbury, LA.

Wilson, Samuel H. Pvt. Co. B. Residence, New Haven, CT. Died of typhoid at Fort Jackson, LA, Aug. 8, 1864. Interred at Fort Jackson Post Cemetery, Plaquemines Parish, LA.

Winn, Abraham. Pvt. Co. L. Residence, Providence. Died of typhoid at Camp Parapet, LA, May 1, 1865. Interred at Shrewsbury Cemetery, Shrewsbury, LA.

Woods, Samuel. Pvt. Co. C. Residence, Baltimore, MD. Died of dysentery at Fort Jackson, LA, Aug. 18, 1864. Interred at Fort Jackson Post Cemetery, Plaquemines Parish, LA.

Woolsey, Austin. Pvt. Co. D. Residence, New Brunswick, NJ. Died of tuberculosis at Fort Jackson, LA, Sept. 5, 1864. Interred at Fort Jackson Post Cemetery, Plaquemines Parish, LA.

Wycoff, Thomas. Pvt. Co. H. Residence, Providence. Died of tuberculosis at Plaquemine, LA, Nov. 12, 1864. Interred at Plaquemine Post Burying Ground, Plaquemine, LA.

Young, Samuel. Pvt. Co. C. Residence, Flatbush, NY. Died of tuberculosis at Fort Jackson, LA, Sept. 7, 1864. Interred at Fort Jackson Post Cemetery, Plaquemines Parish, LA.

Youter, James R. Pvt. Co. M. Residence, Frankfort, KY. Died of dysentery at Camp Parapet, LA, Jan. 25, 1864. Interred at Shrewsbury Cemetery, Shrewsbury, LA.

15

Hospital Guards

Carr, Stephen A. Pvt. Residence, Providence. Drowned in Narragansett Bay, October 24, 1863. Interred at Swan Point Cemetery, Providence, RI.

Higgins, John. Pvt. Residence, Smithfield. Died of disease at Portsmouth Grove Hospital, Portsmouth, RI, Mar. 2, 1863.

Luther, Stephen Gano. Sgt. Residence, Providence. Died of disease contracted in the service at Providence, RI, Jan. 23, 1866. Interred at North Burial Ground, Providence, RI.

Tanner, Charles H. Pvt. Residence, Providence. Died of disease at Portsmouth Grove Hospital, Portsmouth, RI, Jan. 9, 1865.

Taylor, John. Pvt. Residence, Smithfield. Drowned in Narragansett Bay, Dec. 6, 1862. Interred at Slatersville Cemetery, North Smithfield, RI.

Before joining the Hospital Guards, Sergeant Stephen Gano Luther had served in Battery F, First Rhode Island Light Artillery and the Tenth Rhode Island Battery. Like so many Rhode Islanders, he died of the disease he contracted in the army immediately after the war.

16

First Rhode Island Cavalry

Ainsworth, William P. Capt. Co. M. Residence, Nashua, NH. Killed in action at Front Royal, VA, May 30, 1862. Interred at Old Burying Ground, Jaffrey, NH.

Allen, Charles N. Pvt. Co. D. Residence, Providence. Died of disease at Andersonville Prison, Aug. 21, 1864. Interred at Andersonville National Cemetery. Grave 6331.

Allen, Edwin B. Pvt. Co. I. Residence, Lyme, NH. Killed in action at Front Royal, VA, May 30, 1862. Interred at Old Lyme Cemetery, Lyme, NH.

Allen, Henry A. Pvt. Co. A. Residence, Providence. Died of dysentery contracted in the service at Providence, RI, Aug. 11, 1865. Interred at North Burial Ground, Providence, RI.

Angell, Jesse W. Pvt. Co. B. Residence, Smithfield. Killed in action at Berryville, VA, Aug. 13, 1864. Interred at Winchester National Cemetery, Winchester, VA. Grave 3610. Cenotaph at Col. John Angell Lot, Smithfield Cemetery 28, Smithfield, RI.

Austin, John H. Sgt. Co. H. Residence, Providence. Died of disease at Andersonville Prison, GA, July 13, 1864. Interred at Mineral Spring Cemetery, Pawtucket, RI.

Avery, James. Pvt. Co. M. Residence, Cranston. Died of disease at Philadelphia, PA, Nov. 26, 1863.

Babcock, John C. Pvt. Co. K. Residence, Dover, NH. Killed in action at Front Royal, VA, May 30, 1862. Interred at Winchester National Cemetery, Winchester, VA. Grave 3070.

Barnard, Edwin K. Pvt. Co. K. Residence, Manchester, NH. Killed in action at Front Royal, VA, May 30, 1862. Interred at Chestnut Hill Cemetery, Amherst, NH.

Barnard, George G. Pvt. Co. I. Residence, Sutton, NH. Killed in action at Front Royal, VA, May 30, 1862.

Barrows, Rolindo V. Sgt. Co. E. Residence, Johnston. Died of disease while a prisoner of war at Richmond, VA, Feb. 8, 1864. Interred at Richmond National Cemetery, Richmond, VA. Cenotaph at Swan Point Cemetery, Providence, RI.

Bates, Elijah. Pvt. Co. B. Residence, Worcester, MA. Died of disease at Warrenton, VA, April 17, 1862.

Bidmead, John W. Pvt. Co. G. Residence, Providence. Died of disease at Andersonville Prison, GA, June 1, 1864. Interred at Andersonville National Cemetery. Grave 1958. Cenotaph at North Burial Ground, Providence, RI.

Blake, James F. Pvt. Co. M. Residence, Hampstead, NH. Died of disease at Andersonville Prison, GA, June 26, 1864. Interred at Andersonville National Cemetery. Grave 2521.

Bowditch, Isaac. Pvt. Co. F. Residence, Newport. Died of disease as a prisoner of war at Richmond, VA, Jan. 7, 1864. Interred at Richmond National Cemetery, Richmond, VA.

Bowen, Charles L. Pvt. Co. M. Residence, New Hampton, NH. Died of disease at Annapolis, MD, Nov. 22, 1863. Interred at New Hampton Village Cemetery, New Hampton, NH.

Bowley, William J. Pvt. Co. M. Residence, Stratham, NH. Died of disease at Andersonville Prison, GA, June 8, 1864. Interred at Andersonville National Cemetery. Grave 1744.

Brackett, Cyrus A. Pvt. Co. K. Residence, Dover, NH. Killed in action at Front Royal, VA, May 30, 1862.

Brown, James S. Pvt. Co. A. Residence, Providence. Died of disease at New Haven, CT, May 2, 1865.

Brown, John. Corp. Co. A. Residence, Coventry. Died of tuberculosis contracted in the service at Coventry, RI, Dec. 11, 1865. Interred at St. Mary's Cemetery, West Warwick, RI.

Brown, John S. Sgt. Co. B. Residence, Attleboro, MA. Killed in action at Auburn, VA, Oct. 14, 1863.

Brown, William. Pvt. Co. G. Residence, Coventry. Died of typhoid at

Private Cyrus A. Brackett of Company K served in the New Hampshire Battalion of the First Rhode Island Cavalry. A resident of Dover, New Hampshire, he was killed in action at Front Royal, Virginia, on May 30, 1862. Varnum Continentals.

Washington, D.C., Mar. 26, 1862. Interred at Soldier's Home National Cemetery, Washington, D.C.

Buckley, Francis. Pvt. Co. H. Residence, Little Compton. Accidentally shot and killed at Annapolis, MD, Aug. 29, 1863.

Burke, James. Pvt. Co. C. Residence, Smithfield. Died of disease at Andersonville Prison, July 1, 1864. Interred at Andersonville National Cemetery.

Burke, James A. Pvt. Co. B. Residence, New York, NY. Killed in action near Dumfries, VA, Oct. 10, 1863.

Burton, Thomas. Corp. Co. F. Residence, Coventry. Killed in action at Middleburg, VA, June 18, 1863. Interred at Knotty Oak Cemetery, Coventry, RI.

Capwell, Willard T. Pvt. Co. D. Residence, East Greenwich. Died of disease contracted in the service at East Greenwich, RI, Dec. 11, 1867. Interred at Centerville Methodist Cemetery, West Warwick, RI.

Carpenter, Patrick. Co. E. Residence, Boston, MA. Died of disease at Andersonville Prison, GA, May 24, 1864. Interred at Andersonville National Cemetery. Grave 1339.

Caswell, William H. Corp. Co. L. Residence, Hanover, NH. Mortally wounded in action at Cedar Mountain, VA, Aug. 9, 1862. Died of wounds at Piedmont, VA, Aug. 27, 1862. Interred at Culpeper National Cemetery, Culpeper, VA. Grave 147.

Chedell, Joseph A. 2nd Lt. Co. C. Residence, Barrington. Killed in action at Middleburg, VA, June 18, 1863. Interred at North Burial Ground, Providence, RI.

Clarke, George L. Pvt. Co. G. Residence, Warwick. Died of disease at Andersonville Prison, GA, Sept. 27, 1864. Interred at Andersonville National Cemetery. Grave 10847.

Clement, Charles H. Pvt. Co. L. Residence, Alton, NH. Detached to Third Corps Staff. Killed in action July 2, 1863, at Gettysburg, PA.

Collins, James H. Pvt. Co. D. Residence, Boston. Died of disease at Andersonville Prison, GA, April 16, 1865. Interred at Andersonville National Cemetery. Grave 12832.

Colomy, James. Pvt. Co. K. Residence, New Durham, NH. Died of "lung fever" at Concord, NH, Jan. 15, 1862.

Conlin, John. Pvt. Co. G. Residence, Providence. Died of disease at Annapolis, MD Sept. 7, 1863. Interred at Annapolis National Cemetery, Annapolis, MD. Section F, Grave 2283.

Cordon, Benjamin S. Pvt. Co. K. Residence, Dover, NH. Died if disease June 13, 1864 at Andersonville, GA. Interred at Andersonville National Cemetery. Grave 1413.

Corson, Eli. Pvt. Co. K. Residence, Dover, NH. Died of disease at Concord, NH, Dec. 31, 1861.

Cushman, Hartley. Pvt. Co. K. Residence, Portsmouth, NH. Killed in action at Front Royal, VA, May 30, 1862. Interred at Winchester National Cemetery, Winchester, VA. Grave 124.

Dearborn, George. Pvt. Co. M. Residence, Hampton, NH. Died of disease at Andersonville Prison, July 8, 1864. Interred at Andersonville National Cemetery. Grave 3036.

Delanah, Charles B. Sgt. Co. G. Residence, Utica, NY. Died of disease at Andersonville Prison, GA, Oct. 12, 1863. Interred at Andersonville National Cemetery. Grave 651. Cenotaph at Grace Church Cemetery, Providence, RI.

Dix, George H. Pvt. Co. M. Residence, Manchester, NH. Died of disease at Andersonville Prison, GA, May 19, 1864. Interred at Andersonville National Cemetery. Grave 1217.

Durden, Robert. Pvt. Co. F. Residence, Warwick. Died of disease at Andersonville Prison, GA, June 1, 1864. Interred at Andersonville National Cemetery. Grave 4742

Durfee, Andrew. Pvt. Co. D. Residence, Cranston. Died of disease at Salisbury Prison, NC, Mar. 15, 1865. Interred in mass grave at Salisbury National Cemetery, Salisbury, NC.

Elkins, John H. Pvt. Co. M. Residence, Concord, NH. Killed in action at Middleburg, VA, June 18, 1863.

Eustis, George C. Pvt. Co. M. Residence, Nashua, NH. Died of disease at Andersonville Prison, GA, May 1, 1864. Interred at Andersonville National Cemetery.

Fairbanks, Charles. Pvt. Co. M. Residence, Nashua, NH. Killed in action June 18, 1863, at Middleburg, VA.

Fitzgerald, Jeremiah. Sgt. Co. B. Residence, Providence. Killed in action at Kelly's Ford, VA, Mar. 17, 1863.

Flanders, Edward C. Pvt. Co. K. Residence, New Hampton, NH. Died of disease at Washington, D.C., May 10, 1862. Interred at Soldier's Home National Cemetery, Washington, D.C. Grave 1204.

Foster, Horatio. Pvt. Co. E. Residence, Pawtucket. Died of disease at Warrenton, VA, May 23, 1862.

Foster, Jacob B. Pvt. Co. H. Residence, Providence. Died of disease as a prisoner of war at Richmond, VA, Mar. 21, 1864. Interred at Richmond National Cemetery, Richmond, VA.

Freelove, Henry B. Pvt. Co. H. Residence, Cranston. Died of disease at Andersonville Prison, GA, May 7, 1864. Interred at Andersonville National Cemetery. Grave 939.

Gage, George H. Pvt. Co. L. Residence, Dracut, MA. Died of disease at Washington, D.C., May 10, 1864. Interred at Pelham Center Cemetery, Pelham, MA.

Gardiner, Pendleton E. Corp. Co. B. Residence, Johnston. Died of dysentery at Annapolis, MD, May 17, 1865. Interred at Annapolis National Cemetery, Annapolis, MD. Section C, Grave 1117.

Gardner, Joseph W. Pvt. Co. E. Residence, Johnston. Killed in action at Kelly's Ford, VA, Mar. 17, 1863.

Gorton, George W. Corp. Co. D. Residence, West Greenwich. Killed in action at the Battle of Fort Stevens, Washington, D.C., July 11, 1864. Interred at Battle Ground National Cemetery, Washington, D.C.

Gould, Charles E. Pvt. Co. A. Residence, Douglas, MA. Died of disease as a prisoner of war at Richmond, VA, Feb. 25, 1864. Interred at Richmond National Cemetery, Richmond, VA.

Graves, Charles A. Pvt. Co. B. Residence, North Providence. Died of typhoid in camp at Pawtucket, RI, Dec. 26, 1861. Interred at Evergreen Cemetery, Killingly, CT.

Greene, Albert C. Pvt. Co. H. Residence, East Greenwich. Died of disease at Baltimore, MD, May 4, 1864. Interred at Loudoun Park National Cemetery, Baltimore, MD. Section A, Grave 325.

Greene, Henry W. Pvt. Co. E. Residence, Providence. Died of disease at Warrenton, VA, May 22, 1862.

Grove, Lorenzo D. Capt. Co. I. Residence, Hanover, NH. Killed in action at Mountville, VA, Nov. 1, 1862. Interred at Dartmouth College Cemetery, Hanover, NH.

Hall, Theodore A. G. Pvt. Co. C. Residence, Providence. Died of disease at Warrenton, VA, July 30, 1864. Interred at North Burial Ground, Providence, RI.

Hammell, John. Pvt. Co. G. Residence, Providence. Killed in action at Stevensburg, VA, June 7, 1863.

Harris, George W. Sgt. Co. A. Residence, Smithfield. Died of disease at Washington, D.C., May 20, 1864. Interred at Cook Cemetery, Woonsocket, RI.

Healy, Alonzo. Pvt. Co. D. Residence, Newport. Died of disease at Andersonville Prison, GA, June 29, 1864. Interred at Andersonville National Cemetery. Grave 2656.

Henry, Thomas. Pvt. Co. F. Residence, Johnston. Died of disease at Andersonville Prison, GA, June 1, 1864. Interred at Andersonville National Cemetery. Grave 1075.

Hill, Ambrose B. Pvt. Co. C. Residence, Putnam, CT. Died of disease at Washington, D.C., Feb. 2, 1864. Interred at Munyan Cemetery, Putnam, CT.

Hiscox, Benjamin. Pvt. Co. F. Residence, Warren. Died of disease as a prisoner of war at Danville, VA, Oct. 8, 1864. Interred at Danville National Cemetery, Danville, VA. Section B, Grave 498.

Hooker, Anson. Pvt. Co. G. Residence, Providence. Died of disease at Andersonville Prison, GA, Aug. 28, 1864. Interred at Andersonville National Cemetery. Grave 7032.

Hughes, Patrick. Pvt. Co. F. Residence, Pawtucket. Killed in action at Stevensburg, VA, June 7, 1863.

Hunt, Caleb W. Pvt. Co. A. Residence, Cumberland. Died of disease at Andersonville Prison, GA, July 1, 1864. Interred at Andersonville National Cemetery. Grave 2746. Cenotaph at North Burial Ground, Providence, RI.

Ide, Stephen R. Pvt. Co. H. Residence, Foster. Died of disease at Andersonville Prison, GA, May 14, 1864. Interred at Andersonville National Cemetery. Grave 1962. Cenotaph at Hopkins-Ide Lot, Foster Cemetery 26, Foster, RI.

Kane, Charles. Pvt. Co. L. Residence, Manchester, NH. Died of disease at Washington, D.C., Aug. 2, 1862. Interred at Alexandria National Cemetery, Alexandria, VA. Grave 132.

Kenyon, Charles S. Pvt. Co. E. Residence, Westerly. Died of disease at Alexandria, VA, April 21, 1862.

Kenyon, John S. Pvt. Co. A. Residence, Tiverton. Drowned at Washington, D.C., Aug. 28, 1863.

Kettle, James. Pvt. Co. B. Residence, Warwick. Died of disease at Andersonville Prison, GA, July 6, 1864. Interred at Andersonville National Cemetery.

Kiernan, John. Corp. Co. D. Residence, Providence. Mortally wounded in action at Kelly's Ford, VA, Mar. 17, 1863. Died of wounds at Washington, D.C., Mar. 27, 1863.

Kiernan, John. Pvt. Co. F. Residence, Providence. Killed in action at Cedar Mountain, VA, Aug. 9, 1862.

King, Richard E. Pvt. Co. H. Residence, Smithfield. Died of disease at Washington, D.C., Jan. 20, 1863. Interred at Soldier's Home National Cemetery, Washington, D.C.

Lasure, Benjamin C. Pvt. Co. I. Residence, Manchester, NH. Killed in action at Front Royal, VA, May 30, 1862. Interred at Evergreen Cemetery, Strafford, VT.

Lawrence, Benjamin G. Pvt. Co. M. Residence, Concord, NH. Killed in action June 18, 1863 at Middleburg, VA.

Leach, Lyman D. Pvt. Co. F. Residence, Coventry. Died of disease at Andersonville Prison, GA, Sept. 5, 1864. Interred at Andersonville National Cemetery. Grave 7849.

Leighton, Samuel W. Corp. Co. I. Residence, Sanbornton, NH. Died of disease at Annapolis, MD, Sept. 17, 1863.

Leveran, Peter. Pvt. Co. D. Residence, Charlestown. Died of typhoid at Falmouth, VA, Jan. 9, 1863. Interred at Union Cemetery, Laconia, NH.

Lillibridge, Willet R. Blacksmith. Co. H. Residence, Richmond. Died of disease at Washington, D.C., Nov. 1, 1863. Interred at Wood River Cemetery, Richmond, RI.

Lougee, Lorenzo R. Pvt. Co. L. Residence, Dover, NH. Died of typhoid at Winchester, VA, June 7, 1862.

Maine, Charles H. Pvt. Co. F. Residence, Pawtucket. Died of disease at Andersonville Prison, GA, June 27, 1864. Interred at South Cemetery, Brooklyn, CT.

Marden, William R. Pvt. Co. L. Residence, Manchester, NH. Died of disease at Annapolis MD, Sept. 12, 1863. Interred at Francestown Cemetery, Francestown, NH.

McGrath, Peter. Pvt. Co. E. Residence, Pawtucket. Died of disease contracted in the service at Pawtucket, RI, May 18, 1864. Interred at Mineral Spring Cemetery, Pawtucket, RI.

Millington, James W. Pvt. Co. A. Residence, Cumberland. Died of disease at Andersonville Prison, GA, Oct. 27, 1864. Interred at Andersonville National Cemetery. Grave 11564.

Private Willet R. Lillibridge served as a blacksmith in the First Rhode Island Cavalry. He served from Richmond and died of disease.

Minor, Stephen. Pvt. Co. D. Residence, Johnston. Died of disease at Andersonville Prison, GA, June 9, 1864. Interred at Andersonville National Cemetery. Grave 1750.

Moore, Edward F. Corp. Co. L. Residence, Andover, MA. Detached to Third Corps Staff. Killed in action at Gettysburg, PA, July 2, 1863. Interred at Pleasant Street Cemetery, Claremont, NH.

Mulvey, John. Pvt. Co. D. Residence, Cumberland. Killed in action at Cedar Mountain, VA, Aug. 9, 1862.

Nicolai, Henry L. 2nd Lt. Co. M. Residence, Newport. Killed in action at Kelly's Ford, VA, Mar. 17, 1863. Interred at Island Cemetery, Newport, RI.

Northrup, Edward. Pvt. Co. H. Residence, North Kingstown. Died of disease at Andersonville Prison, GA, July 12, 1864. Interred at Andersonville National Cemetery.

Ordway, Levi. Pvt. Co. L. Residence, Providence. Died of disease at Portsmouth Grove Hospital, Portsmouth, RI, Oct. 21, 1862. Interred at Francestown Cemetery, Francestown, NH.

Paine, Allen R. Corp. Co. D. Residence, Providence. Died of disease at Alexandria, VA, July 20, 1862.

Parmenter, Martin L. Sgt. Co. K. Residence, Antrim, NH. Died of disease contracted in the service at Antrim, NH, Jan. 11, 1863. Interred at East Washington Cemetery, Washington, NH.

Peck, Josephus F. Blacksmith. Co. G. Residence, Providence. Died of typhoid at Washington, D.C., July 17, 1862. Interred at Soldier's Home National Cemetery, Washington, D.C.

Perley, John L. 2nd Lt. Co. M. Residence, Laconia, NH. Died of disease at Alexandria, VA, June 9, 1862. Interred at Union Cemetery, Laconia, NH.

Peterson, John R. Sgt. Co. D. Residence, Cranston. Died of disease at Andersonville Prison, GA, April 18, 1864. Interred at Andersonville National Cemetery. Grave 607. Cenotaph at North Burial Ground, Providence, RI.

Petty, Daniel A. Pvt. Co. D. Residence, South Kingstown. Died of disease contracted in the service at Westport, MA, Dec. 24, 1863. Interred at Petty Burial Ground, Westport, MA.

Pierce, George S. Pvt. Co. C. Residence, Bristol. Died of "disease contracted in U.S. Service" at Bristol, RI, Nov. 12, 1869. Interred at North Burial Ground, Bristol, RI.

Potter, George D. Pvt. Co. F. Residence, Cranston. Died of disease at Andersonville Prison, GA, Sept. 16, 1864. Interred at Andersonville National Cemetery.

Pray, John. Pvt. Co. C. Residence, Woonsocket. Died of disease contracted in the service at Woonsocket, RI, Sept. 18, 1865. Interred at Old Aldrich Burial Ground, North Smithfield, RI.

Rathbun, Jeremiah. Pvt. Co. A. Residence, North Kingstown. Died of disease at Andersonville Prison, GA, Aug. 29, 1864. Interred at Andersonville National Cemetery. Grave 1219.

Rawcliffe, Joseph W. Pvt. Co. A. Residence, Wrentham, MA. Died of disease while a prisoner of war at Danville, VA, Dec. 20, 1864. Interred at Danville National Cemetery, Danville, VA. Section D, Grave 574.

Read, Asa K. Pvt. Co. B. Residence, Westport, MA. Died of disease at Baltimore, MD, April 18, 1865. Interred at Loudoun Park National Cemetery, Baltimore, MD. Grave 638.

Reynolds, George T. Pvt. Co. D. Residence, Providence. Died of disease at Richmond, VA, July 7, 1863. Interred at Richmond National Cemetery, Richmond, VA.

Reynolds, Owen. Pvt. Co. G. Residence, Providence. Killed in action at Front Royal, VA, May 25, 1862. Interred at St. Patrick's Cemetery, Providence, RI.

Rounds, Philip J. Pvt. Co. G. Residence, Swansea, MA. Died of disease at New York, NY, Aug. 12, 1864. Interred at North Burial Ground, Providence, RI.

Salisbury, Samuel, Jr. Pvt. Co. A. Residence, Burrillville. Died of typhoid at Falmouth, VA, Dec. 13, 1862. Interred at North Burial Ground, Providence, RI.

Sawyer, Charles A. 2nd Lt. Co. D. Residence, Nashua, NH. Died of disease at Alexandria, VA, Nov. 15, 1863.

Shapley, John H. Sgt. Co. M. Residence, Rye, NH. Died of disease at Waynesboro, VA, Sept. 28, 1864. Interred at Rye Central Cemetery, Rye, NH.

Sheridan, John. Pvt. Co. G. Residence, Providence. Mortally wounded in action at Deep Bottom, VA, July 28, 1864. Died of wounds at New York, NY, Aug. 1, 1864. Interred at St. Patrick's Cemetery, Providence, RI.

Shord, Joseph. Pvt. Co. D. Residence, Tiverton. Died of disease at Annapolis, MD, Oct. 9, 1862.

Slocum, George T. Corp. Co. A. Residence, Middletown. Died of disease at Andersonville Prison, GA, July 4, 1864. Interred at Andersonville National Cemetery. Grave 2859.

Smith, Cyrus. Pvt. Co. E. Residence, Johnston. Died of pneumonia in camp at Pawtucket, RI, Jan. 15, 1862. Interred at Mineral Spring Cemetery, Pawtucket, RI.

Smith, Olney P. Pvt. Co. M. Residence, Bristol, NH. Died of

An Irish immigrant, Pvt. John Sheridan of Providence was mortally wounded at Deep Bottom, Virginia, in July 1864. City of Providence, RI.

disease at Annapolis, MD, Oct. 11, 1862. Interred at Annapolis National Cemetery, Annapolis, MD. Section E, Grave 1779.

Smith, Philip B. Pvt. Co. A. Residence, Newport. Died of disease at Andersonville Prison, GA, July 28, 1864. Interred at Andersonville National Cemetery. Grave 4158.

Spink, Darius. Pvt. Co. H. Residence, East Greenwich. Died of disease at Andersonville Prison, GA, June 27, 1864. Interred at Andersonville National Cemetery. Grave 2562.

Stearns, George W. Pvt. Co. D. Residence, Woonsocket. Died of disease contracted in the service at Woonsocket, RI, Dec. 26, 1864. Interred at Old Town Burial Ground, North Smithfield, RI.

Streeter, George P. Sgt. Co. H. Residence, Providence. Died of disease at Falls Church, VA, June 16, 1862. Interred at Arlington National Cemetery, Arlington, VA. Section 13, Grave 11878.

Sutton, Edward B. Pvt. Co. F. Residence, East Providence. Died of disease contracted in the service at East Providence, RI, June 23, 1864. Interred at Newman Cemetery, East Providence, RI.

Sweet, Marcus W. Pvt. Co. D. Residence, Smithfield. Died of disease at Andersonville Prison, GA, June 23, 1864. Interred at Andersonville National Cemetery. Grave 2382.

Taylor, James P. 2nd Lt. Co. M. Residence, Providence. Died of sunstroke near Cedar Mountain, VA, Aug. 10, 1862. Interred at Culpeper National Cemetery, Culpeper, VA. Grave 448.

Thompson, Leander. Pvt. Co. G. Residence, Douglas, MA. Died of disease contracted in the service at Douglas, MA, Feb. 29, 1864. Interred at South Street Cemetery, Douglas, MA.

Travers, Frank. Pvt. Co. E. Residence, Wrentham, MA. Killed in action at Cedar Mountain, VA, Aug. 9, 1862.

Verguson, Charles H. Pvt. Co. B. Residence, Bristol. Died of disease at Bristol, RI, Aug. 25, 1865. Interred at North Burial Ground, Bristol, RI.

Vincent, Joseph W. Corp. Co. A. Residence, Westerly. Mortally wounded in action at Kelly's Ford, VA, Mar. 17, 1863. Died of wounds at Washington, D.C., Mar. 25, 1863. Interred at River Bend Cemetery, Westerly, RI.

West, George W. Pvt. Co. A. Residence, Warwick. Died of disease at Andersonville Prison, GA, July 31, 1864. Interred at Andersonville National Cemetery. Grave 6322.

West, Hiram. Pvt. Co. A. Residence, Warwick. Died of disease at Andersonville Prison, GA, June 10, 1864. Interred at Andersonville National Cemetery. Grave 1788.

Westcott, Isaac. Pvt. Co. F. Residence, Johnston. Killed in action near Berryville, VA, Aug. 17, 1864.

Wilcox, George S. Wag. Co. E. Residence, Providence. Died of disease at Washington, D.C., April 28, 1862.

Wilcox, Samuel. Pvt. Co. D. Residence, Bellingham, MA. Killed in action at Middleburg, VA, June 18, 1863. Interred at Wilcox Cemetery, Bellingham, MA.

Wilson, Alvin S. Pvt. Co. L. Residence, Gorham, NH. Died of dysentery at Falmouth, VA, Jan. 23, 1863. Interred at Bennett Cemetery, Wilson's Mills, ME.

Winsor, John. Pvt. Co. A. Residence, Smithfield. Died of disease at Manassas, VA July 22, 1862. Interred at Winsor Lot, Smithfield Cemetery 50, Smithfield, RI.

Woodward, Henry. Pvt. Co. L. Residence, Concord, NH. Killed in action at Cedar Mountain, VA, Aug. 9, 1862.

York, Isaac F. Pvt. Co. A. Residence, Westerly. Died of disease as a prisoner of war at Richmond, VA, Feb. 1, 1864. Interred at River Bend Cemetery, Westerly, RI.

17

Second Rhode Island Cavalry

Allen, Horace R. Pvt. Co. B. Residence, Smithfield. Died of disease at New Iberia, LA, Oct. 15, 1863.

Balle, August. Sgt. Co. H. Residence, New York, NY. Died of disease at Baton Rouge, LA, Sept. 7, 1863. Interred at Baton Rouge National Cemetery, Baton Rouge, LA. Section 10, Grave 576.

Besse, William M. Pvt. Co. A. Residence, Westerly. Died of dysentery at Baton Rouge, LA, May 11, 1863. Interred at Oak Grove Cemetery, New Bedford, MA.

Bicknell, George. Pvt. Co. A. Residence, Westerly. Died of disease at Baton Rouge, LA, Aug. 17, 1863.

Boldt, Henry. Pvt. Co. G. Residence New York, NY. Died of disease at St. Louis, MO, Sept. 20, 1863.

Brown, Albert E. Sgt. Co. A. Residence, Providence. Died of disease contracted in the service at Providence, RI, Nov. 7, 1863.

Brown, Charles. Pvt. Co. D. Residence, Coventry. Died of disease at New Orleans, LA, July 3, 1863.

Davis, William. Pvt. Co. H. Residence, Portsmouth. Executed for mutinous behavior at Baton Rouge, LA, Aug. 30, 1863.

Eaton, Charles. Pvt. Co. H. Residence, Johnston. Died of disease at Baton Rouge, LA, Aug. 15, 1863.

Ervin, Thomas. Pvt. Co. E. Residence, Augusta, ME. Killed in action at Donaldsonville, LA, July 1, 1863.

Ewins, Frank C. 1st Sgt. Co. E. Residence, Malden, MA. Died of disease at Brashear City, LA, June 6, 1863.

Garvin, Richard. Pvt. Co. C. Residence, New York, NY. Died of disease at New Orleans, LA, July 3, 1863.

Gibson, George F. Pvt. Co. A. Residence, Burlington, ME. Mortally wounded in action May 2, 1863, near Port Hudson, LA. Died of wounds at Baton Rouge, LA, June 11, 1863.

Greene, Henry. Pvt. Co. A. Residence, Charlestown, MA. Drowned at New Orleans, LA, Feb. 26, 1863.

Hand, Joseph. 1st Sgt. Co. E. Residence, Philadelphia, PA. Mortally wounded in action at Springfield, LA, July 2, 1863. Died of wounds at Baton Rouge, LA, July 6, 1863. Interred at Baton Rouge National Cemetery, Baton Rouge, LA. Grave 492.

Harriman, Joseph W. Pvt. Co. B. Residence, Belfast, ME. Died of disease at Baton Rouge, LA, May 16, 1863. Interred at Grove Cemetery, Belfast, ME.

Hillman, Daniel. Pvt. Co. B. Residence, Saco, ME. Died of disease at New York, NY, Dec. 29, 1862.

Kennon, Charles H. Q.M. Sgt. Residence, Providence. Died of disease at Baton Rouge, LA, May 23, 1863. Interred at North Burial Ground, Providence, RI.

Krause, Charles W. Pvt. Co. E. Residence, New York, NY. Died of disease at Brashear City, LA, July 18, 1863. Interred at Baton Rouge National Cemetery, Baton Rouge, LA. Section 36, Grave 2378.

Lennan, Rudolph. Pvt. Co. F. Residence, Baton Rouge, LA. Died of disease at Baton Rouge, LA, April 14, 1863.

Little, Samuel B. Pvt. Co. C. Residence, Canterbury, NH. Died of disease Memphis, TN, Sept. 16, 1863. Interred at Memphis National Cemetery, Memphis, TN. Section H, Grave 4193.

Lyons, John. Pvt. Co. A. Residence, Cranston. Died of disease at Indianapolis, IN, Sept. 19, 1863.

Mann, William. Pvt. Co. E. Residence, Pawtucket. Died of disease contracted in the service at Pawtucket, RI, July 6, 1863.

Meagan, Edward. Pvt. Co. A. Residence, Providence. Drowned at New Orleans, LA, Feb. 18, 1863.

Myers, John. Pvt. Co. F. Residence, Baton Rouge, LA. Died of disease at Baton Rouge, LA, July 22, 1863. Interred at Baton Rouge National Cemetery, Baton Rouge, LA. Grave 2357.

Moon, Carl. Pvt. Co. H. Residence, New York, NY. Died of disease at New Orleans, LA, Aug. 31, 1864.

Moore, William H. Wag. Co. D. Residence, Boston, MA. Died of disease at New Orleans, LA, June 17, 1863. Interred at Chalmette National Cemetery, New Orleans, LA. Grave 3715.

Neagal, James. Pvt. Co. B. Residence, New York, NY. Drowned at Baton Rouge, LA, Feb. 20, 1863.

Saltonstall, Roswell. Wag. Co. B. Residence, Smithfield. Died of disease at Baton Rouge, LA, June 22, 1863. Interred at Baton Rouge National Cemetery, Baton Rouge, LA. Grave 2494.

Sherman, Clarence. Pvt. Co. F. Residence, Boston. Killed in action at New Iberia, LA, Oct. 23, 1863.

Smith, Charles. Pvt. Co. E. Residence, Providence. Died of disease at New Orleans, LA, Feb. 5, 1864.

Smith, Richard F. Pvt. Co. F. Residence, Boston, MA. Executed for mutinous behavior at Baton Rouge, LA, Aug. 30, 1863.

Taylor, John. Pvt. Co. A. Residence, Providence. Killed in action at Port Hudson, LA, April 20, 1863.

Theune, Hugo. Pvt. Co. G. Residence, New York, NY. Died of disease at New Orleans, LA, July 8, 1863.

Waters, John F. Pvt. Co. C. Residence, Sutton, MA. Died as a prisoner of war at Alexandria, LA, July 20, 1864.

Weber, Otto. Pvt. Co. F. Residence, New York, NY. Died of disease at Baton Rouge, LA, Sept. 10, 1863.

Westley, John G. Pvt. Co. B. Residence, Boston, MA. Mortally wounded in action at Springfield, LA, July 2, 1863. Died of wounds at Baton Rouge, LA, Sept. 12, 1863.

Williams, John. Pvt. Co. C. Residence, Boston, MA. Killed in action at Crow Bayou, LA, Nov. 3, 1863. Interred at Baton Rouge National Cemetery, Baton Rouge, LA.

Wright, Maurice. Pvt. Co. A. Residence, New York, NY. Died of disease as a prisoner of war at Andersonville, GA, Mar. 6, 1864. Interred at Andersonville National Cemetery. Grave 19.

Zivanger, William. Pvt. Co. C. Residence New York, NY Killed in action at Port Hudson, LA, Mar. 25, 1863.

18

Third Rhode Island
Cavalry

Alexander, Smith A. Pvt. Co. G. Residence, Cumberland. Died of dysentery at New Orleans LA, Sept. 23, 1864. Interred at Chalmette National Cemetery, New Orleans, LA. Grave 5422.

Angell, Smith A. Pvt. Co. G. Residence, Coventry. Died of diphtheria at Jamestown, RI, Mar. 29, 1864. Interred at John Parker Lot, Scituate Cemetery 159, Scituate, RI.

Baggs, Nathan L. Pvt. Co. B. Residence, Smithfield. Drowned in the sinking of the *North America* off Florida, Dec. 22, 1864.

Barnes, Norman K. Pvt. Co. H. Residence, North Providence. Died of disease at Jamestown, RI, April 20, 1864. Interred at Wrentham Center Cemetery, Wrentham, MA.

Barton, Lewis. Mus. Co. A. Residence, Cumberland. Died of disease at Napoleonville, LA, Oct. 20, 1864.

Benedict, Joseph B. Pvt. Co. G. Residence, Pawtucket. Died of disease at Napoleonville, LA, Dec. 10, 1864. Interred at Mineral Spring Cemetery, Pawtucket, RI.

Benford, Augustus. Pvt. Co. F. Residence, Smithfield. Died of disease at New Orleans, LA, Sept. 23, 1864.

Bleavins, William A. Pvt. Co. E. Residence, Westerly. Died of disease at Vicksburg, MS, April 1, 1865. Interred at Vicksburg National Cemetery, Vicksburg, MS.

Bowen, Frank. Pvt. Co. C. Residence, Cumberland. Died of disease at Camp Parapet, LA, Sept. 7, 1864. Interred at Shrewsbury Cemetery, Shrewsbury, LA.

Brenno, Alexander. Pvt. Co. I. Residence, Smithfield. Drowned "at sea" Aug. 23, 1864.

Brown, Calvin M. Pvt. Co. H. Residence, Millbury, MA. Died of sunstroke at Greenville, LA, Sept. 21, 1865. Interred at Chalmette National Cemetery, New Orleans, LA. Grave 7456.

Brown, Henry. Pvt. Co. I. Residence, New Bedford, MA. Died of disease at New Orleans, LA, July 28, 1864. Interred at Chalmette National Cemetery, New Orleans, LA. Grave 4093.

Brown, Pardon B. Pvt. Co. B. Residence, Brooklyn, CT. Died of disease at New Orleans, LA, Oct. 29, 1864. Interred at Chalmette National Cemetery, New Orleans, LA. Grave 5499. Cenotaph at South Cemetery, Brooklyn, CT.

Brown, William A. Pvt. Co. A. Residence, Providence. Died of disease at Vicksburg, MS, April 1, 1865.

Burnett, William. Pvt. Co. E. Residence, South Hadley, MA. Died of disease at New York, NY, Oct. 14, 1864.

Burnham, Daniel W. Pvt. Co. A. Residence, Woonsocket. Died of disease contracted in the service at Woonsocket, RI, April 7, 1866. Interred at Oak Hill Cemetery, Woonsocket, RI.

Burrows, Simeon A. Pvt. Co. C. Residence, Cranston. Died as a prisoner of war at Camp Tyler, TX, July 15, 1864. Interred at Alexandria National Cemetery, Pineville, LA. Grave 1053.

Cain, Philip. Corp. Co. D. Residence, Providence. Died of disease at Napoleonville, LA, Nov. 26, 1864.

Campbell, Frederick. Pvt. Co. I. Residence, Smithfield. Died of disease at Napoleonville, LA, Aug. 14, 1865. Interred at Old Willimantic Cemetery, Windham, CT.

Carolin, Thomas. Blacksmith. Co. E. Residence, Pawtucket. Died of disease at Napoleonville, LA, Oct. 15, 1864. Interred at Chalmette National Cemetery, New Orleans, LA. Grave 5464.

Carr, Isaac. Pvt. Co. H. Residence, Providence. Died of disease at New Orleans LA, Nov. 8, 1864. Interred at Chalmette National Cemetery, New Orleans, LA. Grave 5501.

Chaffee, William H. Pvt. Co. G. Residence, Providence. Drowned in the sinking of the *North America* off Florida, Dec. 22, 1864.

Clapp, Albert. 1st Lt. Co. I. Residence, New Haven, CT. Accidentally shot and killed on picket duty at Napoleonville, LA, Jan. 19, 1865. Interred at Westfield Cemetery, Killingly, CT.

Clarke, John H. Pvt. Co. F. Residence, Wrentham, MA. Died of disease at New Orleans, LA, June 13, 1864. Interred at Chalmette National Cemetery, New Orleans, LA. Grave 4054.

Cleveland, Israel A. Pvt. Co. M. Residence, West Greenwich. Died of disease at Napoleonville, LA, Nov. 12, 1864.

Cleverly, Ebenezer. Pvt. Co. F. Residence, Quincy, MA. Died of disease at Camp Parapet, LA, July 22, 1864. Interred at Mt. Wollaston Cemetery, Quincy, MA.

Cleverly, John M., Jr. Pvt. Co. F. Residence, Hull, MA. Died of disease at Camp Parapet, LA, May 29, 1864. Interred at Chalmette National Cemetery, New Orleans, LA. Grave 4562.

Collins, Moses W. 2nd Lt. Co. A. Residence, Coventry. Died of disease contracted in the service at Coventry, RI, Dec. 17, 1865. Interred at Greenwood Cemetery, Coventry, RI.

Commerford, Peter. Pvt. Co. E. Residence, Providence. Died of disease at Napoleonville, LA, May 4, 1865.

Connelly, John. Pvt. Co. D. Residence, Burrillville. Killed in action at Grand Levee, LA, May 24, 1864.

Cooke, Joseph. Pvt. Co. G. Residence, Casco, ME. Died of disease at New Orleans, LA, Sept. 11, 1864. Interred at Chalmette National Cemetery, New Orleans, LA. Grave 1927.

Coyne, Patrick. Pvt. Co. I. Residence, Pawtucket. Drowned in the sinking of the *North America* off Florida, Dec. 22, 1864.

Demers, Richard. Pvt. Co. M. Residence, Cumberland. Died of disease at Napoleonville, LA, Jan. 20, 1865.

Devine, Bartholomew. Pvt. Co. H. Residence, Providence. Died of disease at New Orleans, LA, Oct. 18, 1864. Interred at Chalmette National Cemetery, New Orleans, LA. Grave 5931.

Devlin, John. Pvt. Co. D. Residence, Cumberland. Died of disease at Donaldsonville, LA, Nov. 30, 1864.

Dinsmore, Trescott. Pvt. Co. I. Residence, Cranston. Died of disease at Napoleonville, LA, Nov. 28, 1864.

Dodge, John T. Pvt. Co. G. Residence, New Shoreham. Died of disease at Napoleonville, LA, June 22, 1865.

Dolan, Patrick. Pvt. Co. G. Residence, Providence. Drowned in the sinking of the *North America* off Florida, Dec. 22, 1864.

Douglas, James L. Corp. Co. F. Residence, North Kingstown. Died of dysentery at New Orleans, LA, Sept. 15, 1864. Interred at Chalmette National Cemetery, New Orleans, LA.

Drown, William A. Pvt. Co. H. Residence, Barrington. Died of disease at Donaldsonville, LA, Dec. 3, 1864. Interred at Prince's Hill Burial Ground, Barrington, RI.

Dunply, Lawrence. Pvt. Co. H. Residence, Springfield, MA. Died of disease at Donaldsonville, LA, Oct. 15, 1864.

Early, Michael. Pvt. Co. I. Residence, North Bridgewater, MA. Died of disease at Camp Parapet, LA, Sept. 29, 1864.

Ellis, Stillman W. Corp. Co. L. Residence, Providence. Died of disease at Napoleonville, LA, July 19, 1865. Cenotaph at North Burial Ground, Providence, RI.

Felix, George. Pvt. Co. B. Residence, Danielson, CT. Died of disease at New Orleans LA, Mar. 22, 1864. Interred at Chalmette National Cemetery, New Orleans, LA.

Fisher, Augustus. Pvt. Co. I. Residence, Providence. Died of disease at New Orleans, LA, Sept. 10, 1864. Interred at Chalmette National Cemetery, New Orleans, LA. Grave 3843.

Fiske, William A. Sgt. Co. G. Residence, Providence. Drowned in the sinking of the *North America* off Florida, Dec. 22, 1864.

Fitts, Henry C. Capt. Co. H. Residence, East Douglas, MA. Died of disease at Donaldsonville LA, Dec. 19, 1864. Interred at South Sutton Cemetery, Sutton, MA.

Fly, Peter. Pvt. Co. F. Residence, Cumberland. Died of disease at Napoleonville, LA, Oct. 13, 1864.

Forrester, Thomas. Pvt. Co. E. Residence, Cumberland. Died of disease at New Orleans, LA, Oct. 25, 1864. Interred at Chalmette National Cemetery, New Orleans, LA. Grave 5252.

Fox, William. Pvt. Co. G. Residence, Pawtucket. Died of disease at New Orleans, LA, Sept. 19, 1864. Interred at Chalmette National Cemetery, New Orleans, LA. Grave 5230.

Galligan, Bernard. Pvt. Co. C. Residence, Providence. Killed in action at Terrebonne Station, LA, May 17, 1865.

Gannon, Mattias. Sgt. Co. D. Residence, Boston, MA. Died of disease at Napoleonville, LA, Aug. 14, 1865.

Gilroy, Peter. Corp. Co. D. Residence, Smithfield. Died of disease at Greenville, LA, July 19, 1864. Interred at Shrewsbury Cemetery, Shrewsbury, LA.

Goodnough, Wallis E. Sgt. Co. I. Residence, Brandon, VT. Drowned "at sea" Oct. 25, 1865.

Gould, Daniel E. Pvt. Co. H. Residence, East Douglas, MA. Died of disease at St. Louis, MO, May 25, 1865. Interred at Jefferson Barracks National Cemetery, St. Louis, MO. Grave 1383.

Greene, William B. Pvt. Co. L. Residence, Providence. Drowned in the sinking of the *North America* off Florida, Dec. 22, 1864. Cenotaph at Capt. Randall Holden Lot, Warwick Cemetery 68, Warwick, RI.

Greenman, Walter P. Corp. Co. F. Residence, Providence. Died of disease Baton Rouge, LA, Sept. 17, 1864. Interred at Baton Rouge National Cemetery, Baton Rouge, LA. Grave 2249.

Grey, Thomas. Pvt. Co. A. Residence, New York, NY. Died of disease at Napoleonville, LA, Mar. 22, 1865.

Hall, Dudley D. Pvt. Co. M. Residence, West Greenwich. Drowned in the sinking of the *North America* off Florida, Dec. 22, 1864.

Hammett, Charles D. 2nd Lt. Co. E. Residence, Jamestown. Died of disease at New Orleans, LA, Sept. 13, 1864. Interred at Island Cemetery, Newport, RI.

Hansen, Hans. Pvt. Co. K. Residence, New York, NY. Died of disease at New Orleans, LA, Sept. 6, 1864.

Harris, William. Pvt. Co. M. Residence, Tiverton. Died of typhoid contracted in the service at Providence, RI, Nov. 15, 1865.

Hart, Patrick. Pvt. Co. G. Residence, Providence. Died of disease at Napoleonville, LA, Aug. 12, 1865.

Harvey, Edward. Pvt. Co. I. Residence, Warwick. Drowned in the sinking of the *North America* off Florida, Dec. 22, 1864.

Hawkins, John H. Corp. Co. I. Residence, Pawtucket. Mortally wounded in action at Simmesport, LA, May 17, 1864. Died of wounds at New Orleans, LA, July 31, 1864. Cenotaph at Pocasset Cemetery, Cranston, RI.

Hewitt, George. Pvt. Co. G. Residence, Providence. Died of disease at New Orleans, LA, Sept. 5, 1864. Interred at Chalmette National Cemetery, New Orleans, LA. Grave 5959.

Higgins, Maurice. Pvt. Co. H. Residence, Worcester, MA. Drowned in the sinking of the *North America* off Florida, Dec. 22, 1864.

Hill, Edward. Pvt. Co. L. Residence, Tiverton. Drowned in the sinking of the *North America* off Florida, Dec. 22, 1864.

Hoar, Isaac. Pvt. Co. D. Residence, Bristol. Killed in action on picket duty at Napoleonville, LA April 21, 1864. Cenotaph at North Burial Ground, Bristol, RI.

Holmes, Thomas H. Pvt. Co. D. Residence, Cumberland. Drowned in the Mississippi River, Nov. 13, 1865.

Horan, John. Pvt. Co. B. Residence, Uxbridge, MA. Died of disease at New Orleans, LA, Oct. 14, 1864. Interred at Chalmette National Cemetery, New Orleans, LA. Grave 5461.

Horton, Benjamin S. Pvt. Co. M. Residence, Burrillville. Died of disease at New Orleans, LA, Sept. 8, 1865. Interred at Chalmette National Cemetery, New Orleans, LA. Grave 10934. Cenotaph at Acotes Hill Cemetery, Glocester, RI.

Ingraham, David. Pvt. Co. H. Residence, Cumberland. Killed in action at Bayou Goula, LA, Jan. 26, 1865. Interred at Lambremont Plantation, Iberville, LA. Cenotaph at Rockland Cemetery, Scituate, RI.

Johnson, James H. Pvt. Co. D. Residence, Mansfield, CT. Died of disease at New Orleans, LA, May 15, 1864. Interred at Chalmette National Cemetery, New Orleans, LA.

Johnson, Walter H. Veterinary Surgeon. Residence, Jamestown, NY. Died of disease at New Orleans, LA, Oct. 19, 1864. Interred at Chalmette National Cemetery, New Orleans, LA. Grave 7040.

Keith, Henry S. Sgt. Co. E. Residence, Springfield, MA. Mortally wounded in action at the Red River, near Alexandria, LA, April 30, 1864. Died of wounds May 1, 1864.

Kenney, Thomas. Pvt. Co. B. Residence, Providence. Died of disease at Philadelphia, PA, June 18, 1865. Interred at Mt. Moriah Cemetery, Philadelphia, PA.

Kittridge, Martin. Pvt. Co. E. Residence, Providence. Died of tuberculosis at Napoleonville, LA, Nov. 1, 1864.

Lamb, George R. Pvt. Co. L. Residence, Providence. Died of disease at New Orleans, LA, Sept. 14, 1864. Interred at Chalmette National Cemetery, New Orleans, LA. Grave 5197.

Larkin, James. Pvt. Co. F. Residence, Westerly. Died of disease at Napoleonville, LA, Dec. 9, 1864.

Leavitt, Charles F. Pvt. Co. F. Residence, Quincy, MA. Drowned in the sinking of the *North America* off Florida, Dec. 22, 1864.

Letheran, Antoine. Pvt. Co. M. Residence, New York, NY. Died of disease at New Orleans, LA, Sept. 10, 1864. Interred at Chalmette National Cemetery, New Orleans, LA.

Llufrio, Washington B. Pvt. Co. D. Residence, North Kingstown. Died of disease at New York, NY, Sept. 17, 1864. Interred at Elm Grove Cemetery, North Kingstown, RI.

Loeffel, Augustus. Pvt. Co. K. Residence, New York, NY. Killed in action near Napoleonville, LA, Mar. 24, 1865.

Loeffler, Severin. Corp. Co. K. Residence, New York, NY. Died of disease at New Orleans, LA, Nov. 18, 1865. Interred at Chalmette National Cemetery, New Orleans, LA. Grave 6786.

Logue, Edward. Corp. Co. F. Residence, Providence. Killed in action at Donaldsonville, LA, May 26, 1864.

Lund, Merrill. Pvt. Co. I. Residence, Providence. Died of disease at Grand Ecore, LA, April 17, 1864.

Magee, Thomas M. Corp. Co. H. Residence, Douglas, MA. Drowned in the sinking of the *North America* off Florida, Dec. 22, 1864.

Mallon, Barney. Pvt. Co. E. Residence, North Providence. Died of disease at New Orleans, LA, Dec. 24, 1864.

Masterson, Patrick. Saddler. Co. E. Residence, Providence. Drowned in the sinking of the *North America* off Florida, Dec. 22, 1864. Cenotaph at St. Patrick's, East Greenwich, RI.

Matteson, Calvin Rhodes. Pvt. Co. A. Residence, Coventry. Drowned in the sinking of the *North America* off Florida, Dec. 22, 1864. Cenotaph at Large Maple Root Cemetery, Coventry, RI.

Matteson, Daniel E. Pvt. Co. D. Residence, Putnam, CT. Died of disease at New Orleans, LA, Oct. 30, 1864.

Matteson, George H. Pvt. Co. A. Residence, Coventry. Drowned in the sinking of the *North America* off Florida, Dec. 22, 1864.

McCarthy, John. Corp. Co. I. Residence, Cranston. Drowned in the sinking of the *North America* off Florida, Dec. 22, 1864.

McCormack, James. QM. Sgt. Co. B. Residence, Providence. Died of disease at Napoleonville, LA, July 1, 1865.

McCoullers, Charles. Pvt. Co. B. Residence, Portsmouth. Killed in action at Alexandria, LA, May 1, 1864.

McElroy, John. Pvt. Co. A. Residence, Providence. Died of disease at Memphis, TN, Aug. 19, 1864. Interred at Memphis National Cemetery, Memphis, TN. Grave 4194.

McGovern, John. Pvt. Co. H. Residence, Cumberland. Died of disease at New Orleans, LA, Oct. 26, 1864. Interred at Chalmette National Cemetery, New Orleans, LA. Grave 5256.

McKenna, Charles. Pvt. Co. I. Residence, Cumberland. Died of disease at New Orleans, LA, Feb. 8, 1864. Interred at Chalmette National Cemetery, New Orleans, LA. Grave 6193.

McLaughlin, Thomas. Pvt. Co. B. Residence, Providence. Died of disease at New Orleans, LA, Sept. 10, 1864. Interred at Chalmette National Cemetery, New Orleans, LA. Grave 1026.

McManus, James. Pvt. Co. E. Residence, Providence. Died of disease at Napoleonville, LA, Oct. 1, 1864.

McMinnemee, Michael. Pvt. Co. E. Residence, North Providence. Killed in action at the Red River, LA, April 22, 1864.

Millard, Benjamin F. Pvt. Co. H. Residence, New Shoreham. Died of disease at Jamestown, RI, April 20, 1864. Interred at Island Cemetery, Jamestown, RI.

Moffitt, Leonard T. Corp. Co. E. Residence, East Providence. Drowned at Napoleonville, LA, May 23, 1864.

Mooney, Thomas. Pvt. Co. M. Residence, Providence. Died of disease at New Orleans, LA, Aug. 31, 1864.

Mowry, Augustus. Sgt. Co. C. Residence, Pawtucket. Died of disease at Alexandria, LA, April 8, 1864.

Murray, Charles. Corp. Co. G. Residence, Providence. Drowned in the sinking of the *North America* off Florida, Dec. 22, 1864.

O'Brien, John. Pvt. Co. M. Residence, Scituate. Drowned in the sinking of the *North America* off Florida, Dec. 22, 1864.

Olds, William H. Pvt. Co. L. Residence, Providence. Drowned in the sinking of the *North America* off Florida, Dec. 22, 1864. Cenotaph at Common Burying Ground, Newport, RI.

O'Sullivan, Patrick. Pvt. Co. G. Residence, Blackstone, MA. Died of disease at Greenville, LA, June 30, 1864. Interred at Chalmette National Cemetery, New Orleans, LA. Grave 7122.

Parker, John M. Sgt. Co. D. Residence, Smithfield. Died of illness contracted in the service April 15, 1865, at Smithfield, RI. Interred at Slatersville Cemetery, North Smithfield, RI.

Parkes, William. Pvt. Co. M. Residence, Stonington, CT. Died of disease at New Orleans, LA, Aug. 24, 1864. Interred at Chalmette National Cemetery, New Orleans, LA. Grave 4515.

Pearson, David B. Pvt. Co. F. Residence, Providence. Drowned in the sinking of the *North America* off Florida, Dec. 22, 1864.

Peck, George W. Pvt. Co. C. Residence, Providence. Drowned in the sinking of the *North America* off Florida, Dec. 22, 1864. Cenotaph at Pawtuxet Cemetery, Warwick, RI.

Peck, William E. 1st Lt. Co. F. Residence, East Greenwich. Died of disease at Napoleonville, LA, Aug. 13, 1865. Interred at First Cemetery, East Greenwich, RI.

Perry, Amos. Corp. Co. G. Residence, Pawtucket. Killed by "a band of guerrillas" at Bayou Goula, LA, Jan. 14, 1865. Interred at Chalmette National Cemetery, New Orleans, LA. Grave 2208. Cenotaph at North Burial Ground, Providence, RI.

Pettis, George A. Pvt. Co. G. Residence, Providence. Died of

A prominent lawyer from East Greenwich, First Lieutenant William E. Peck died of malaria four months after Appomattox, while engaged in early Reconstruction duties in Louisiana.

disease at New Orleans, LA, Oct. 19, 1864. Interred at Swan Point Cemetery, Providence, RI.

Pike, Henry. Pvt. Co. D. Residence, Philadelphia, PA. Died of disease at Napoleonville, LA, Jan. 12, 1865.

Pollard, John. Pvt. Co. C. Residence, Providence. Died of disease at New Orleans, LA, Dec. 14, 1864.

Powers, George A. Pvt. Co. G. Residence, Stonington, CT. Died of disease at Greenville, LA, July 27, 1864. Interred at Elm Grove Cemetery, North Kingstown, RI.

Read, Alonzo S. Pvt. Co. B. Residence, Little Compton. Died of disease at New Orleans, LA, Sept. 11, 1864.

Reynolds, Philip. Pvt. Co. F. Residence, Providence. Died of disease at New Orleans, LA, Oct. 19, 1864. Interred at Chalmette National Cemetery, New Orleans, LA. Grave 5484.

Rice, Santa Anna. Pvt. Co. B. Residence, Killingly, CT. Died of disease at Napoleonville, LA, Oct. 1, 1864. Interred at Grove Street Cemetery, Putnam, CT.

Richmond, Almond C. Pvt. Co. L. Residence, Scituate. Drowned in the sinking of the *North America* off Florida, Dec. 22, 1864. Cenotaph at Chappell Lot, Scituate Cemetery 215, Scituate, RI.

Ryan, Thomas. Pvt. Co. I. Residence, Providence. Died of disease at Napoleonville, LA, Sept. 2, 1865. Interred at Chalmette National Cemetery, New Orleans, LA.

Santor, Francis. Pvt. Co. A. Residence, New York, NY. Died of disease at New Orleans, LA, Aug. 30, 1864. Interred at Chalmette National Cemetery, New Orleans, LA. Grave 5325.

Sayles, Lyman M. Pvt. Co. M. Residence, Mendon, MA. Died of disease at New Orleans, LA, Dec. 4, 1865. Interred at Chalmette National Cemetery, New Orleans, LA. Grave 7487.

Scannell, Michael. Pvt. Co. D. Residence, Providence. Drowned in the sinking of the *North America* off Florida, Dec. 22, 1864. Cenotaph at St. John's Cemetery, Worcester, MA.

Schroeder, Heinrich. Pvt. Co. K. Residence, New York, NY. Died of disease at Napoleonville, LA, Jan. 19, 1865.

Sheldon, Charles B. Pvt. Co. E. Residence, Sterling, CT. Died of sun stroke at New Orleans, LA, July 31, 1865.

Sherman, Clark E. Pvt. Co. L. Residence, Barrington, NH. Died of disease at Napoleonville, LA, June 18, 1865.

Slater, Albert H. Pvt. Co. H. Residence, Warwick. Died of disease at Napoleonville, LA, Aug. 9, 1864. Interred at Chalmette National Cemetery, New Orleans, LA. Grave 4483.

Smith, Francis. Pvt. Co. D. Residence, Warwick. Died of dysentery at New Orleans, LA, Sept. 13, 1864.

Smith, Franklin. Pvt. Co. G. Residence, South Kingstown. Died of disease at Napoleonville, LA, Nov. 26, 1864. Interred at Chalmette National Cemetery, New Orleans, LA. Grave 4794. Cenotaph at Oak Dell Cemetery, South Kingstown, RI.

Smith, Thomas. Pvt. Co. H. Residence, Providence. Died of disease at New Orleans, LA, Dec. 15, 1864. Interred at Chalmette National Cemetery, New Orleans, LA. Grave 5939.

Spinney, Nathaniel. Pvt. Co. I. Residence, Elliot, ME. Drowned at New Orleans, LA, Oct. 7, 1865.

Stanley, Adolphus. Mus. Co. M. Residence, Dublin, NH. Died of disease at New Orleans, LA, Oct. 3, 1864. Cenotaph at West Lebanon Cemetery, Lebanon, NH.

Steele, William. Pvt. Co. D. Residence, Providence. Died of disease at Napoleonville, LA, Oct. 20, 1864.

Sullivan, John. Pvt. Co. I. Residence, Exeter. Drowned "at sea" Oct. 20, 1865.

Sullivan, Peter M. Sgt. Maj. Residence, Boston, MA. Died of disease at New Orleans, LA, Aug. 10, 1865. Interred at Chalmette National Cemetery, New Orleans, LA.

Sunderland, Henry A. Sgt. Co. F. Residence, Warwick. Died of tuberculosis at Napoleonville, LA, Feb. 22, 1865.

Swan, William. 1st Sgt. Co. K. Residence, Providence. Died of disease contracted in the service at Providence, RI, Mar. 29, 1866. Interred at North Burial Ground, Providence, RI.

Sweetland, Nathan J. Corp. Co. E. Residence, Providence. Died of disease at Greenville, LA, July 16, 1864.

Symonds, Charles H. Corp. Co. H. Residence, Springfield, MA. Died of disease at Jamestown, RI, April 18, 1864. Interred at Springfield Cemetery, Springfield, MA.

Tatro, Isaac. Pvt. Co. L. Residence, Cumberland. Died of disease at New Orleans, LA, Sept. 13, 1864.

Taylor, Henry D. Pvt. Co. M. Residence, North Providence. Drowned in the sinking of the *North America* off Florida, Dec. 22, 1864.

Teacher, Alfred. Saddler. Co. K. Residence, New York, NY. Died of disease at Grand Ecore, LA, April 16, 1864.

Tefft, William A. 2nd Lt. Co. C. Residence, South Kingstown. Died of disease contracted in the service at South Kingstown, RI, June 10, 1865. Interred at Elm Grove Cemetery, North Kingstown, RI.

Tennant, Ezra A. Sgt. Co. H. Residence, East Greenwich. Drowned in the sinking of the *North America* off Florida, Dec. 22, 1864. Cenotaph at First Cemetery, East Greenwich, RI.

Thayer, Richard. Pvt. Co. M. Residence, Burrillville. Died of disease at New Orleans, LA, Oct. 14, 1864. Interred at Chalmette National Cemetery, New Orleans, LA. Grave 5460.

Von Sjoestien, Tino. Pvt. Co. K. Residence, New York, NY. Died of disease at New Orleans, LA, Aug. 31, 1864.

Walker, William H. Corp. Co. H. Residence, East Providence. Drowned in the sinking of the *North America* off Florida, Dec. 22, 1864. Cenotaph at Lakeside-Carpenter Cemetery, East Providence, RI.

Warburton, James. Pvt. Co. G. Residence, East Greenwich. Died of disease at New Orleans, LA, Sept. 17, 1864.

Wehrens, Eugene. Pvt. Co. K. Residence, New York, NY. Died of disease at Washington, LA, Sept. 18, 1865.

Weigel, Christopher. Pvt. Co. A. Residence, New York, NY. Died of disease at New Orleans, LA, Sept. 1, 1864. Interred at Chalmette National Cemetery, New Orleans, LA. Grave 5398.

Whipple, Patrick. Pvt. Co. F. Residence, Providence. Died of disease at New Orleans, LA, Oct. 9, 1864.

Wilcox, William H. Corp. Co. H. Residence, East Douglas, MA. Drowned in the sinking of the *North America* off Florida, Dec. 22, 1864.

Williams, William C. Pvt. Co. C. Residence, Boston, MA. Died of disease at New Orleans, LA, Oct. 19, 1864.

Witherell, Benjamin O. Pvt. Co. L. Residence, Providence. Killed in action at the Red River, LA, April 23, 1864.

19

Seventh Squadron
of Cavalry

Colwell, Henry C. Pvt. Co. A. Residence, Glocester. Died of typhoid contracted in the service at Glocester, RI, Nov. 3, 1862. Interred at Acotes Hill Cemetery, Glocester, RI.

Coombs, Arthur W. Pvt. Co. B. Residence, Thetford, VT. Died of typhoid at Winchester, VA, Aug. 19, 1862. Interred at Pleasant Ridge Cemetery, Thetford, VT.

20

Battery A, First Rhode Island Light Artillery

Bosworth, Joseph T. Pvt. Residence, Providence. Killed in action at Antietam, MD, Sept. 17, 1862. Interred at Antietam National Cemetery, Sharpsburg, MD. Rhode Island Section, Grave 2834.

Bourne, William E. Pvt. Residence, Providence. Killed in an accidental explosion of a gun limber at Washington, D.C., July 9, 1861. Interred at Swan Point Cemetery, Providence, RI.

Brown, Clovis T. Pvt. Residence, Douglas, MA. Died of disease at Washington, D.C., Aug. 28, 1861. Interred at South Street Cemetery, Douglas, MA.

Bupp, Frederick. Pvt. Residence, Providence. Killed in action at Bull Run, VA, July 21, 1861.

Chaffee, George W. Pvt. Residence, Providence. Died of dysentery at Providence, RI, Jan. 13, 1863. Interred at North Burial Ground, Providence, RI.

Church, Norris L. Pvt. Residence, Hopkinton. Killed in action at Shallow Creek, VA, May 31, 1864. Cenotaph at Pine Grove Cemetery, Hopkinton, RI.

Dickerson, Joseph C. Pvt. Residence, Providence. Died of cholera contracted in the service at North Providence, RI, September 13, 1865. Interred at North Burial Ground, Providence, RI.

Gladding, Olney D. Pvt. Residence, Providence. Mortally wounded in action at Bull Run, VA, July 21, 1861. Died of wounds at Washington, D.C., Aug. 3, 1861. Interred at Swan Point Cemetery, Providence, RI.

Higgins, John. Pvt. Residence, Newport. Mortally wounded in action July 3, 1863, at Gettysburg, PA. Died of wounds at Gettysburg, PA, July 8, 1863. Interred at Gettysburg National Cemetery, Gettysburg, PA. Rhode Island Section.

Hunt, Peter. 1st Lt. Residence, East Providence. Mortally wounded in action at Shallow Creek, VA, May 31, 1864. Died of wounds at Washington, D.C., June 14, 1864. Interred at Hunt's Mills Cemetery, East Providence, RI.

Keene, Seth H. Corp. Residence, Providence. Died of disease at Washington, D.C., Sept. 11, 1863. Interred at Arlington National Cemetery, Arlington, VA. Section 13, Grave 9185.

Lannegan, Patrick. Pvt. Residence, Providence. Killed in action at Gettysburg, PA, July 3, 1863. Interred at Gettysburg National Cemetery, Gettysburg, PA. Rhode Island Section.

Lawrence, Charles A. Pvt. Residence, Providence. Killed in action at the Wilderness, VA, May 6, 1864.

Lawrence, John H. Pvt. Residence, Providence. Killed in action at Antietam, MD, Sept. 17, 1862. Interred at Antietam National Cemetery, Sharpsburg, MD. Rhode Island Section. Grave 2835. Cenotaph in Grace Church Cemetery, Providence, RI.

First Lieutenant Peter Hunt of Battery A was mortally wounded two weeks before he was due to return home to East Providence in May 1864.

Marcy, Albourne W. Pvt. Residence, Providence. Drowned in the sinking of the *Vanderbilt*, July 21, 1862. Interred at Hampton National Cemetery, Hampton, VA.

Moran, John. Pvt. Residence, Providence. Mortally wounded in action at Bristoe Station, VA, Oct. 14, 1863. Died of wounds at Alexandria, VA, Oct. 28, 1863.

Morse, Nathan T. Corp. Residence, Providence. Killed in an accidental explosion of a gun limber at Washington, D.C., July 9, 1861. Interred at Swan Point Cemetery, Providence, RI.

Reed, Charles M. Sgt. Residence, Providence. Killed in action at Antietam, MD, Sept. 17, 1862. Interred at Swan Point Cemetery, Providence, RI.

Private John H. Lawrence was killed in the horrific fighting near Dunker Church at Antietam. A resident of Providence, he was interred at Antietam National Cemetery. Antietam National Battlefield.

Salisbury, William. Pvt. Residence, Cranston. Died of dysentery at Fairfax, VA, Oct. 14, 1863.

Slocum, Moses F. Pvt. Residence, Providence. Died of typhoid at Warwick, RI, April 17, 1863. Interred at Pawtuxet Burial Yard, Warwick, RI.

Stone, Edwin. Pvt. Residence, Johnston. Killed in action at Antietam, MD, Sept. 17, 1862. Interred at Antietam National Cemetery, Sharpsburg, MD. Rhode Island Section. Grave 2833.

Swain, Reuben C. Pvt. Residence, Providence. Died of typhoid contracted in the service at Providence, RI, Dec. 24, 1863. Interred at North Burial Ground, Providence, RI.

Vose, Warren L. Pvt. Residence, Providence. Killed in action at Bull Run, VA, July 21, 1861.

Walker, Arnold A. Corp. Residence, Coventry. Died of dysentery at Coventry, RI, Feb. 19, 1863. Interred at Walker Lot, Coventry Cemetery 14, Coventry, RI.

Worsely, Hiram B. Pvt. Residence, Providence. Died of typhoid at Providence, RI, Aug. 8, 1862. Interred at North Burial Ground, Providence, RI.

Zimala, John. Pvt. Residence, Providence. Killed in action July 3, 1863, at Gettysburg, PA. Interred at Gettysburg National Cemetery, Gettysburg, PA. Rhode Island Section.

21

Battery B, First Rhode Island Light Artillery

Adams, Charles H. 1st Sgt. Residence, Providence. Killed in action at Ream's Station, VA, Aug. 25, 1864.

Austin, George R. Pvt. Residence, East Greenwich. Died of typhoid at Fort Monroe, VA, Aug. 31, 1862. Interred at Austin Lot, North Kingstown Cemetery 5, North Kingstown, RI.

Ballou, Henry H. Corp. Residence, Pawtucket. Mortally wounded in action at Gettysburg, PA, July 2, 1863. Died of wounds at Gettysburg, PA, July 4, 1863. Interred at Gettysburg National Cemetery, Gettysburg, PA. Rhode Island Section. Cenotaph at Mineral Spring Cemetery, Pawtucket, RI.

Barber, Henry J. Pvt. Residence, Exeter. Died of typhoid at Falmouth, VA, Dec. 2, 1862. Interred at Wood River Cemetery, Richmond, RI.

Breene, John. Pvt. Residence, Cumberland. Mortally wounded in action at Gettysburg, PA, July 3, 1863. Died of wounds at Gettysburg, PA, July 16, 1863. Interred at Gettysburg National Cemetery, Gettysburg, PA. Rhode Island Section.

Brown, Fenner A. Pvt. Residence, Scituate. Died of disease at New York, NY, Aug. 6, 1864. Interred at Grace Church Cemetery, Providence, RI.

Burton, Hazard W. Pvt. Residence, Hopkinton. Died disease at Washington, D.C., Oct. 15, 1862. Interred at White Brook Cemetery, Richmond, RI.

Burton, Joseph C. Pvt. Residence, Hopkinton. Died of typhoid at Falmouth, VA, Dec. 17, 1862. Interred at White Brook Cemetery, Richmond, RI.

Chapman, John H. Pvt. Residence, Providence. Killed in action at Ream's Station, VA, Aug. 25, 1864.

Clark, Charles. Pvt. Residence, Providence. Mortally wounded in action at Bristoe Station, VA, Oct. 14, 1863. Died of wounds at Washington, D.C., Oct. 21, 1863.

Dennis, William. Pvt. Residence, Providence. Killed in action at the Po River, VA, May 9, 1864.

Dickerson, William A. Corp. Residence, North Kingstown. Died of typhoid at Harpers Ferry, WV, Oct. 31, 1862. Interred at Elm Grove Cemetery, North Kingstown, RI.

Gardiner, Alfred G. Pvt. Residence, Swansea, MA. Killed in action July 3, 1863, at Gettysburg, PA. Cenotaph at Gettysburg National Cemetery, Gettysburg, PA. Interred at Gardiner Cemetery, Swansea, MA.

Glynn, John. Pvt. Residence, Providence. Killed in action at Ream's Station, VA, Aug. 25, 1864.

Greene, Caleb H. H. Pvt. Residence, West Greenwich. Mortally wounded in action at Fredericksburg, VA, Dec. 13, 1862. Died of wounds at West Greenwich, RI, Dec. 25, 1864. Interred at Benjamin Greene Lot, West Greenwich Cemetery 14, West Greenwich, RI.

Hamilton, William. Pvt. Residence, Pawtucket. Died of disease at Frederick, MD, Dec. 4, 1862.

Hendrick, Albert E. Pvt. Residence, Exeter. Mortally wounded in action at Fredericksburg, VA, Dec. 13, 1862. Died of wounds at Falmouth, VA, Dec. 23, 1862. Interred at Chestnut Hill Cemetery, Exeter, RI.

Private Alfred G. Gardiner was killed during Pickett's Charge on July 3, 1863, while working on the cannon later called the Gettysburg Gun. In a rare case, his remains were brought back home and interred in the family plot in Swansea, Massachusetts. The alleged grave in Gettysburg National Cemetery is a cenotaph. Gettysburg National Military Park.

Herman, Frederick H. Pvt. Residence, Boston, MA. Captured at Ream's Station, VA, Aug. 25, 1864. Died of disease at Salisbury, NC, Nov. 4, 1864. Interred at Mass Grave, Salisbury National Cemetery, Salisbury, NC.

Hunt, Chester F. Pvt. Residence, North Kingstown. Killed in action at Bristoe Station, VA, Oct. 14, 1863. Interred at Hunt-Hall Cemetery, North Kingstown Cemetery 1, North Kingstown, RI.

Jones, William. Pvt. Residence, Boston, MA. Killed in action at Gettysburg, PA, July 3, 1863. Interred at Gettysburg National Cemetery, Gettysburg, PA. Rhode Island Section.

King, David B. Pvt. Residence, Scituate. Killed in action at Gettysburg, PA, July 2, 1863. Interred at Gettysburg National Cemetery, Gettysburg, PA. Rhode Island Section. Cenotaph at Smithville Cemetery, Scituate, RI.

Luther, Joseph C. Pvt. Residence, Providence. Mortally wounded at Fredericksburg, VA, Dec. 13, 1862. Died of wounds at Washington, D.C., Feb. 24, 1863. Interred at Intervale Cemetery, North Providence, RI.

Milne, Joseph S. 2nd Lt. Residence, Providence. Detached to Battery A, 4th U.S. Artillery. Mortally wounded in action July 3, 1863, at Gettysburg, PA. Died of wounds at Gettysburg, PA, July 8, 1863. Interred at Oak Grove Cemetery, Fall River, MA.

Moffitt, Thomas. Pvt. Residence, Providence. Died of typhoid at Washington, D.C., Nov. 9, 1864. Interred at Grace Church Cemetery, Providence, RI.

Olney, Luther C. Corp. Residence, Providence. Mortally wounded in action at Ball's Bluff, VA, Oct. 21, 1861. Captured and Paroled. Died of wounds at Providence, Oct. 22, 1862. Interred at Grace Church Cemetery, Providence, RI.

Pearce, Harvey. Pvt. Residence, Richmond. Died of disease contracted in the service at Richmond, RI, April 28, 1864. Interred at Wood River Cemetery, Richmond, RI.

Pearce, William. Pvt. Residence, Richmond. Died of disease contracted

Private David B. King of Scituate was killed in action at Gettysburg on July 2, 1863. He is interred at Gettysburg National Cemetery. Gettysburg National Military Park.

Detached to Battery A, Fourth United States Artillery, Second Lieutenant Joseph S. Milne of Rhode Island's Battery B was mortally wounded during Pickett's Charge at Gettysburg. His final words were, "Comfort my mother and tell her I died doing my duty."

in the service at Richmond, RI, March 13, 1863. Interred at Wood River Cemetery, Richmond, RI.

Perrin, William S. 1st Lt. and Bvt. Capt. Residence, Providence. Mortally wounded in action August 25, 1864, at Ream's Station, VA. Left leg amputated. Captured and mustered out April 1865. Became a morphine addict after the war due to loss of leg. Died of a morphine overdose directly attributable to his Ream's Station injury Aug. 13, 1876, in Pawtucket, RI. Interred at Riverside Cemetery, Pawtucket, RI.

Phillips, Albert A. Pvt. Residence, Foster. Died of dysentery at Alexandria, VA, Dec. 15, 1862. Interred at Oak Grove Cemetery, Pawtucket, RI.

Sanford, Herbert D. Pvt. Residence, Providence. Died of disease near Warrenton, VA, July 18, 1863.

Remembered as a hero for his actions at Gettysburg, Sergeant Albert Straight of Exeter died of dysentery in November 1863. Gettysburg National Military Park.

Seamans, Ezekiel W. Pvt. Residence, North Providence. Died of dysentery at Providence, RI, Dec. 16, 1862. Interred at Swan Point Cemetery, Providence, RI.

Sisson, John J. Pvt. Residence, Exeter. Died of disease contracted in the service at Exeter, RI, Dec. 15, 1865. Interred at Plain Meeting Cemetery, West Greenwich, RI.

Smith, Francis A. 2nd Lt. Residence, Providence. Died of bronchitis contracted in the service at Providence, RI, Feb. 9, 1862. Interred at North Burial Ground, Providence, RI.

Straight, Albert. Sgt. Residence, Exeter. Died of dysentery at Fairfax, VA, Nov. 16, 1863. Interred at Plain Meeting Cemetery, West Greenwich, RI.

Tanner, William M. Corp. Residence, West Greenwich. Killed in action at Ball's Bluff, VA, Oct. 21, 1861. Cenotaph at Plain Meeting Cemetery, West Greenwich, RI.

Trescott, John. Pvt. Residence, Providence. Died of tuberculosis at Poolesville, MD, Mar. 29, 1862.

Winsor, William W. Pvt. Residence, Scituate. Captured at Ream's Station, VA, Aug. 25, 1864. Died of pneumonia at Salisbury Prison, NC, Feb. 22, 1865. Cenotaph at Abraham Winsor Lot, Smithfield Cemetery 31, Smithfield, RI.

22

Battery C, First Rhode Island Light Artillery

Baker, Henry M. Pvt. Residence, Providence. Died of typhoid at Washington, D.C., January 13, 1863.

Blanchard, Sheldon L. Pvt. Residence, Foster. Died of disease contracted in the service at Foster, RI, Sept. 11, 1867. Interred at Blanchard Lot, Foster Cemetery 84, Foster, RI.

Donohoe, Hugh. Pvt. Residence, Providence. Killed in a train accident, Mar. 11, 1862. Interred at Soldier's Home National Cemetery, Washington, D.C.

Ham, George W. Pvt. Residence, Little Compton. Killed in action at Gaines Mill, VA, June 27, 1862. Cenotaph at Swan Point Cemetery, Providence, RI.

Hanna, Augustus S. Sgt. Residence, Pawtucket. Killed in action at Chancellorsville, VA, May 3, 1863. Interred at Mineral Spring Cemetery, Pawtucket, RI.

Hewitt, Henry. Pvt. Residence, Providence. Died of disease at Washington, D.C., July 20, 1862. Interred at Soldier's Home National Cemetery, Washington, D.C. Section C, Grave 3957.

Holden, George W. Pvt. Residence, Foster. Died of disease at Washington, D.C., Sept. 17, 1862. Interred at Soldier's Home National Cemetery, Washington, D.C. Grave 912. Cenotaph at Clayville Cemetery, Foster, RI.

Irving, William. Pvt. Residence, Providence. Killed in action at Gaines Mill, VA, June 27, 1862. Cenotaph at North Burial Ground, Providence, RI.

Lamphier, Thomas. Pvt. Residence, Richmond. Killed in action at Cold Harbor, VA, June 3, 1864. Interred at Cold Harbor National Cemetery, Mechanicsville, VA. Grave 60.

Lovely, Judson A. Pvt. Residence, Providence. Died of epilepsy at Baltimore, MD, Aug. 4, 1862.

Matteson, James A. Pvt. Residence, Scituate. Killed in action at Cedar Creek, VA, Oct. 19, 1864. Interred at Winchester National Cemetery, Winchester, VA.

McVeigh, Hugh. Pvt. Residence, Providence. Accidentally run over and killed by a caisson at Washington, D.C., Oct. 7, 1861.

Montgomery, Frank. Pvt. Residence, Plainfield, CT. Killed in action at Fredericksburg, VA, Dec. 13, 1862. Interred at Union Cemetery, Plainfield, CT.

Moyes, Frederic S. Pvt. Residence, Pawtucket. Killed in action at Chancellorsville, VA, May 3, 1863.

Mullen, Francis. Pvt. Residence, Cumberland. Killed in action at Malvern Hill, VA, July 1, 1862.

Nason, Henry. Pvt. Residence, Providence. Died of disease at Brandy Station, VA, Jan. 13, 1864.

O'Brien, Patrick. Pvt. Residence, Warwick. Died of typhoid at Providence, RI, Aug. 13, 1863.

Parker, Gideon B. Pvt. Residence, Coventry. Killed in action at Gaines Mill, VA, June 27, 1862.

Perry, George A. Sgt. Residence, Pawtucket. Mortally wounded in action at Cedar Creek, VA, Oct. 19, 1864. Died of wounds at Baltimore, MD, Nov. 1, 1864. Interred at Oak Grove Cemetery, Pawtucket, RI.

Reynolds, John T. Pvt. Residence, Richmond. Killed in action at Yorktown, VA, April 1, 1862. Interred at Wood River Cemetery, Richmond, RI.

Ryan, Daniel. Pvt. Residence, Providence. Killed in action at Cedar Creek, VA, Oct. 19, 1864.

Swan, John J. Pvt. Residence, Providence. Killed in action at Gaines Mill, VA, June 27, 1862. Interred at St. Francis Cemetery, Pawtucket, RI.

Terry, David. Pvt. Residence, North Kingstown. Killed in action at Gaines Mill, VA, June 27, 1862. Interred at Terry Lot, North Kingstown Cemetery 121, North Kingstown, RI.

Testen, Henry E. Pvt. Residence, Blackstone, MA. Killed in action at Gaines Mill, VA, June 27, 1862. Interred at Oak Hill cemetery, Woonsocket, RI.

Thayer, Elisha D. Pvt. Residence, Smithfield. Killed in action at Malvern Hill, VA, July 1, 1862.

Thompson, William B. Corp. Residence, Pawtucket. Killed in action at Malvern Hill, VA, July 1, 1862.

Towne, Samuel. Pvt. Residence, North Providence. Died of "dysentery contracted in the Chickahominy" at North Providence, RI, Feb. 13, 1863. Interred at Hunts Corner Cemetery, Albany, ME.

Watson, George H. Corp. Residence, South Kingstown. Killed in action at Malvern Hill, VA, July 1, 1862. Interred at Elisha Watson Lot, South Kingstown Cemetery 22, South Kingstown, RI.

Young, George W. Pvt. Residence, Providence. Killed in action at Malvern Hill, VA, July 1, 1862. Interred at North Burial Ground, Providence, RI.

23

Battery D, First Rhode Island Light Artillery

Burt, Everett B. Pvt. Residence, Providence. Mortally wounded in action at Antietam, MD, Sept. 17, 1862. Sent to hospital at Washington, D.C., and died there of wounds June 27, 1863.

Caesar, Daniel. Pvt. Residence, Smithfield. Died of typhoid at Hampton, VA, Mar. 19, 1863. Interred at Hampton National Cemetery, Hampton, VA. Grave 2505.

Carroll, Edward. Pvt. Residence, Warwick. Killed in action at Antietam, MD, Sept. 17, 1862. Interred at St. Mary's Cemetery, West Warwick, RI.

Doran, Hugh. Pvt. Residence, Warwick. Killed in action at Second Manassas, VA, Aug. 28, 1862.

Eldred, George A. Corp. Residence, Coventry. Killed in action at Second Manassas, VA, Aug. 28, 1862. Interred at Manchester Cemetery, Coventry, RI.

French, John S. Pvt. Residence, Providence. Died of disease at Sharpsburg, MD, Oct. 24, 1862. Interred at Antietam National Cemetery, Sharpsburg, MD. Rhode Island Section, Grave 2838.

Galloughly, John. Pvt. Residence, Warwick. Killed in action at Antietam, MD, Sept. 17, 1862. Interred in unknown plot at Antietam National Cemetery, Sharpsburg, MD.

Gilmore, Solomon. Pvt. Residence, Providence. Died of disease contracted in the service at Providence, RI, April 11, 1867. Interred at North Burial Ground, Providence, RI.

Green, John T. Pvt. Residence, Coventry. Died of measles at Hampton, VA, Mar. 6, 1863. Interred at Hopkins Hollow Cemetery, Coventry, RI.

Hawkins, Richard S. Pvt. Residence, Coventry. Died of typhoid contracted in the service at Coventry, RI, Mar. 27, 1862. Interred at Hawkins Lot, Coventry Cemetery 22, Coventry, RI.

Hicks, Otis F. Pvt. Residence, Providence. Killed in action at Second Manassas, VA, Aug. 28, 1862.

Hopkins, Daniel. Pvt. Residence, Foster. Died of disease at Annapolis, MD, Nov. 10, 1862. Interred at Annapolis National Cemetery, Annapolis, MD. Section E, Grave 1736.

Kennison, Charles H. Sgt. Residence, Providence. Died of disease contracted in the service at Providence, RI, June 27, 1864. Interred at Swan Point Cemetery, Providence, RI.

Kilburn, Bernard. Pvt. Residence, Providence. Killed in action at Antietam, MD, Sept. 17, 1862.

Kimball, Charles H. Sgt. Residence, Scituate. Died of disease at Knoxville, TN, Dec. 13, 1863. Interred at Smithville Cemetery, Scituate, RI.

McGovern, John. Pvt. Residence, Providence. Killed in action at Antietam, MD, Sept. 17, 1862.

Norris, Bradley J. Pvt. Residence, Albany, VT. Died of typhoid at Knoxville, TN, Jan. 3, 1864. Interred at Knoxville National Cemetery, Knoxville, TN. Section D, Grave 1868. Cenotaph at Albany Village Cemetery, Albany, VT.

Oakes, William A. Pvt. Residence, Providence. Mortally wounded in action at Knoxville, TN, Nov. 27, 1863. "Died of effects of wounds" at Providence, RI, Dec. 28, 1864. Interred at North Burial Ground, Providence, RI.

Peckham, William S. Pvt. Residence, South Kingstown. Died of dysentery contracted in the service at South Kingstown, RI, April 1, 1863. Interred at Riverside Cemetery, South Kingstown, RI.

Potter, Frank A. Pvt. Residence, Providence. Killed in action at Antietam, MD, Sept. 17, 1862.

Robbins, Duty. Pvt. Residence, Warwick. Killed in action at Antietam, MD, Sept. 17, 1862.

Russell, Francis. Pvt. Residence, Providence. Killed in action at Antietam, MD, Sept. 17, 1862.

Smith, David. Pvt. Residence, Westerly. Killed in action at Antietam, MD, Sept. 17, 1862.

Webb, Edward J. Pvt. Residence, North Providence. Died of disease at Somerset, KY, June 2, 1863. Interred at Mill Spring National Cemetery, Somerset, KY.

24

Battery E, First Rhode Island Light Artillery

Beard, William. Pvt. Residence, Johnston. Killed in action at Gettysburg, PA, July 2, 1863. Interred at Gettysburg National Cemetery, Gettysburg, PA. Rhode Island Section.

Bennett, Jeremiah. Pvt. Residence, Providence. "Died after discharge" of disease contracted in the service at Providence, RI, April 2, 1864. Interred at North Burial Ground, Providence, RI.

Braman, John. Pvt. Residence, Providence. Killed in action at Groveton, VA, Aug. 27, 1862.

Colvin, John. Pvt. Residence, Scituate. Died of typhoid at Harrison's Landing, VA, July 5, 1862. Interred at Glenford Cemetery, Scituate, RI.

Colwell, Albert N. Pvt. Residence, Scituate. Killed in action at Kelly's Ford, VA, Nov. 7, 1863. Interred at Smithville Cemetery, Scituate, RI.

Corp, Stephen. Pvt. Residence, Foster. Mortally wounded in action at Glendale, VA, June 30, 1862. Died of wounds at Foster, RI, Dec. 24, 1866.

Fiske, George W. Pvt. Residence, Coventry. Died of disease at Fair Oaks, VA, June 28, 1862. Interred at Seven Pines National Cemetery, Richmond, VA. Grave 582. Cenotaph at Fiske-Andrews Lot, Coventry Cemetery 10, Coventry, RI.

Galvin, Edward. Pvt. Residence, Providence. Killed in action at Second Manassas, VA, Aug. 29, 1862.

Greene, Lemuel A. Pvt. Residence, Scituate. Killed in action at Second Manassas, VA, Aug. 29, 1862. Interred at Manchester Cemetery, Coventry, RI.

Harrop, Joseph. Pvt. Residence, Warwick. Killed in action at Malvern Hill, VA, July 1, 1862.

Higgins, George. Pvt. Residence, Providence. Died in an accident at Bull Run, VA, Nov. 22, 1862.

Jordan, John. Pvt. Residence, Providence. Captured at Chancellorsville, VA, May 3, 1863. Died as a prisoner of war at Richmond, VA, Aug. 31, 1863.

King, William H. Pvt. Residence, North Providence. Died of disease at Point Lookout, MD, Sept. 5, 1862.

Leavens, Martin M. Pvt. Residence, Providence. Died of disease at Falmouth, VA, Mar. 8, 1863.

Mason, William. Pvt. Residence, Warwick. Killed in action at Fredericksburg, VA, Dec. 13, 1862. Interred in unknown grave at Fredericksburg National Cemetery, Fredericksburg, VA.

Mathewson, John B. Corp. Residence, Barrington. Died of typhoid at Fort Lyon, VA, Jan. 22, 1862. Interred at Prince's Hill Burial Ground, Barrington, RI.

Matteson, Edwin A. Pvt. Residence, West Greenwich. Died of typhoid at Falmouth, VA, Dec. 13, 1862. Interred at David Matteson Lot, West Greenwich Cemetery 8, West Greenwich, RI.

McCaffery, Edward. Pvt. Residence, Plainfield, CT. Died of dysentery at City Point, VA, Oct. 28, 1864.

Medbury, Louis A. Pvt. Residence, Scituate. Died of typhoid at Washington, D.C., Mar. 30, 1864. Interred at Glenford Cemetery, Scituate, RI.

Moore, Charles. Pvt. Residence, Pawtucket. Mortally wounded in action at Chancellorsville, VA, May 2, 1863. Died of wounds at Washington, D.C., July 2, 1863. Interred at Soldier's Home National Cemetery, Washington, D.C. Section D, Grave 5327.

Potter, Elisha E. Pvt. Residence, Scituate. Killed in action at Chancellorsville, VA, May 3, 1863. Interred at Glenford Cemetery, Scituate, RI.

Potter, Thomas H. Pvt. Residence, Scituate. Died of disease contracted in the service at Scituate, RI, May 12, 1863. Interred at Glenford Cemetery, Scituate, RI.

Pratt, James F. Pvt. Residence, Providence. Died of disease at Falmouth, VA, Dec. 2, 1862.

Rose, Richard. Pvt. Residence, Bristol. Mortally wounded in action at Gettysburg, PA, July 2, 1863. Died of wounds at Bristol, RI, Dec. 15, 1863. Interred at North Burial Ground, Bristol, RI.

Sayles, Crawford A. Pvt. Residence, Glocester. Died of disease at City Point, VA, Aug. 27, 1864. Interred at City Point National Cemetery, Hopewell, VA. Grave 1521.

Shaw, Thomas. Pvt. Residence, Providence. Died of disease at Washington, D.C., Aug. 29, 1863. Interred at Soldier's Home National Cemetery, Washington, D.C. Section H, Grave 2170.

Simpson, Ernest. Pvt. Residence, Providence. Killed in action at Gettysburg, PA, July 2, 1863. Interred at Gettysburg National Cemetery, Gettysburg, PA. Rhode Island Section.

Slaven, John. Pvt. Residence, Providence. Died of disease in hospital at Chester, PA, Aug. 23, 1863.

Sullivan, Cornelius. Pvt. Residence, Providence. Killed in action at Fredericksburg, VA, Dec. 13, 1862.

Sutcliffe, Robert. Pvt. Residence, Warwick. Died of disease at Washington, D.C., June 27, 1862.

Trescott, Albert H. Corp. Residence, Providence. Died of dysentery at Harrison's Landing, VA, July 28, 1862.

Williams, Henry. Pvt. Warwick. Died of disease contracted in the service at Warwick, RI, Aug. 22, 1863. Interred at Brayton Cemetery, Warwick, RI.

Winslow, Charles S. 1st Sgt. Residence, Providence. Shot in back and sent to hospital at Gettysburg, PA, July 2, 1863. Transferred to Veterans Reserve Corps. Mustered out Sept. 30, 1864. "He died of consumption Dec. 30, 1873. His death was hastened, doubtless by the wound received at Gettysburg." Interred at North Burial Ground, Providence, RI.

First Sergeant Charles S. Winslow was severely wounded at Gettysburg on July 2, 1863. The veterans of Battery E considered his 1873 death a direct result of the wounds he received ten years prior.

Battery F, First Rhode Island Light Artillery

Bartlett, John E. Pvt. Residence, New Bedford, MA. Died of "brain fever" at Beaufort, NC, June 29, 1862. Interred at New Bern National Cemetery, New Bern, NC. Grave 1868.

Baten, Nathan. Pvt. Residence, Coventry. Died of disease contracted in the service at Coventry, RI, Feb. 10, 1865. Interred at Greenwood Cemetery, Coventry, RI.

Baxter, Henry H. Pvt. Residence, Pawtucket. Died of disease at Annapolis, MD, Feb. 5, 1862. Interred at Oak Grove Cemetery, Pawtucket, RI.

Benway, Thomas. Pvt. Residence, Providence. Died of dysentery at Fort Monroe, VA, Oct. 7, 1864. Interred at Hampton National Cemetery, Hampton, VA. Grave 1365.

Connor, James. Pvt. Residence, Providence. Died of tuberculosis at New Bern, NC, 1863. Interred at New Bern National Cemetery, New Bern, NC. Grave 1862.

Daley, David. Pvt. Residence, Coventry. Killed in action at Proctor's Creek, VA, May 12, 1864.

Davis, James C. Pvt. Residence, Providence. Mortally wounded in action at Proctor's Creek, VA, May 16, 1864. Died of wounds at Richmond, VA, May 30, 1864.

Davis, William M. Pvt. Residence, Westerly. Died of dysentery at New Bern, NC, Aug. 27, 1862.

Day, Henry F. Pvt. Residence, Westerly. Died of disease at New Bern, NC, Aug. 27, 1862. Interred at River Bend Cemetery, Westerly, RI.

Draper, Benjamin H. Sgt. Residence, Providence. Died after being kicked by horse, resulting in amputation, at New Bern, NC, May 27, 1862. Interred at Swan Point Cemetery, Providence, RI.

Easterbrooks, Sylvester. Pvt. Residence, Warren. Mortally wounded in action at Proctor's Creek, VA, May 12, 1864. Died of wounds at Hampton,

VA, May 24, 1864. Interred at Hampton National Cemetery, Hampton, VA. Section C, Grave 1605. Cenotaph at Oak Dell Cemetery, South Kingstown, RI.

Gavitt, James L. Pvt. Residence, Westerly. Killed in action at Whitehall, NC, Dec. 16, 1862. Interred at River Bend Cemetery, Westerly, RI.

Goff, Amasa R. Pvt. Residence, Coventry. Died of disease at Petersburg, VA, June 28, 1865. Interred at Daniel Goff Lot, Coventry Cemetery 41, Coventry, RI.

Hall, Henry. Pvt. Residence, Thompson, CT. Mortally wounded in action at Drewry's Bluff, VA, May 13, 1864. Died of wounds at Brattleboro Hospital, Brattleboro, VT, Sept. 28, 1864. Interred at Wilsonville Cemetery, Thompson, CT.

Hazard, Job. Pvt. Residence, South Kingstown. Died of diphtheria at New Bern, NC, Dec. 20, 1862. Interred at Wakefield Baptist Cemetery, South Kingstown, RI.

Healy, William B. Pvt. Residence, Providence. Died of typhoid at Roanoke Island, NC, Mar. 19, 1862.

Horton, Alonzo C. Pvt. Residence, Providence. Died of disease at Hatteras, NC, Feb. 19, 1862. Interred at North Burial Ground, Providence, RI.

Horton, Henry R. Pvt. Residence, Westerly. Mortally wounded in action at Petersburg, VA, June 24, 1864. Died of wounds at Fort Monroe, VA, July 4, 1864. Interred at River Bend Cemetery, Westerly, RI.

Kenyon, Welcome W. Pvt. Residence, South Kingstown. Died of disease at Baltimore, MD, Sept. 12, 1864.

Larkin, Reuben E. Pvt. Residence, Richmond. Died of typhoid at New Bern, NC, June 11, 1862. Interred at Wood River Cemetery, Richmond, RI.

Martindale, Benjamin. Corp. Residence, East Greenwich. Killed in action while on picket duty near New Bern, NC, May 2, 1862. Interred at New Bern National Cemetery, New Bern, NC. Grave 1900.

McCabe, Patrick. Pvt. Residence, Providence. Killed in action at Drury's Bluff, VA, May 15, 1864.

McComb, John. Pvt. Residence, Providence. Died of yellow fever at New Bern, NC, Aug. 31, 1862. Interred at New Bern National Cemetery, New Bern, NC. Grave 1971.

Nesbit, William. Pvt. Residence, Westerly. Killed in action at Whitehall, NC, Dec. 16, 1862.

Nye, Jonathan. Pvt. Residence, South Kingstown. Died of diphtheria at New Bern, NC, Aug. 2, 1862. Interred at New Bern National Cemetery, New Bern, NC. Grave 1944.

Schmid, Casper I. Sgt. Residence, Providence. Mortally wounded in action at Petersburg, VA, Aug. 9, 1864. Died of wounds at Philadelphia, PA, Oct. 7, 1864.

Sheldon, Nehemiah K. Pvt. Residence, Woonsocket. Died of "disease contracted in the service" at Woonsocket, RI, Mar. 25, 1866. Interred at Oak Hill Cemetery, Woonsocket, RI.

Slocum, Elisha A. Corp. Residence, Pawtucket. Died of disease contracted in the service at Pawtucket, RI, April 1, 1862. Interred at Mineral Spring Cemetery, Pawtucket, RI.

Stanley, Milton. Pvt. Residence, Providence. Died of bronchitis at Willett's Point, NY, Dec. 6, 1864.

Whitham, Benjamin. Pvt. Residence, Providence. Captured at Drury's Bluff, VA, May 16, 1864. Died of disease while a prisoner of war at Andersonville, GA, Sept. 19, 1864. Interred at Andersonville National Cemetery. Grave 9273.

Young, Edward S. Pvt. Residence, Scituate. Died of disease at Petersburg, VA, July 9, 1864. Interred at Stephen Young Lot, Scituate Cemetery 66, Scituate, RI.

26

Battery G, First Rhode Island Light Artillery

Baker, William A. Pvt. Residence, Providence. Died of disease contracted in the service at Providence, RI, July 21, 1865. Interred at Knotty Oak Cemetery, Coventry, RI.

Bowen, George W. Pvt. Residence, Providence. Mortally wounded in action at Cedar Creek, VA, Oct. 19, 1864. Died of wounds at Baltimore, MD, Dec. 3, 1864. Interred at Swan Point Cemetery, Providence, RI.

Braman, James. H. Pvt. Residence, South Kingstown. Died of typhoid at Philadelphia, PA, Sept. 11, 1862. Interred at Philadelphia National Cemetery, Philadelphia, PA. Section B, Grave 249.

Brennan, Patrick. Pvt. Residence, North Providence. Mortally wounded in action at Second Fredericksburg, May 3, 1863. Died of wounds at Providence, RI, April 28, 1864.

Briggs, Edward C. Pvt. Residence, Coventry. Died of disease at Washington, D.C., Sept. 28, 1862. Interred at Soldier's Home National Cemetery, Washington, D.C. Grave 3733.

Brown, Eleazer H. Pvt. Residence, Providence. Died of pneumonia at Washington, D.C., Mar. 22, 1862. Interred at Soldier's Home National Cemetery, Washington, D.C. Section B, Grave 1428.

Callahan, James. Pvt. Residence, Pawtucket. Captured at Spotsylvania Court House, VA, May 12, 1864. Died at Andersonville, GA, July 23, 1864. Interred at Andersonville National Cemetery. Grave 3810.

Canning, John. Pvt. Residence, Providence. Died of disease Dec. 22, 1862, at Washington, D.C.

Carringan, Patrick. Pvt. Residence, Providence. Died after being kicked by a horse at Falmouth, VA, Dec. 17, 1862.

Chace, Henry E. Corp. Residence, Westerly. Killed in action at Cedar Creek, VA, Oct. 19, 1864. Interred at Winchester National Cemetery, Winchester, VA. Grave 3622.

Coffery, Michael. Pvt. Residence, Providence. Died of typhoid at Harpers Ferry, WV, Oct. 18, 1862. Interred at Winchester National Cemetery, Winchester, VA. Grave 3624.

Cole, James. A. Corp. Residence, Scituate. Died of typhoid at Fort Monroe, VA, Sept. 18, 1862. Interred at Pine Grove Cemetery, Coventry, RI.

Conley, William. Pvt. Residence, Providence. Died of disease at Washington, D.C., Oct. 3, 1863.

Connery, John. Pvt. Residence, Providence. Died of disease at Washington, D.C., Dec. 23, 1862. Interred at Soldier's Home National Cemetery, Washington, D.C. Grave 3376.

Douglas, William C. Pvt. Residence, Westerly. Killed in action at Cedar Creek, VA, Oct. 19, 1864. Interred at Winchester National Cemetery, Winchester, VA. Grave 3600.

Farnsworth, Henry. Pvt. Residence, Tiverton. Died of disease at Hampton, VA, Sept. 20, 1862. Interred at Hampton National Cemetery, Hampton, VA. Section D, Grave 2609.

Gardner, Charles G. Pvt. Residence, Barrington. Killed in action at Cedar Creek, VA, Oct. 19, 1864. Interred at Winchester National Cemetery, Winchester, VA. Grave 3611.

Horton, James H. Pvt. Residence, Glocester. Died of disease at Washington, D.C., Aug. 24, 1862. Interred at Acotes Hill Cemetery, Glocester, RI.

Hudson, Charles W. Pvt. Residence, Smithfield. Died of typhoid at Philadelphia, PA, Aug. 23, 1862. Interred at Union Village Cemetery, North Smithfield, RI.

Johnston, John K. Pvt. Residence, Charlestown. Killed in action at Second Fredericksburg, VA, May 3, 1863.

Kelley, Benjamin E. 2nd Lt. Residence, Providence. Mortally wounded in action at Second Fredericksburg, VA, May 3, 1863. Died of wounds at Falmouth, VA, May 4, 1863. Interred at Swan Point Cemetery, Providence, RI.

Kent, Jacob V. Sgt. Residence, Warwick. Died of tuberculosis contracted in the service Dec. 5, 1862, at Warwick, RI. Interred at Swan Point Cemetery, Providence, RI.

Lewis, William H. Mus. Residence, Providence. Mortally wounded in action at Cedar Creek, VA, Oct. 19, 1864. Died of wounds at Middletown, VA, Oct. 21, 1864. Interred at Winchester National Cemetery, Winchester, VA. Grave 3589.

Mars, Thomas E. Mus. Residence, Tiverton. Mortally wounded in action at the Second Battle of Fredericksburg, May 3, 1863. Died of wounds May 9, 1863, at Washington, D.C. Interred at Soldier's Home National Cemetery, Washington, D.C. Grave 3526.

McDonald, James. Pvt. Residence, Providence. Mortally wounded in action at Cedar Creek, VA, Oct. 19, 1864. Died of wounds at Winchester, VA, Nov. 1, 1864. Interred at Winchester National Cemetery, Winchester, VA. Grave 4015.

McManus, Charles. Art. Residence, New York, NY. Died of disease at Washington, D.C., Sept. 21, 1863.

Norton, George R. Pvt. Residence, Providence. Died of disease contracted in the service at Providence, RI, Feb. 22, 1869. Interred at North Burial Ground, Providence, RI.

Pomeroy, Elijah. Pvt. Residence, Providence. Died of disease at Portsmouth Grove Hospital, Portsmouth, RI, Sept. 12, 1862. Interred at Grace Church Cemetery, Providence, RI.

Rice, Charles H. Pvt. Residence, Coventry. Died of disease contracted in the service at Coventry, RI, Jan. 20, 1868. Interred at Hopkins Hollow Cemetery, Coventry, RI.

Salpaugh, Jacob H. Pvt. Residence, New York, NY. Died of typhoid at Falmouth, VA, Dec. 11, 1862.

Scott, Charles V. 2nd Lt. Residence, Providence. Mortally wounded in action at Cedar Creek, VA, Oct. 19, 1864. Died of wounds at Winchester, VA, Jan. 21, 1865. Interred at Grace Church Cemetery, Providence, RI.

Starboard, Simeon H. Pvt. Residence, Davisville, ME. Mortally wounded in

Bugler William H. Lewis wore this magnificent coat when he was shot in the chest at Cedar Creek trying to save a gun from being captured; he died two days later. Connecticut State Library.

The grave of Bugler William Henry Lewis at Winchester National Cemetery in Virginia.

action at Cedar Creek, VA, Oct. 19, 1864. Died of wounds Jan. 1, 1865, at Winchester, VA

Stephens, George W. Pvt. Residence, Charlestown. Died of typhoid at Washington, D.C., Sept. 9, 1862.

Sullivan, Edward G. Sgt. Residence, Coventry. Died of disease at Petersburg, VA, Mar. 22, 1865. Interred at Poplar Grove National Cemetery, Petersburg, VA. Grave 1598.

Sunderland, Joseph W. Pvt. Residence, South Kingstown. Mortally wounded in action at Second Fredericksburg, May 3, 1863. Died of wounds at Washington, D.C., April 20, 1864.

Tabor, William O. Pvt. Residence, Richmond. Died of typhoid at Washington, D.C., Jan. 27, 1863. Interred at Wood River Cemetery, Richmond, RI.

Taft, John. Pvt. Residence, Providence. Died of disease at Washington, D.C., Jan. 24, 1862. Interred at Soldier's Home National Cemetery, Washington, D.C. Grave 3292.

Prior to promotion and reassignment to Battery G, Second Lieutenant Charles V. Scott had served in Battery A as a private and saved the Bull Run Gun from capture. He was mortally wounded at Cedar Creek trying to save one of Battery G's guns from capture.

Tanner, Charles. Pvt. Residence, Providence. Died of typhoid at Washington, D.C., Sept. 25, 1862.

Travers, Augustus F. Residence, Providence. Killed in action at Cedar Creek, VA, Oct. 19, 1864. Interred at Winchester National Cemetery, Winchester, VA. Grave 3633.

Wilbur, William B. Art. Residence, Providence. Died of disease at Warrenton, VA, Aug. 10, 1863.

Williams, Jason L. Pvt. Residence, Scituate. Died of disease at Portsmouth Grove Hospital, Portsmouth, RI, July 31, 1862. Interred at Williams Lot, Scituate Cemetery 71, Scituate, RI.

27

Battery H, First Rhode Island Light Artillery

Arnold, Henry N. Pvt. Residence, Coventry. Committed suicide at Washington, D.C., Feb. 12, 1864. Interred at Hopkins Hollow Cemetery, Coventry, RI.

Bennett, Samuel. Pvt. Residence, Richmond. Died of tuberculosis contracted in the service at Providence, RI, Oct. 29, 1863. Interred at North Burial Ground, Providence, RI.

Booth, James. Pvt. Residence, Burrillville. Died of disease at Washington, D.C., Oct. 11, 1864.

Carpenter, George P. Sgt. Residence, Providence. Died of typhoid at Washington, D.C., Mar. 1, 1863.

Carter, Thomas. Pvt. Residence, Providence. Killed in action at Petersburg, VA, April 2, 1865. Interred at Cumberland Cemetery, Cumberland, RI.

Goff, Thomas I. Mus. Residence, Warren. Died of typhoid at Fairfax, VA, Feb. 1, 1863. Interred at South Burial Ground, Warren, RI.

Manchester, William G. Pvt. Residence, Providence. Died of disease at Fairfax, VA, Feb. 13, 1863.

Phillips, John. Pvt. Residence, Providence. Died of disease at Fairfax, VA, Mar. 1, 1863.

Phinney, Henry. Pvt. Residence, Warwick. Died of disease at Alexandria, VA, April 24, 1864. Interred at Arlington National Cemetery, Arlington, VA. Section 13, Grave 7516.

Tracy, George E. Art. Residence, Providence. Died of disease at Fairfax, VA, Feb. 1, 1863.

Turner, Andrew. Pvt. Residence, Warwick. Died of tuberculosis contracted in the service at Warwick, RI, Oct. 14, 1863. Interred at Cottrell Cemetery, Scituate, RI.

Vaslett, Charles. Pvt. Residence, Providence. Killed in action at Petersburg, VA, April 2, 1865. Interred at Poplar Grove National Cemetery Petersburg, VA. Grave 1590.

Webster, Clement. 1st Lt. Residence, Providence. Died of disease contracted in the service at Providence, RI, Oct. 16, 1864. Interred at Grace Church Cemetery, Providence, RI.

Williams, George A. Pvt. Residence, Providence. Died of disease at Washington, D.C., May 30, 1864.

28

Tenth Rhode Island
Battery

Flate, James. Corp. Residence, New York, NY. Killed when struck by a limber pole while engaged in a cannon drill at Washington, D.C., Aug. 8, 1862. Interred at Sloatsburg Cemetery, Sloatsburg, NY.

29

United States Army

Alger, Joseph. Pvt. Co. G, 15th U.S. Infantry. Residence, Bristol. Died of disease contracted in the service at Bristol, RI, Sept. 27, 1867. Interred at North Burial Ground, Bristol, RI.

Barnes, George O. Pvt. Co. H, 14th U.S. Infantry. Killed in action at Gaines Mill, VA, June 27, 1862.

Beaman, William. Pvt. Co. H, 3rd Battalion, 15th U.S. Infantry. Died of disease at Mobile, AL, Mar. 18, 1866. Interred at Mobile National Cemetery, Mobile, AL. Section 2, Grave 324.

Bell, Samuel R. Pvt. Co. F, 2nd Battalion, 15th U.S. Infantry. Died of disease at Chattanooga, TN, Oct. 28, 1864. Interred at Chattanooga National Cemetery, Chattanooga, TN. Section G, Grave 8214.

Beverley, Albert W. Pvt. U.S. Signal Corps. Died of disease at Georgetown Hospital, Washington, D.C., Sept. 1, 1864.

Blanding, Jabez B. Capt. 21st Veteran Reserve Corps. Residence, Providence. Murdered by the Ku Klux Klan at Grenada, MS, April 30, 1866. Interred at North Burial Ground, Providence, RI.

Bowen, John. Pvt. Co. G, 2nd Battalion, 15th U.S. Infantry. Died of disease at Rome, GA, Dec. 26, 1867.

Britt, Thomas. Pvt. Co. H, 2nd Battalion, 15th U.S. Infantry. Died of disease at Vicksburg, MS, Aug. 26, 1866. Interred at Vicksburg National Cemetery, Vicksburg, MS. Section E, Grave 16469.

Brown, Christopher C. Pvt. 15th U.S. Infantry. Died of disease at Chattanooga, TN, Jan. 9, 1865. Interred at Jonathan Arnold Lot, Lincoln Cemetery 26, Lincoln, RI.

Burchard, Francis. Corp. Co. H, 14th U.S. Infantry. Residence, Burrillville. Mortally wounded in action at Gettysburg, PA, July 2, 1863. Died of wounds at Gettysburg, PA, July 15, 1863. Interred at Gettysburg National Cemetery, Gettysburg, PA. U.S. Regular Section.

Callary, John H. Pvt. Co. C, 2nd Battalion, 15th U.S. Infantry. Died of disease at Mobile, AL, Aug. 28, 1867.

Campbell, Joseph. Pvt. Co. H, 3rd Battalion, 15th U.S. Infantry. Died of disease at Mobile, AL, Nov. 9, 1865. Interred at Mobile National Cemetery, Mobile, AL. Section 2, Grave 388.

Card, Archaleus. Pvt. Co. C, 15th U.S. Infantry. Killed in action at Marietta, GA, July 4, 1864. Cenotaph at North Burial Ground, Bristol, RI.

Cassidy, Thomas E. Pvt. Co. C, 2nd Battalion, 15th U.S. Infantry. Died of disease at Vicksburg, MS, Aug. 22, 1866.

Cavanaugh, Daniel. Pvt. Co. G, 14th U.S. Infantry. Killed in action at Gettysburg, PA, July 2, 1863.

Charnley, John. Pvt. Co. H, 14th U.S. Infantry. Died of disease at Harrison's Landing, VA, July 10, 1862. Interred at Intervale Cemetery, North Providence, RI.

Clark, John A. 2nd Lt. 2nd U.S. Infantry. Captured at Bull Run July 21, 1861, as a member of the 1st R.I.D.M. Commissioned Aug. 5, 1861. Died while a prisoner of war at Tuscaloosa, AL, May 17, 1862.

Clarke, Charles P. Pvt. Co. H, 14th U.S. Infantry. Died of disease while a prisoner of war at Salisbury, NC, Dec. 10, 1864. Interred in a mass grave at Salisbury National Cemetery, Salisbury, NC.

Collins, Andrew J. Pvt. Co. B, 15th U.S. Infantry. Killed in action near Atlanta, GA, July 30, 1864. Interred at Marietta National Cemetery, Marietta, GA. Cenotaph at Cedar Lot, Johnston Cemetery 7, Johnston, RI.

Corcoran, William C. Pvt. Co. F, 2nd Battalion, 15th U.S. Infantry. Died of disease at Vicksburg, MS, April 20, 1867. Interred at Vicksburg National Cemetery, Vicksburg, MS. Section E, Grave 16510.

Cory, Nicholas H. Pvt. Co. H, 14th U.S. Infantry. Committed suicide at Perryville, MD, Feb. 13, 1862.

Crawford, William. Pvt. Co. D, 11th U.S. Infantry. Killed in action at Gaines Mill, VA, June 27, 1862.

Cronin, Michael. Pvt. Co. G, 2nd Battalion, 15th U.S. Infantry. Accidentally killed in a railroad accident near Chattanooga, TN, April 18, 1866. Interred at Chattanooga National Cemetery, Chattanooga, TN. Section H, Grave 11103.

Crowell, John. Pvt. Co. H, 3rd Battalion, 15th U.S. Infantry. Died of disease at Mobile, AL, Oct. 10, 1866.

Cull, James S. Pvt. U.S. Signal Corps. Residence, Cumberland. Died of dysentery at Vicksburg, MS, August 7, 1866.

Damiens, Joseph. Pvt. Co. A, 2nd Battalion, 15th U.S. Infantry. Died of disease at Vicksburg, MS, Aug. 30, 1866.

Degnan, Patrick. Pvt. Co. G, 14th U.S. Infantry. Killed in action July 2, 1863, at Gettysburg, PA.

Diamon, Thomas. Pvt. Co. G, 14th U.S. Infantry. Killed in action at Chancellorsville, VA, May 1, 1863.

Downs, Dennis. Pvt. 15th U.S. Infantry. Died of disease at Fort Adams, Newport, RI, Mar. 12, 1865. Interred at Fort Adams Cemetery, Newport, RI.

Duffee, William. Pvt. Co. M, 3rd U.S. Artillery. Residence, Providence. Died of typhoid fever at Cincinnati, OH, Aug. 27, 1863. Interred at Spring Grove National Cemetery, Cincinnati, OH. Section 21, Grave 533.

Duvillard, John Antoine. 1st Lt. 12th U.S. Infantry. Died of disease at Fort Hamilton, New York, NY, May 8, 1865. Interred at St. John's Episcopal Cemetery, Cape Vincent, NY.

Elliot, James E. Pvt. U.S. Signal Corps. Died of disease at Fort Leavenworth, KS, Feb 2, 1865.

Fenner, George D. Pvt. Co. I, 2nd U.S. Infantry. Residence, Johnston. Killed in action at Spotsylvania Court House, VA, May 12, 1864.

Field, Gustavus H. U.S. Signal Corps. Died of disease at New Orleans, LA, Feb. 6, 1865. Interred at Swan Point Cemetery, Providence, RI.

Fisher, Xavier D. Pvt. Co. B, 3rd Battalion, 15th U.S. Infantry. Died of disease at Mobile, AL, Oct. 11, 1866.

Fitts, Patrick. Pvt. Co. F, 2nd Battalion, 15th U.S. Infantry. Died of disease at Nashville, TN, June 28, 1864.

Fitzgibbon, Michael. Pvt. Co. B, 11th U.S. Infantry. Mortally wounded in action July 2, 1863, at Gettysburg, PA. Died of wounds at Gettysburg, PA, Aug. 29, 1863.

Foy, Michael J. Pvt. Co. G, 2nd Battalion, 14th U.S. Infantry. Residence, Providence. Died of pneumonia at Providence, RI, May 2, 1863.

Griffin, John. Sgt. Co. F, 2nd Battalion, 15th U.S. Infantry. Died of disease at Vicksburg, MS, Aug. 20, 1866. Interred at Vicksburg National Cemetery, Vicksburg, MS. Section E, Grave 16462.

Grover, Stephen A. Pvt. Co. E, 2nd Battalion, 15th U.S. Infantry. Died of disease at Mobile, AL, April 21, 1866. Interred at Mobile National Cemetery, Mobile, AL. Section 2, Grave 411.

Hannah, Thomas. Pvt. Co. H, 14th U.S. Infantry. Killed in action at Second Manassas, VA, Aug. 30, 1862.

Harney, John. Pvt. Co. H, 2nd Battalion, 15th U.S. Infantry. Died of disease at Macon, GA, Mar. 8, 1867.

Harold, John. Pvt. Co. D, 14th U.S. Infantry. Killed in action at Gaines Mill, VA, June 27, 1862.

Hatch, Roswell. Pvt. Co. H, 14th U.S. Infantry. Died of disease at Philadelphia, PA, April 8, 1862. Interred at Philadelphia National Cemetery, Philadelphia, PA. Section E, Grave 38.

Hopkins, William H. Pvt. 3rd U.S. Artillery. Residence, Foster. Died of disease at Washington, D.C., April 21, 1865. Interred at Spears Cemetery, Foster, RI.

Howard, Edmund W. Pvt. Co. G, 14th U.S. Infantry. Mortally wounded in action at Gettysburg, PA, July 2, 1863. Died of wounds at Gettysburg, PA, July 15, 1863. Interred at Gettysburg National Cemetery, Gettysburg, PA. U.S. Regular Section.

Howland, Franklin. Pvt. Co. G, 3rd Battalion, 15th U.S. Infantry. Died of disease at Macon, GA, Sept. 29, 1866.

Johnson, Fernando M. Pvt. U.S. Signal Corps. Residence, Foster. Died of disease at Fort Monroe, VA, Sept. 9, 1864. Interred at Moosup Valley Cemetery, Foster, RI.

Johnson, Samuel M. U.S. Signal Corps. Died of disease at Knoxville, TN, Jan. 21, 1864. Interred at Knoxville National Cemetery, Knoxville, TN. Section C, Grave 355.

Jones, Henry. Pvt. Co. G, 3rd Battalion, 15th U.S. Infantry. Died of disease at Chattanooga, TN, July 17, 1865.

Kennedy, John. Pvt. Co. G, 2nd Battalion, 15th U.S. Infantry. Died of disease at Vicksburg, MS, Aug. 15, 1866.

Kenyon, Owen. Pvt. Co. G, 3rd Battalion, 15th U.S. Infantry. Died of disease at Chattanooga, TN, July 22, 1865.

Knight, Nathan. Pvt. Co. H, 2nd Battalion, 15th U.S. Infantry. Residence, West Greenwich. Died of tuberculosis at Mobile, AL, Dec. 24, 1865. Interred at Mobile National Cemetery, Mobile, AL. Section 2, Grave 541.

Latham, Charles M. Pvt. U.S. Signal Corps. Died of wounds received in action against hostile Indians at Fort Leavenworth, KS, Nov. 6, 1865. Interred at Robert Latham Lot, Smithfield Cemetery 41, Smithfield, RI.

Loyall, David. Pvt. Co. H, 14th U.S. Infantry. Mortally wounded in action at Second Manassas, VA, Aug. 30, 1862. Died of wounds at Washington, D.C., Sept. 10, 1862. Interred at Soldier's Home National Cemetery, Washington, D.C. Section B, Grave 970.

Lucas, Abraham. Pvt. Co. G, 2nd Battalion, 15th U.S. Infantry. Died of disease at Vicksburg, MS, Aug. 31, 1866. Interred at Vicksburg National Cemetery, Vicksburg, MS. Section E, Grave 16478.

Martin, James. Pvt. Co. B, 11th U.S. Infantry. Killed in action at Gaines Mill, VA, June 27, 1862.

Mayo, Peter. Pvt. Co. A, 3rd Battalion, 15th U.S. Infantry. Accidentally killed in building collapse at Fort Adams, Newport, RI, Feb. 5, 1864. Interred at Fort Adams Cemetery, Newport, RI.

McCabe, Michael. Pvt. Co. B, 3rd Battalion, 15th U.S. Infantry. Killed in action at Jonesboro, GA, Aug. 13, 1864.

McCarty, Florence. Pvt. Co. A, 2nd Battalion, 15th U.S. Infantry. Killed in action at Atlanta, GA, Aug. 7, 1864.

McQuade, Owen. Pvt. Co. H, 3rd Battalion, 15th U.S. Infantry. Died of disease at Chattanooga, TN, July 25, 1865.

Meagher, Daniel. Pvt. Co. F, 2nd Battalion, 15th U.S. Infantry. Died of disease at Fort Adams, Newport, RI, Dec. 12, 1863. Interred at Fort Adams Cemetery, Newport, RI.

Mehan, James. Pvt. Co. B, 11th U.S. Infantry. Died of disease at Philadelphia, PA, April 25, 1864.

Moies, John E. 1st Lt. 10th USCT. Residence, Smithfield. Died of disease at Galveston, TX, Oct. 19, 1865. Interred at Mineral Spring Cemetery, Pawtucket, RI.

Mooney, Bernard. Pvt. Co. G, 2nd Battalion, 15th U.S. Infantry. Died of disease Aug. 11, 1866, at Vicksburg, MS.

Moran, William. Pvt. Co. D, 14th U.S. Infantry. Killed in action at Gaines Mill, VA, June 27, 1862.

Occleston, William B. Capt. 15th U.S. Infantry. Died of disease contracted in the service at Newport, RI, Aug. 24, 1867. Interred at Island Cemetery, Newport, RI.

Ogden, Frederick C. Adjutant. 1st U.S. Cavalry. Killed in action at Trevilian Station, VA, June 11, 1864. Interred at Island Cemetery, Newport, RI.

Pickford, John. Pvt. Co. D, 15th U.S. Infantry. Committed suicide by jumping overboard from the *Evening Star,* Jan. 8, 1866.

Pulsifer, Moses R. Corp. Co. H, 3rd Battalion, 15th U.S. Infantry. Died of disease at Mobile, AL, April 5, 1866. Interred at Mobile National Cemetery, Mobile, AL. Section 2, Grave 381.

Roberts, Edmund. Pvt. Co. G, 3rd Battalion, 15th U.S. Infantry. Died of disease at Macon, GA, Oct. 24, 1866.

Robinson, Timothy W. Pvt. Co. H, 14th U.S. Infantry. Died of disease at Philadelphia, PA, Mar. 30, 1862. Interred at Woodlands Cemetery, Philadelphia, PA.

Searles, Amos P. Pvt. Co. E, 2nd U.S. Dragoons. Enlisted April 4, 1858. Mustered out Sept. 23, 1861 after serving three years on the Texas Frontier. Reenlisted in 3rd Massachusetts Cavalry Nov. 15, 1861. Died of disease at New Orleans, LA, Nov. 12, 1862. Interred at Upper Cemetery, Philipston, MA.

Seaver, William H. Pvt. Veteran Reserve Corps. Died of disease contracted in the service at Providence, RI, June 17, 1865. Interred at Grace Church Cemetery, Providence, RI.

Shawcross, Beiston. Pvt. Co. H, 3rd Battalion, 15th U.S. Infantry. Died of disease at Chattanooga, TN, Aug. 25, 1866.

Sherman, George. Pvt. 14th U.S. Infantry. Residence, South Kingstown. Died of typhoid at Washington, DC, Feb. 26, 1862.

Simmons, Levi. Pvt. 15th U.S. Infantry. Residence, Woonsocket. Died of disease at Chattanooga, TN, Aug. 24, 1865. Interred at Chattanooga National Cemetery, Chattanooga, TN. Section H, Grave 10649.

Skinion, Frank. Pvt. Co. H, 14th U.S. Infantry. Died of disease at Aquia Creek, VA, Feb. 26, 1863.

Smith, James W. Pvt. Co. H, 14th U.S. Infantry. Residence, Providence. Killed in action at Gaines Mill, VA, June 27, 1862. Cenotaph at North Burial Ground, Providence, RI.

Smith, Ranson L. Sgt. 17th U.S. Infantry. Mortally wounded in action, shot in elbow, at Gettysburg, PA, July 2, 1863. Died of wounds at Baltimore, MD, July 26, 1863. Interred at Grace Church Cemetery, Providence, RI.

Smith, Samuel S. Pvt. Co. H, 14th U.S. Infantry. Residence, Providence. Killed in action at Gaines Mill, VA, June 27, 1862. Cenotaph at North Burial Ground, Providence, RI.

Suddard, Edwin. Pvt. Co. H, 2nd Battalion, 15th U.S. Infantry. Died of disease at Vicksburg, MS, Aug. 28, 1866. Interred at Vicksburg National Cemetery, Vicksburg, MS. Section E, Grave 16471.

Suddard, Thomas J. Pvt. Co. H, 2nd Battalion, 15th U.S. Infantry. Died of disease at Vicksburg, MS, Aug. 27, 1866. Interred at Vicksburg National Cemetery, Vicksburg, MS. Section E, Grave 16452.

Swindles, Robert. Pvt. Co. H, 14th U.S. Infantry. Mortally wounded in action at Second Manassas, VA, Aug. 30, 1862. Died of wounds at Fairfax, VA, Sept. 10, 1862. Interred at Greenwood Cemetery, Coventry, RI.

Taylor, Charles H. Pvt. Battery E, 3rd U.S. Artillery. Killed in action at Charleston, SC, April 22, 1864. Interred at Beaufort National Cemetery, Beaufort, SC. Section 1, Grave 9.

Tye, Frederick. Pvt. Co. G, 3rd Battalion, 15th U.S. Infantry. Died of disease at Chattanooga, TN, June 29, 1866. Interred at Chattanooga National Cemetery, Chattanooga, TN. Section H, Grave 11057.

Tyler, Benoid. Pvt. Co. G, 2nd Battalion, 15th U.S. Infantry. Died of disease at Vicksburg, MS, Nov. 4, 1866.

Vining, Edward. Pvt. Co. H, 14th U.S. Infantry. Killed in action at Spotsylvania Court House, VA, May 12, 1864.

Walker, John. Pvt. Co. G, 2nd Battalion, 15th U.S. Infantry. Died of disease at Vicksburg, MS, Aug. 1, 1866.

Wallace, Dennis. Pvt. Battery I, 5th U.S. Art. Killed in action at Gettysburg, PA, July 2, 1863. Interred at Gettysburg National Cemetery, Gettysburg, PA. U.S. Regular Section.

Wares, John. Pvt. Co. B, 2nd Battalion, 15th U.S. Infantry. Died of sunstroke at Huntsville, AL, July 18, 1868.

Watson, George. Pvt. Co. H, 14th U.S. Infantry. Mortally wounded in action at Gaines Mill, VA, June 27, 1862. Died of wounds at Alexandria, VA, Nov. 5, 1862.

Weller, Henry. Pvt. Co. A, 2nd Battalion, 15th U.S. Infantry. Died of disease at Vicksburg, MS, Oct. 17, 1866. Interred at Vicksburg National Cemetery, Vicksburg, MS. Section E, Grave 16486.

Wender, Joseph. Pvt. Co. E, 14th U.S. Infantry. Killed in action at Spotsylvania Court House, VA, May 12, 1864.

Westcott, Bowen. Pvt. Co. B, 2nd Battalion, 15th U.S. Infantry. Died of disease at Grenada, MS, Nov. 7, 1868.

Whittier, Horace. Pvt. Co. G, 3rd Battalion, 15th U.S. Infantry. Died of disease at Macon, GA, July 28, 1866.

Whittier, Leroy M. Pvt. Co. G, 3rd Battalion, 15th U.S. Infantry. Died of disease at Chattanooga, TN, Aug. 5, 1865. Interred at Chattanooga National Cemetery, Chattanooga, TN. Section H, Grave 10643.

30

United States Navy

Adams, Frank G. Ensign. Residence, Providence. Served onboard U.S.S. *Chenango.* Died of dysentery at Key West, FL, May 23, 1865. Interred at North Burial Ground, Providence, RI.

Atkinson, Martin L. Landsman. Served onboard U.S.S. *Nipsic.* Died of disease while prisoner of war, Feb. 26, 1864.

Bailey, Ira E. Seaman. Residence, Cranston. Served onboard U.S.S. *Somerset.* Died of disease July 29, 1862.

Bannon, John E. Landsman. Served onboard U.S.S. *Keystone State.* Killed in action off Charleston, SC, Jan. 31, 1863.

Barney, Miller L.B. Ordinary Seaman. Residence, Warren. Served onboard U.S.S. *Clifton.* Drowned Sept. 8, 1863.

Bartlett, Horace. Seaman. Served onboard U.S.S. *Somerset.* Died of disease Dec. 27, 1862.

Blaisdell, Joel B. 1st class fireman. Residence, Providence. Served on board U.S.S. *Kearsarge.* Died of disease contracted in the service at Cranston, RI, Jan. 13, 1867. Interred at Locust Grove Cemetery, Providence, RI.

Blake, James. Ordinary Seaman. Served onboard U.S.S. *Lodona.* Killed in action at Charleston, SC, Sept. 8, 1863.

Boss, William A. Seaman. Residence, Newport. Served onboard U.S.S. *Cairo.* Died of disease at Memphis, TN, July 10, 1862. Interred at Island Cemetery, Newport, RI.

Ensign Frank Adams of Providence died of dysentery at Key West, Florida, serving in the United States Navy. His brother was Captain George W. Adams of Battery G, First Rhode Island Light Artillery.

Bowen, Edward A. Coal Heaver. Served onboard U.S.S. *Vermont.* Died of disease May 23, 1863.

Brown, Edward S. Landsman. Residence, Burrillville. Served onboard U.S.S. *Perry.* Died of disease June 20, 1864.

Bullock, James W. Landsman. Residence, North Kingstown. Died of disease onboard U.S.S. *Connecticut* at Fort Monroe, VA, May 29, 1865. Interred at Elm Grove Cemetery, North Kingstown, RI.

Burlingame, William A. Landsman. Served onboard U.S.S. *Red Rover.* Residence, East Greenwich. Died of disease at Memphis, TN, July 1, 1863. Interred at First Cemetery, East Greenwich, RI.

Burns, James. Ordinary Seaman. Served onboard U.S.S. *Benton.* Died of disease Feb. 28, 1863.

Butler, Michael. Landsman. Residence, South Kingstown. Served onboard U.S.S. *Mohawk.* "Died of disease contract in US service during the Great Rebellion" at South Kingstown, RI, Dec. 7, 1865. Interred at Old St. Francis Cemetery, South Kingstown, RI.

Butts, Noah. Seaman. Residence, Tiverton. Died of measles at New York, NY, Feb. 9, 1862.

Cage, Henry. Ordinary Seaman. Served onboard U.S.S. *Minnesota.* Died of disease at Roanoke, NC, July 5, 1862.

Campbell, Walker. Landsman. Served onboard U.S.S. *Southfield.* Lost at sea April 19, 1864.

Canty, John. Landsman. Served onboard U.S.S. *Lafayette.* Died of disease July 4, 1864.

Carroll, Thomas. Seaman. Served onboard U.S.S. *Montauk.* Died of disease June 30, 1863.

Cassidy, James L. Seaman. Residence, Providence Served onboard U.S.S. *Osage.* Died of disease Mar. 31, 1864.

Cole, George W. Master's Mate. Residence, Providence. Killed in action at Fort Jackson, LA, April 24, 1862. Served onboard U.S.S. Iroquois. Interred at Swan Point Cemetery, Providence, RI.

Collins, Charles. Signal QM. Residence, Hopkinton. Served onboard U.S.S. *Eastport.* Died of disease "on the Mississippi," Nov. 7, 1863. Cenotaph at Dr. Isaac Collins Lot, Hopkinton Cemetery 40, Hopkinton, RI.

Collins, John. Seaman. Served onboard U.S.S. *Wabash.* Died of disease at Washington, D.C., Nov. 4, 1861.

Collins, Owen. Landsman. Served onboard U.S.S. *Beauregard.* Died of disease June 1, 1863.

Connolly, Edward. Served onboard U.S.S. *Ohio.* Died of disease Mar. 19, 1865.

Cook, Brenton B. Acting 3rd Asst. Engineer. Served onboard U.S.S. *Princeton.* Died Dec. 31, 1862.

Coty, Henry. Ordinary Seaman. Served onboard U.S.S. *Connecticut.* Died of disease Feb. 27, 1863.

Crane, James. 2nd Class Fireman. Served onboard U.S.S. *Ohio.* Died Mar. 4, 1865.

Davis, Frederick E. Acting Ensign. Served onboard U.S.S. *DeKalb.* Died of disease Mar. 16, 1863. Interred at Vicksburg National Cemetery, Vicksburg, MS. Section Q, Grave 9595. Cenotaph at Swan Point Cemetery, Providence, RI.

Denning, Henry. Seaman. Residence, Providence. Served onboard U.S.S. *Relief.* Died of disease Aug. 30, 1863.

Dexter, William H. Seaman. Served onboard U.S.S. *Pensacola.* Died of tuberculosis contracted in the service at Cranston, RI, May 9, 1865.

Drowne, Edgar. Seaman. Served onboard U.S.S. *Cairo.* Died of disease at Cairo, IL, Nov. 18, 1862. Interred at Drown Lot, Foster Cemetery 6, Foster, RI.

Earle, James H. Asst. Paymaster. Served onboard U.S.S. *Underwriter.* Died of disease at Andersonville Prison, Aug. 1, 1864. Interred at Andersonville National Cemetery. Grave 4462.

Farrell, Edward. Coal Heaver. Served onboard U.S.S. *Bienville.* Died of disease onboard Oct. 22, 1866.

Finan, Patrick. Coal Heaver. Served onboard U.S.S. *Wabash.* Died of disease April 6, 1864.

Fish, Spencer. Ordinary Seaman. Residence, Warwick. Killed in action Mar. 8, 1862, aboard U.S.S. *Congress.*

Foster, James. Seaman. Served onboard U.S.S. *Santee.* Died of disease April 18, 1865.

Franklin, Ira. Seaman. Residence, Westerly. Died of disease July 27, 1862 at New Orleans, LA.

Franks, George. Seaman. Died at Baltimore, MD, Nov. 12, 1865.

Galligan, Edward. Ordinary Seaman. Served onboard U.S.S. *Roebuck.* Died of disease July 27, 1864.

George, James. Ordinary Seaman. Served onboard U.S.S. *Sea Foam.* Died May 7, 1862.

Gladding, John H. Ordinary Seaman. Served onboard U.S.S. *Mystic.* Died of disease Jan. 21, 1864.

Goff, Elijah Warren. Landsman. Served onboard U.S.S. *Dacotah.* Died of disease contracted in the service, Aug. 10, 1864. Interred at Oak Grove Cemetery, Pawtucket, RI.

Greely, John. Landsman. Served onboard U.S.S. *Kennebec.* Died of disease Sept. 12, 1865.

Greene, Lewis A. Ordinary Seaman. Lost in the sinking of the U.S.S. *Sumter*, June 25, 1863.

Greene, Nathaniel C. Landsman. Residence, Coventry. Served onboard U.S.S. *Southfield*. Died of disease at Andersonville Prison, Aug. 2, 1864. Interred at Large Maple Root Cemetery, Coventry, RI.

Griffin, James. Seaman. Served onboard U.S.S. *Cincinnati*. Died of disease May 27, 1863.

Hamill, Henry. Ordinary Seaman. Died of disease off of Florida Oct. 6, 1863.

Hancock, John. Seaman. Served onboard U.S.S. *Portsmouth*. Died of disease April 26, 1862.

Hanley, John. Landsman. Served onboard U.S.S. *Montgomery*. Died of disease Aug. 9, 1863.

Hardman, William. Ordinary Seaman. Died of cancer at Newport, RI, Aug. 1, 1865.

Harrington, John. Seaman. Killed in action Mar. 8, 1862, onboard U.S.S. *Cumberland*.

Harrington, Timothy. Ordinary Seaman. Killed in action Mar. 8, 1862, onboard U.S.S. *Cumberland*.

Henson, William C. Seaman. Served onboard U.S.S. *Ohio*. Committed suicide onboard the *Ohio*, Oct. 26, 1863.

Horton, Stephen A. Seaman. Served onboard U.S.S. *Ohio*. Died of disease, Sept. 22, 1862.

Horton, William H. Ordinary Seaman. Served onboard U.S.S. *Galena*. Killed in action at Drewry's Bluff, VA, May 15, 1862.

Hurley, Patrick. Landsman. Served onboard U.S.S. *North Carolina*. Died of disease in hospital at New York, NY, Oct. 30, 1863.

Ives, Thomas P. Lt. Commander. Residence, Warwick. Died at Havre, France of tuberculosis contracted in the service, Nov. 17, 1865. Interred at North Burial Ground, Providence, RI.

Jacques, Peleg M. Landsman. Residence, Hopkinton. Died of typhoid contracted in the service at Hopkinton, RI, November 23, 1864. Interred at Rockville Cemetery, Hopkinton, RI.

Jackson, Thomas. Ordinary Seaman. Served onboard U.S.S. *Mystic*. Died of disease Dec. 21, 1861.

Johnson, George P. Landsman. Residence, Attleboro, MA. Served onboard U.S.S. *Nipsic*. Died of dysentery at Andersonville Prison, Sept. 8, 1864. Interred at Andersonville National Cemetery. Grave 8291. Cenotaph at Woodlawn Cemetery, Attleboro, MA.

Kelly, Robert L. Acting Master. Killed in action aboard U.S.S. *Mississippi* Mar. 14, 1863. Cenotaph at Swan Point Cemetery, Providence, RI.

Kerrigan, Patrick. Landsman. Served onboard U.S.S. *Whitehead.* Died of disease May 17, 1862.

Kettle, Henry G. Ordinary Seaman. Residence, Coventry. Killed in an accident falling from the rigging onboard U.S.S. *Minnesota,* Dec. 29, 1861. Interred at Irwin-Hines Lot, Coventry Cemetery 81, Coventry, RI.

Mallahan, Thomas. Acting Third Assistant Engineer. Residence, Providence. Served onboard Gunboat *Eagle.* Killed in action April 15, 1863 during the Siege of Little Washington, NC.

Manchester, David W. 2nd Class Boy. Served onboard U.S.S. *South Carolina.* Died of disease Nov. 25, 1861.

Mason, John. 1st Class Fireman. Lost in the sinking of the U.S.S. *Patapsco,* Dec. 31, 1864.

Mayer, Henry. Ordinary Seaman. Served onboard U.S.S. *Alleghany.* Died of disease May 2, 1864.

McCabe, Hugh. 2nd Class Fireman. Served onboard U.S.S. *Westfield.* Died of disease at Galveston, TX, Jan. 1, 1863.

McDonald, Jeremiah. Seaman. Served onboard U.S.S. *Ethan Allen.* Died of disease April 11, 1865.

McGowan, John. Seaman. Served onboard U.S.S. *Louisville.* Died of disease in hospital at Mound City, IL, Oct. 10, 1862.

McGuire, William. Seaman. Served onboard U.S.S. *Southfield.* Died of disease May 14, 1862.

McLaughlin, Charles. Seaman. Served onboard U.S.S. *Ironsides.* Died of disease June 1, 1863.

McQuade, James. Ordinary Seaman. Served onboard U.S.S. *Niagara.* Drowned May 9, 1864.

Myrick, John. Gunner. Died of disease contracted in the service at Mamaroneck, NY Sept. 17, 1862. Interred at Old Mamaroneck Burial Ground, Mamaroneck, NY.

Newcomb, Henry S. Commander. Residence, Providence. Died of disease at Key West, FL while in command of the U.S.S. *Tioga* Oct. 24, 1863. Interred at North Burial Ground, Providence, RI.

Nugent, Robert. Ordinary Seaman. Served onboard U.S.S. *Weehawken.* Died of disease Dec. 5, 1863.

O'Brien, John. Seaman. Killed in action onboard U.S.S. *Cumberland,* Mar. 8, 1862.

Ornell, Frank T. Landsman. Residence, Providence. Died of dysentery at Providence, RI, Jan. 24, 1863.

Paine, Amasa. Capt. Died of disease contracted in the service at Providence, RI, July 27, 1863. Interred at Swan Point Cemetery, Providence, RI.

Peck, Edwin H. Landsman. Served onboard U.S.S. *Mount Vernon*. Killed in action on blockade duty Aug. 1, 1863.

Phillips, Albert. Seaman. Served onboard U.S.S. *Oneida*. Died of disease Aug. 5, 1864.

Phillips, Edward. Ordinary Seaman. Died of disease Dec. 19, 1861.

Pierson, James. Seaman. Served onboard U.S.S. *Constitution*. Died of disease Oct. 22, 1866.

Pinkham, Edward S. Gunner's Mate. Served onboard U.S.S. *Santee*. Died of disease April 24, 1867.

Pomeroy, Philip L. Seaman. Served onboard U.S.S. *Ohio*. Died of disease July 21, 1863.

Price, James. Landsman. Served onboard U.S.S. *Constitution*. Died of disease Feb. 8, 1864.

Purkins, Francis. Ordinary Seaman. Served onboard U.S.S. *Nightingale*. Died of disease Sept. 24, 1863.

Putnam, George. Ordinary Seaman. Killed in action onboard U.S.S. *Cumberland,* Mar. 8, 1862.

Remington, Albert H. Ordinary Seaman. Served onboard U.S.S. *Santiago*. Drowned Sept. 2, 1862.

Remington, William E. Seaman. Residence, Warwick. Served onboard U.S.S. *Ohio*. Died of disease at New York, NY, April 27, 1864.

Reynolds, Henry. Landsman. Killed in action at Fort Henry, TN, Feb. 6, 1862, while serving onboard U.S.S. *Essex*.

Rhodes, Robert. Lt. Residence, Warwick. Killed in action onboard U.S.S. *Clifton* at Sabine Pass, TX, Sept. 10, 1863. Interred at Grace Church Cemetery, Providence, RI.

Richardson, George W. Landsman. Served onboard U.S.S. *Winnipeg*. Died of disease Mar. 24, 1865.

Rose, John E. Landsman. Lost in the sinking of the U.S.S. *Bainbridge,* Aug. 21, 1863.

Rose, Leonard E. Landsman. Served onboard U.S.S. *Nita*. Died of yellow fever at Key West, FL. July 4, 1864. Interred at Key West, FL.

Rourke, Andrew. Seaman. Served onboard U.S.S. *Scioto*. Drowned April 18, 1863.

Seatle, Henry B. 1st Class Boy. Served onboard U.S.S. *Mahaska*. Died of disease Feb. 17, 1865.

Sherman, Robert. Died of disease contracted in the service at Providence, RI Nov. 23, 1865. Interred at North Burial Ground, Providence, RI.

Stebbins, Joseph. Seaman. Served onboard U.S.S. *J.S. Chambers*. Died of disease Aug. 9, 1864.

Stirling, Thomas. Seaman. Served onboard U.S.S. *Marion*. Died of disease April 7, 1867.

Stock, Louis. Seaman. Served onboard U.S.S. *Constitution*. Died of disease Feb. 27, 1865.

Thomas, Augustus. Seaman. Served onboard U.S.S. *Hartford*. Killed in action at New Orleans, LA, April 25, 1862.

Tillinghast, Henry. Seaman. Residence, Providence. Died of tuberculosis at Providence, RI, June 30, 1864.

Trim, James J. Ordinary Seaman. Served onboard U.S.S. *Pensacola*. Died of disease at Washington, D.C., Jan. 28, 1862.

Wilkey, Peter W. Seaman. Residence, Newport. Served onboard U.S.S. *Iroquois*. Died of disease June 9, 1864.

Williams, John. Residence, North Kingstown. Served onboard U.S.S. *Ohio*. Died of disease April 11, 1862.

Lieutenant Robert Rhodes of Warwick was killed in the Battle of Sabine Pass, Texas, on September 10, 1863.

Williams, John G. Served onboard U.S.S. *Eastport*. Died of disease at White River, AR, Nov. 7, 1863.

Wilson, Henry. Seaman. Residence, South Kingstown. Served onboard U.S.S. *Alabama*. Died of disease at Cape Haytien, Haiti, July 19, 1863.

31

Regiments of Other States

Angell, Abel S. Pvt. Co. A, 25th MA. Died of typhoid at Hampton, VA, June 28, 1864. Interred at Hampton National Cemetery, Hampton, VA. Grave 1431.

Arnold, George H. Pvt. Co. A, 115th IL. Died of disease at Danville, KY. Mar. 7, 1863. Interred at Danville National Cemetery, Danville, KY. Section 31, Grave 135.

Barber, Alden E. Pvt. Co. K, 39th IL. Mortally wounded in action and captured May 16, 1864, near Drewry's Bluff, VA. Died of wounds at Richmond, VA, June 18, 1864. Interred at Richmond National Cemetery, Richmond, VA.

Burnett, Charles R. Pvt. Co. K, 31st IL. Killed in action June 20, 1863 at Vicksburg, MS. Interred at Vicksburg National Cemetery, Vicksburg, MS. Section G, Grave 4519.

Butts, Edwin W. Sgt. Co. C, 5th IL Cav. Died of disease at Vicksburg, MS, Aug. 17, 1864. Interred at Swan Point Cemetery, Providence, RI.

Chaffee, Daniel K. Pvt. Co. I, 2nd MA Cav. Died of disease at Washington, D.C., June 15, 1863. Interred at North Burial Ground, Providence, RI.

Clarke, Richard D. Pvt. Co. G, 2nd MA Heavy Art. Captured at Plymouth, NC, April 20, 1864. Died of disease at Florence, SC, Oct. 17, 1864. Cenotaph at North Burial Ground, Providence, RI.

Clarke, William P. Pvt. Co. G, 8th CT. Residence, Hopkinton. Died of typhoid at Newport News, VA, Aug. 3, 1862. Interred at Oak Grove Cemetery, Hopkinton, RI.

Clegg, William. Pvt. Co. B, 24th IN. Residence, Newport. Died of disease at Otterville, MO, Jan. 25, 1862. Interred at Island Cemetery, Newport, RI.

Cleveland, John A. Pvt. Co. F, 114th NY. Died of disease at Brashear City, LA, June 1, 1863.

Eddy, Benjamin T. Pvt. Co. C. 22nd MA. Killed in action at Savage's Station, VA, June 29, 1862.

Eldridge, Samuel A. Pvt. Co. E, 3rd MN. Died of disease at Pine Bluff, AR, Aug. 7, 1864.

Ferris, Frank B. Capt. Co. I, 12th IL. Mortally wounded in action April 6, 1862, at Shiloh, TN. Died of wounds at Shiloh, TN, April 18, 1862. Interred at Oakland Cemetery, Princeton, IL.

Fessenden, Charles H. Co. D, 49th MA. Died of disease contracted in the service c. 1865. Interred at Swan Point Cemetery, Providence, RI.

Grace, Thomas W. Sgt. Co. H, 26th CT. Died of disease contracted in the service at Providence, RI, Oct. 8, 1863. Interred at North Burial Ground, Providence, RI.

Gray, Franklin S. Corp. Co. E, 58th MA. Residence, Little Compton. Killed in action at Cold Harbor, VA, June 3, 1864. Interred at Congregational Cemetery, Tiverton, RI.

Greene, Anthony H. Pvt. Co. B, 10th CT. Died of disease at Beaufort, SC, Oct. 23, 1863. Interred at Capt. Randall Holden Lot, Warwick Cemetery 68, Warwick, RI.

Greene, Howard. Capt. Co. B, 24th WI. Killed in action during the storming of Missionary Ridge, Chattanooga, TN, Nov. 25, 1863. Interred at Forest Home Cemetery, Milwaukee, WI.

Gunn, William. Wag. Co. G, 5th CT. Residence, Westerly. Killed in action at Cedar Mountain, VA, Aug. 9, 1862.

Hill, Sylvester G. Col. 35th IA. Residence, East Greenwich. Killed in action at Nashville, TN, Dec. 15, 1864. Interred at Greenwood Cemetery, Muscatine, IA.

Hodges, George F. Adjutant. 18th MA. Residence, Providence. Died of typhoid at Hall's Hill, VA, Jan. 31, 1862. Interred at Forest Hills Cemetery, Boston, MA.

Hodges, William T. Capt. Co. I, 4th MA Cav. Residence, Providence. Killed in action at Burkesville, VA, April 6, 1865. Interred at Forest Hills Cemetery, Boston, MA.

Hough, William. Pvt. Co. A, 5th CT. Died of disease contracted in the service at Cumberland, RI, Sept. 23, 1865. Interred at Oak Grove Cemetery, Pawtucket, RI.

Jenckes, John B. Residence, Cumberland. Pvt. Co. C, 12th MA. Mortally wounded in action at Antietam, MD, Sept. 17, 1862. Died of wounds Oct. 6, 1862. Interred at Ballou Cemetery, Cumberland, RI.

Kenyon, Isaac D. Capt. Co. B, 21st CT. Residence, Richmond. Mortally wounded at Petersburg, VA, Aug. 18, 1864. Died of wounds at Petersburg, VA, Sept. 1, 1864. Interred at Kenyon Cemetery, Richmond Cemetery 34, Richmond, RI.

Kibbe, Edward. Pvt. Co. G, 3rd CA. Died of disease at Camp Douglas, Utah, April 5, 1864.

Kilton, Benjamin Briggs. Pvt. Co. E, 58th IL. Residence, Coventry. Died of disease at Cairo, IL, Jan. 6, 1864. Interred at Knotty Oak Cemetery, Coventry, RI.

Lane, George F. Corp. Co. G, 5th CT. Residence, Westerly. Killed in action at Cedar Mountain, VA, Aug. 9, 1862.

McDermott, Peter. Pvt. Co. G, 58th MA. Residence, Burrillville. Killed in action at Spotsylvania Court House, VA, May 11, 1864. Interred at St. Patrick's Cemetery, Burrillville, RI.

Moore, Thomas A. Pvt. Co. A, 19th IL. Killed in action at Stone's River, TN, Dec. 31, 1862. Interred at South Burial Ground, Warren, RI.

Niles, William H. Pvt. Co. G, 54th MA. Residence, South Kingstown, RI. Died of disease at Jacksonville, FL, Mar. 9, 1864.

Parker, Jefferson M. Sgt. Co. E, 85th NY. Captured May 31, 1862, at Fair Oaks, VA. Died as a prisoner of war at Richmond, VA, July 23, 1862. Cenotaph at Weaver Settlement Cemetery, Allegany, NY.

Payne, George H. Pvt. Co. G, 64th NY. Mortally wounded in action at Petersburg, VA, Sept. 15, 1864. Died of wounds at Beverley, NJ, Dec. 4, 1864. Interred at Swan Point Cemetery, Providence, RI.

Randall, James B. Pvt. Co. L, 2nd MA Cav. Died of disease at Andersonville Prison, July 15, 1864. Interred at Andersonville National Cemetery. Grave 3358.

Read, George P. Pvt. Co. H, 2nd MA Heavy Art. Died of disease at Andersonville, GA, Sept. 6, 1864. Interred at Union Cemetery, Plainfield, CT.

Ripley, Albert G. 2nd Lt. Co. K, 3rd CA. Died of disease contractes in the service c. 1867 at Santa Clara, CA.

Sayles, Moses M. Pvt. Co. K, 86th IL. Died of dysentery at Chattanooga, TN, Dec. 7, 1863. Interred at Chattanooga National Cemetery, Chattanooga, TN. Section D, Grave 12395. Cenotaph at Sayles-Newell Lot, Smithfield Cemetery 55, Smithfield, RI.

Southwick, Stephen H. 1st Lt. Co. B, 24th IN. Killed in action at Shiloh, TN, April 7, 1862. Interred at Island Cemetery, Newport, RI.

Waite, Albert F. Pvt. Co. F, 15th MA. Mortally wounded in action at Ball's Bluff, VA, Oct. 21, 1861. Died of wounds at Baltimore, MD, Sept. 24, 1862. Interred at Nichols-Waite Lot, Warwick Cemetery 46, Warwick, RI.

Wales, Selden D. 1st Sgt. Co. A, 5th NY Cav. Killed in action at Hanover, PA, June 30, 1863.

Warren, E. Julian. Sgt. Co. A, 176th NY. Died of disease at Bonne Carre, LA, Dec. 2, 1863. Interred at Mineral Spring Cemetery, Pawtucket, RI.

Weld, John D. Pvt. Co. F, 24th IL. Died of disease June 14, 1865. Interred at Col. Abraham Winsor Lot, Smithfield Cemetery 31, Smithfield, RI.

Wheeler, George. Corp. Co. D, 61st NY. Died of disease in hospital at New York, NY, Sept. 18, 1864. Interred at First Hopkinton Cemetery, Hopkinton, RI.

Whitehouse, J. Crocker. Pvt. Co. I, 16th NY. Killed in action June 27, 1862, at Gaines Mill, VA. Interred at Common Burying Ground, Newport, RI.

Wildman, Henry H. Commissary Sgt. 16th IL Cav. Died of disease at Washington, D.C., Oct. 12, 1864. Interred at Arlington National Cemetery, Arlington, VA. Grave 9313.

Appendix

Total Deaths by Regiment

Regiment	Battle	Other Causes	Total
Gens & Staff	5	2	7
1st RIDM	20	16	36
2nd RIV	124	96	220
3rd RIHA	46	100	146
4th RIV	80	82	162
5th RIHA	8	120	128
7th RIV	105	138	243
9th RIV	0	6	6
10th RIV	0	3	3
11th RIV	0	18	18
12th RIV	22	50	72
14th RIHA	3	341	344
Hospital Guards	0	5	5
1st RI Cav	36	102	138
2nd RI Cav	8	32	40
3rd RI Cav	12	147	159
7th Squadron	0	2	2
Battery A	14	12	26
Battery B	18	19	37
Battery C	19	10	29
Battery D	13	11	24
Battery E	14	20	34
Battery F	10	21	31
Battery G	13	27	40
Battery H	2	12	14
10th Battery	0	1	1
U.S. Army	30	68	98
U.S. Navy	16	93	109
Marine Corps	0	0	0
Other States	19	26	45
Total	**637**	**1,580**	**2,217**

Chapter Notes

Chapter 1

1. *New York Times*, April 2, 2012.

2. William F. Fox, *Regimental Losses in the American Civil War: 1861–1865* (Albany: Albany Publishing Company, 1889), preface, 526, 533.

3. Harold R. Barker, *History of the Rhode Island Combat Units in the Civil War: 1861–1865* (Providence: NP, 1964), 307–308.

4. For more on the Rhode Island Soldiers' and Sailors' Monument, refer to *Report on the Committee on a Monument to the Rhode Island Soldiers' and Sailors' who Perished in Suppressing the Rebellion Made to the General Assembly, January Session, 1867* (Providence: Providence Press, 1867) and *Proceedings at the Dedication of the Soldiers' and Sailors' Monument in Providence* (Providence: A. Crawford Greene, 1871).

5. Elisha Dyer, *Annual Report of the Adjutant General of the State of Rhode Island and Providence Plantations for the Year 1865. Corrected, Revised, and Republished in Accordance with the Provisions of Chapters 705 and 767 of the Public Laws. Volume I* (Providence: E.L. Freeman, 1893), i. This book, the official listing of Rhode Island's Civil War soldiers is more commonly referred to as *The Revised Register of Rhode Island Volunteers*. Volume One covers those who served in the infantry, while Volume Two covers the cavalry, artillery, Regulars, and U.S. Navy. In the mid-1990s Kenneth Carlson of the Rhode Island State Archives began a meticulous project to finally catalog all of the Civil War papers from Rhode Island. Today, the papers, at the Rhode Island State Archives contain the best records of Rhode Island's Civil War soldiers.

6. *Names of the Officers, Soldiers, and Seamen in Rhode Island Regiment, or Belonging to the State of Rhode Island, and Serving in the Regiments of other States and in the Regular Army and Navy of the United States, who lost their live in the Defence of their Country in the Suppression*

of the Late Rebellion (Providence: Providence Press, 1869).

7. Fox, *Regimental Losses*, 434:473.

8. *Manufacturers and Farmers' Journal*, January 3, 1870 and *Newport Mercury*, January 1, 1870. William P. Hopkins, *The Seventh Regiment Rhode Island Volunteers in the Civil War: 1862–1865* (Providence: Snow & Farnum, 1903), 322. As stated above, my recording of casualty figures has been exhaustively researched from all available soldiers' letters and journal entries, pension and service files at the National Archives, death listings in town hall records, as well as cemetery visits.

9. Zenas Randall Bliss, *The Reminiscences of Major General Zenas R. Bliss: 1854–1876*, ed. Thomas T. Smith, Jerry D. Thompson, Robert Wooster, and Ben E. Pingenot (Austin: Texas State Historical Association, 2007), 324–330; Hopkins, *Seventh Rhode Island*, 47–59. Company A, Seventh Rhode Island Monthly Returns, December 1862, Author's Collection. Richard Weeden, Pension Files, National Archives. William P. Hopkins gave the Seventh's casualty figures as thirty-nine dead and 120 wounded for a total loss of 159. My figure includes men who later died of wounds and those whose injuries were recorded in myriad of sources including newspapers, letters, journals, and pension records.

10. Joseph B. Curtis to William Sprague, September 22, 1862, *Providence Journal*, September 25, 1862. Rhode Island State Archives.

11. George H. Allen, *Forty-Six Months in the Fourth Rhode Island Volunteers* (Providence: J.A. & R.A. Reid, 1887), 371–389; *Revised Register: Volume One*, 301. *Proceedings at the Dedication*, 9–10; John Michael Priest, *Antietam: The Soldiers Battle* (Oxford: Oxford University Press, 1994), 277–278: 351.

12. Death Records for Burrillville, Coventry, Glocester, Little Compton, Providence, Scituate, Warwick, Westerly, contained in the clerk's offices in those communities.

13. Register of Death entry for Samuel Towne, 1863 North Providence Death Returns, Pawtucket City Hall, Pawtucket, RI.

14. Joseph K. Barnes, *The Medical and Surgical History of the War of the Rebellion* (Washington, DC: Government Printing Office, 1875), 201.

15. Alpheus Salisbury, Pension File, National Archives. *Proceedings at the Dedication,* 55.

16. Harvey and William Pearce Headstones, Wood River Cemetery, Richmond, RI. *Revised Register: Volume II,* 784.*Proceedings at the Dedication,* 61–62.

17. Register of Death entry for Henry C. Colwell, 1862 Death Returns, Glocester Town Hall, Chepachet, RI. *Revised Register: Volume II,* 305–310. *Proceedings at the Dedication,* 63–65.

18. Frederic Denison, *Shot and Shell: The Third Rhode Island Heavy Artillery Regiment in the Rebellion, 1861–1865* (Providence: J.A. & R.A. Reid, 1879) Register of Death entry for Ira E. Cole, 1865 Death Returns, Foster Town Hall, Foster, RI. *Proceedings at the Dedication,* 50.

19. Hopkins, *Seventh Rhode Island,* 522. Register of Death entry for Ira Cornell, Jr., 1867 Death Returns, Coventry Town Hall, Coventry, RI.

20. Register of Death entry for Ira Cornell, April 1, 1863, Coventry Town Hall. Hopkins, *Seventh Rhode Island,* 69–70.

21. Thomas Williams Bicknell, *The History of the State of Rhode Island and Providence Plantations: Volume II* (New York: American Historical Society), 820–821.

Annotated Bibliography

The following published sources will allow the reader to find additional resources that were used to compile the data presented in this book, as well as books from which these names were extracted. Most importantly were the regimental histories, as well as the *Revised Register of Rhode Island Volunteers*. Readers should consult the individual regimental histories for additional information on each soldier before they became a casualty of the war.

Aldrich, Thomas M. *The History of Battery A, First Regiment Rhode Island Light Artillery in the War to Preserve the Union, 1861–1865.* Providence: Snow & Farnum, 1904.

The last published battery history and the only one to be illustrated with photographs rather than engravings. Aldrich's history of Battery A is well regarded, however one must compare Aldrich against other sources, such as *Diary of Battery A*. Aldrich often placed himself at the center of the action, such as at Bull Run and Gettysburg when he was actually in the rear with the supply train. This book provides a very good view of Battery A's actions at Antietam.

Allen, George H. *Forty-Six Months with the Fourth R.I. Volunteers, in the War of 1861 to 1865 Comprising a History of Its Marches, Battles, and Camp Life. Compiled from Journals Kept While on Duty in the Field and Camp, by Corp. Geo. H. Allen.* Providence: J.A. & R.A. Reid, 1887.

Originally published as his memoirs, this book was later adopted by the Fourth Rhode Island as their official regimental history. A corporal from Providence, Allen kept a meticulous journal during the war. This volume provides one of the best accounts of the Battle of New Bern, as well as the Fourth's actions at Antietam and the Crater at Petersburg. Highly readable, Allen wrote clearly and with a sense of preserving the deeds of his regiment for posterity. The book also provides details regarding the bitter feud between the Fourth and Seventh Rhode Island Regiments.

Bartlett, John Russell. *Memoirs of Rhode Island Officers, Who Were Engaged in the Service of Their Country During the Great Rebellion of the South: Illustrated with Thirty-Four Portraits.* Providence: Sidney S. Rider, 1867.

One of the best and most important books ever written about Rhode Island and the Civil War. Written by Secretary of State John Russell Bartlett, a noted bibliophile who began collecting books on the Civil War immediately after the conflict started, this volume contains biographies of every Rhode Island officer who commanded a regiment or battery during the Civil War. Even more important are the biographies of those officers who died in the war; these sketches were written by family members and include many fine quotations from their private letters. The book is also enhanced by thirty-four engravings of the officers.

Bicknell, Thomas W. *A History of Barrington Rhode Island.* Providence: Snow & Farnum, 1898. Pp. 498–511.

A detailed history of Barrington written by a well-known local historian. Bicknell details the actions of the local town council during the conflict and includes a detailed roster of all the men from the town who served in the Civil War.

Burgess, Gideon A. *The Owen Soldier's Monument North Scituate, R.I.: Dedicated August 20, 1913.* North Scituate: E.F. Sibley & Co., 1913.

Dedicated in 1913, the Civil War monument in Scituate was one of the last to be dedicated in Rhode Island. This very detailed sketch, published for the dedication ceremony provides detailed information regarding the role of Scituate in the Civil War, as well as providing details and a list of the men from Scituate who died in the army.

Burlingame, John K. *History of the Fifth Regiment of Rhode Island Heavy Artillery During Three Years and a Half of Service in North Carolina. January 1862–June 1865.* Providence: Snow & Farnum, 1892.

The first published regimental history under the 1892 act, the Fifth Rhode Island was unique in that they spent their entire wartime service in North Carolina. The regiment spent most of the war on garrison duty and only engaged in occasional raids along the Carolina coast. Despite not being a "combat" regiment, this book is filled with interesting details regarding the Burnside Expedition, interactions with southern civilians in the New Bern area, as well as the prison experiences of those sent to Andersonville. The book is well illustrated with many engravings of both officers and men.

Busey, John W. *These Honored Dead: The Union Casualties at Gettysburg.* Hightstown, NJ: Longstreet House, 1996.

An important resource that lists the Union soldiers who died at Gettysburg.

Cady, John Hutchins. *Rhode Island Boundaries: 1636–1936.* Providence: Rhode Island Tercentenary Commission, 1936.

A must-read book to understand the physical boundaries during the Civil War era. The town boundaries of the state have changed dramatically since the Civil War; as such this book provides important information regarding the geography of Rhode Island during the Civil War era.

Chase, Philip S. *Battery F, First Regiment Rhode Island Light Artillery in the Civil War, 1861–1865.* Providence: Snow & Farnham, 1892.

The only battery to not spend any of its service in the Army of the Potomac, Battery F spent the majority of the war in North Carolina and joined the Army of the James in Virginia in 1864. This book provides an interesting look into combat in the North Carolina theater, as well as the participation of Battery F in several smaller engagements along the coast. Illustrated with engravings and includes a useful roster.

Chenery, William H. *The Fourteenth Regiment Rhode Island Heavy Artillery (Colored), In the War to Preserve the Union, 1861–1865.* Providence: Snow & Farnum, 1898.

A comprehensive history of the Fourteenth, this book provides details of their service in Louisiana and Texas during the war. Chenery focused more on the white officer corps of the regiment, rather than the black enlisted men. As such, the book is filled with excellent biographical sketches of the officers, as well as many photographs.

Dailey, Charlotte F. *Report Upon the Disabled Rhode Island Soldiers: Their Names, Condition, and in What Hospital They Are. Made to His Excellency Gov. Sprague, and Presented to the General Assembly of Rhode Island, January Session, 1863.* Providence: A. Anthony, 1863.

Following the Battle of Fredericksburg in January 1863, Governor Sprague sent Charlotte Dailey of Providence to Washington to visit each hospital to find and identify Rhode Island soldiers needing treatment. Dailey found nearly 500 Rhode Islanders suffering from wounds or illness requiring treatment; this is the report of her findings and provides a detailed view of the sufferings endured by Rhode Island's soldiers.

"Dedication of the Soldiers and Sailors Monument at Riverside Cemetery South Kingstown, R.I., June 10, 1886." *The Narragansett Historical Register: Volume 5.* Pp. 81–125.

Proportionally no town lost more men than South Kingstown; one out of every three men who served in the Seventh Rhode Island died, and the losses were equal in other units. This sketch, which was also later published as a separate pamphlet chronicles the efforts to build a memorial to the soldiers of South Kingstown. The planning for the monument is included, as are the dedication exercises, and a list of the men from the town who died in the war.

Denison, Frederic. *Sabres and Spurs: The First Regiment Rhode Island Cavalry in the Civil War, 1861–1865. Its Origins, Marches, Scouts, Skirmishes, Raid, Battles, Sufferings, Victories, and Appropriate Official Papers; with The Roll of Honor and Roll of the Regiment.* Central Falls: E.L. Freeman, 1876.

One of the finest cavalry regimental histories, *Sabres and Spurs* was written by the regimental chaplain, Frederic Denison, who also wrote the history of the Third Rhode Island Heavy Artillery. Exceptionally well written, the book is filled with the personal narrative of the officers and men of the regiment, as well as Denison's wartime poetry. Serving throughout the war in the Army of the Potomac, the book heavily focuses on the role of the regiment in the Shenandoah Valley in 1862 and 1864, as well as the disastrous Battle of Middleburg. Of particular note is that the

Third Battalion of the regiment was originally made up of soldiers from New Hampshire; these men later became the nucleus of the First New Hampshire Cavalry. As that regiment never had a history, *Sabres and Spurs* serves as the history of both.

Denison, Frederic. *Shot and Shell: The Third Rhode Island Heavy Artillery Regiment in the Rebellion, 1861–1865: Camps, Forts, Batteries, Garrisons, Marches, Skirmishes, Sieges, Battles, and Victories, Also, the Roll of Honor and Roll of the Regiment: Illustrated with Portrait, Maps, and Scenes.* Providence: J.A. & R.A. Reid, 1879.

One of the best books written about a heavy artillery regiment, Denison's volume is a fantastic regimental history. He covers provides information on each of the twelve batteries of the regiment and their varied service from Florida to Virginia. Highly readable, *Shot and Shell* also includes information on the effectiveness of heavy artillery during the war, as well as the recruiting of the regiment.

Fenner, Earl. *The History of Battery H, First Regiment Rhode Island Light Artillery, in the War to Preserve the Union, 1861–1865.* Providence: Snow & Farnham, 1894.

Battery H spent much of the war in garrison duty around Washington and only went to the front lines at Petersburg late in the war. This regimental history is most useful for understanding how the First Rhode Island Light Artillery was recruited. This book is also illustrated with engravings and enlightened with detailed biographical sketches.

Grandchamp, Robert. *The Boys of Adams' Battery G: The Civil War Through the Eyes of a Union Light Artillery Unit.* Jefferson, NC: McFarland Publishing, 2009.

In this masterful study, Robert Grandchamp writes a full regimental history of Battery G; one of the few units never to publish a history. Based on intense, in-depth research, Grandchamp chronicles the organization, campaigns, and personalities of the battery and the many battles they took part in. Well illustrated with many images of battery members, this book follows Battery G's path as they took part in every major battle with the Army of the Potomac. One of the finest books ever written about Rhode Island and the Civil War.

Griswold, S.S. *Historical Sketch of the Town of Hopkinton, From 1757–1876, Comprising a Period of 119 Years.* Hope Valley: L.W.A. Cole, Job Printers, 1877. Pp. 46–51.

A small-town history, the few pages devoted to the Civil War list bounties paid by the town, as well as a roster of those who served. One out of every six men from Hopkinton died in the service, a casualty rate unseen in any Rhode Island town excepting South Kingstown.

Groeling, Meg. *The Aftermath of Battle: The Burial of the Civil War Dead.* El Dorado Hills, CA: Savas Beatie, 2015.

A detailed history of the burial of Civil War dead, the establishment of National Cemeteries, and mortuary practices during the war. The book also provides a detailed understanding of how the new number of 750,000 military deaths was reached. A very detailed source.

Hopkins, William P. *The Seventh Regiment Rhode Island Volunteers in the Civil War, 1862–1865.* Providence: Snow & Farnum, 1903.

The most impressive of the post-war regimental histories published in Rhode Island, this book has often been cited as the most impressive regimental history ever published. Taking nearly a decade to research and write, the book follows the campaigns of the Seventh from its recruitment, to service with the Ninth Corps in Virginia and Mississippi, including the Battle of Fredericksburg where the regiment sustained forty percent casualties. Of particular use are the many biographies written about members of the regiment, filled with genealogical details and their service during the war. The book is heavily illustrated with hundreds of photographs of Seventh Rhode Island soldiers.

Lewis, George. *The History of Battery E, First Regiment Rhode Island Light Artillery, in the War of 1861 and 1865, to Preserve the Union.* Providence: Snow & Farnham, 1892.

Perhaps the best of the six published battery histories from Rhode Island, Lewis' history of Battery E is a model history. Heavily illustrated with engravings, the book includes the detailed memoirs of several members, as well as excellent biographical details of battery members. Lewis does an excellent job of placing Battery E's actions within the context of the Army of the Potomac's campaigns.

Neff, John R. *Honoring the Civil War Dead: Commemoration and the Problem of Reconciliation.* Lawrence: University Press of Kansas, 2005.

A fantastic study that provides an excellent reference to the ways that Civil War veterans remembered their fallen comrades in the years after the war.

Pfanz, Donald C. *Where Valor Proudly Sleeps: A History of Fredericksburg National Cemetery, 1866–1933.* Carbondale: Southern Illinois University Press, 2018.

The landscape around Fredericksburg, Virginia is the bloodiest in the United States. Over 100,000 men were killed or wounded at Fredericksburg, Chancellorsville, the Wilderness, and Spotsylvania Court House. Furthermore, thousands died of disease or other illness in camps in the vicinity. After the war, many of the Union dead were reinterred at Fredericksburg National Cemetery, located on Marye's Heights in the city. Twenty known Rhode Islanders are buried at the cemetery, most from the Seventh Rhode Island, while doubtless dozens more will rest forever under a headstone marked as Unknown. This book provides a detailed overview of the establishment of the cemetery and the history of commemoration there.

Rhodes, John H. *The History of Battery B, First Regiment Rhode Island Light Artillery, in the War to Preserve the Union, 1861–1865.* Providence: Snow & Farnham, 1894.

One of the better battery histories from Rhode Island, Rhodes provides a detailed narrative of Battery B's service in the Army of the Potomac. The book includes much minutiae relating to the life of a Union artilleryman. Illustrated with engravings, this book provides much relevant information on Battery B's actions at Gettysburg and the Gettysburg Gun, now on display at the Rhode Island State House.

Spicer, William A. *History of the Ninth and Tenth Regiments Rhode Island Volunteers, and the Tenth Rhode Island Battery, in the Union Army in 1862.* Providence: Snow & Farnum, 1892.

An anecdotal history of the Ninth and Tenth Regiments during their three months of service in the defenses of Washington in the summer of 1862. Hastily raised and sent to the front, these two regiments accomplished little during their term of service. Spicer's history is a good history of life in camp, the trials of soldier life, and the interesting people the soldiers encountered. The book is well illustrated, largely with engravings copied from the book *Si Klegg and His Pard.* Also includes the activities of the veteran's associations of the Ninth and Tenth.

Sumner, George C. *Battery D, First Rhode Island Light Artillery, in the Civil War, 1861–1865.* Providence: Rhode Island Printing Company, 1897.

One of the smaller battery histories. Sumner died in the middle of writing this book and it was finished by an unknown colleague. This factor, combined with the loss of Battery

D's official papers which were captured at Cedar Creek make this one of the poorer battery histories. Of value however is the detailed roster. For specifics on Battery D's campaigns, readers should consult the several publications from Battery D veterans published by the Soldiers and Sailors Historical Society.

Tillinghast, Pardon E. *History of the Twelfth Regiment Rhode Island Volunteers in the Civil War 1862–1863.* Providence: Snow & Farnum, 1904.

The history of the Twelfth Rhode Island was written by a committee of members of the regiment and edited by Tillinghast. Rather than being a flowing narrative, the book is the memoirs of several different soldiers arranged by chapter. The format, while different from other regimental histories allows more than one voice to tell the story of the regiment. The history of the Twelfth is well illustrated and tells the story of the regiment at Fredericksburg and during their term of service in the West. While most Rhode Island soldiers wrote home that the Twelfth broke and ran under fire at Fredericksburg, this book presents a heroic version on their actions at the battle.

Woodbury, Augustus. *A Narrative of the Campaign of the First Rhode Island Regiment, in the Spring and Summer of 1861.* Providence: Sidney S. Rider, 1862.

As stated in the introduction, this book was the very first regimental history to be published about a Civil War unit. Highly detailed, Woodbury's account set the standard by which all future histories would be written. This book chronicles Rhode Island's response to the Civil War in April 1861, as well as the First's actions at Bull Run. Woodbury includes biographical sketches of the fallen members of the regiment, as well as a list of those who had reenlisted in other units. An excellent account of the First Rhode Island.

Woodbury, Augustus. *The Second Rhode Island Regiment: A Narrative of Military Operations in Which the Regiment Was Engaged from the Beginning to the End of the War for the Union.* Providence: Valpey, Angell, and Co., 1875.

Woodbury's second published regimental history, this volume is a detailed history of the Second Rhode Island and its service in all the actions of the Army of the Potomac from Bull Run to Appomattox. Based on the memoirs and letters of several veterans, this stout volume covers the history of this gallant regiment. Of utmost importance are detailed biographical sketches of every soldier in the regiment who lost his life while serving in the Second Rhode Island.

Woodbury, Augustus, and Sarah Helen Whitman. *Proceedings at the Dedication of the Soldiers' and Sailors' Monument: Erected in Providence by the State of Rhode Island: with the Oration by the Rev. Augustus Woodbury, and the Memorial Hymn by Mrs. Sarah Helen Whitman: to Which Is Appended a List of the Deceased Soldiers and Sailors Whose Names Are Sculptured Upon the Monument.* Providence: A. Crawford Greene, 1871.

Erected in Exchange Place in Providence in 1871, the Rhode Island Soldiers and Sailors Monument is the state's official Civil War memorial. On the large monument are engraved the names of every known Rhode Islander who died in the Civil War at that time, although current research indicates that more names should be on the monument. This book chronicles the building of the monument, as well as providing a detailed report of the dedication services. In addition, it includes a list of the names on the monument. A very important volume.

Index